DATE DUE

Plain Diversity

Young Center Books in Anabaptist & Pietist Studies
Donald B. Kraybill, *Series Editor*

Plain Diversity

Amish Cultures and Identities

STEVEN M. NOLT

and

THOMAS J. MEYERS

DONALD TLAMB

The Johns Hopkins University Press

Baltimore

The Johns Hopkins University Press
2715 North Charles Street
Baltimore, Maryland 21218-4363
www.press.jhu.edu

Library of Congress Cataloging-in-Publication Data
Nolt, Steven M. 1968–
Plain diversity: Amish cultures and identities / Steven M. Nolt
and Thomas J. Meyers.
p.   cm. — (Young center books in anabaptist and pietist studies)
Includes bibliographical references and index.
ISBN-13: 978-0-8018-8605-8 (hardcover : alk. paper)
ISBN-10: 0-8018-8605-8 (hardcover : alk. paper)
1. Amish—Indiana—Social life and customs. 2. Amish—Indiana—
Social conditions. 3. Amish—Indiana—Ethnic identity. 4. Community
life—Indiana. 5. Indiana—Social life and customs. 6. Indiana—Social
conditions. 7. Indiana—History, Local. I. Meyers, Thomas J., 1952– II. Title.
F535.M45N65.2007
305.8009772—dc22
2006025985

A catalog record for this book is available from the British Library.

Contents

Preface

Before sunup an Old Order Amish family in northeastern Indiana rises to begin the tasks of another day. They dress by gas lamps, their home devoid of public utility electricity. Over breakfast they might plan a horse-and-buggy trip to town or discuss the anticipated construction of a new Amish school. Then they head to the shop behind their house to spend the day manufacturing and shipping carefully tooled metal products to industrial clients around the country, including the National Aeronautics and Space Administration Visitor's Center in Houston, Texas.

By 7:00 a.m. the family's routine has both confirmed and called into question popular notions of Amish identity predicated on simple separation from the world. On the one hand, they work without alternating current or direct telephone service, yet on the other, they cast and lathe precision and decorative pieces for a wide array of products, including some they might be banned from buying themselves.

But charting the cultural contours of their community and its members involves more than making sense of technological choices. Uncomplicated notions of Amish culture isolate and essentialize. Instead, careful consideration of cultural identity situates its subject in relationships with neighbors—historical and contemporary, Amish and non-Amish, near and far away. For example, what is the significance of the fact that intercultural interaction in northeastern Indiana comes not via inquisitive tourists supposing exotic Amish distinctiveness so much as through sales representatives assuming a shared commercial language of quality, volume, and price—not to mention that these Old Orders live on the outskirts of Fort Wayne, a bustling city of a quarter million people? Then, too, what does it mean that being Amish in this place also involves being different from *other* Amish who live only a few miles to the northwest, who speak a strikingly different dialect, and who prescribe different patterns of practice—and with whom there is relatively little interaction?

Indeed, the more one considers Amish life in detail, the more it defies the easy distinctions that have often—even if sometimes unwittingly—explained Amish culture in both popular presentations and academic studies. We find the image of a mosaic helpful as we explore and represent Amish cultural identity because it connotes both diversity and unity. The image of the mosaic functions on several levels. First, Amish separation does not demand withdrawal, and their culture cannot be understood in isolation. Just as the shade and color intensity of a mosaic tile differs, depending on the contrasting and complementary hues of adjacent tiles, Old Orders interact with local environments, area economies, and civic officials in ways that color Amish identity in creative—and not merely reactive—ways. In short, the Amish cannot be understood apart from broader contexts.

At the same time, it is problematic to speak of *the* Amish, as if they constituted a single swatch on the cultural color palette. Instead, the closer one looks, the more it seems that Amish culture is itself a mosaic. Amish people have disparate histories and contrasting collections of prohibitions and prescriptions, and they think about the world in different ways. Some attend public schools, some vacation in Florida, and some resist immunization—diverse practices that are as curious to other Amish people as they are to outsiders.

But mosaics also reveal larger patterns despite—or rather because of—their varied pieces. In that sense, we offer the Amish mosaic in yet a third way, as an invitation to step back and ask questions of Amish unity and cultural coherence in light of the diversity that makes simple generalization impossible but promises a richer representation.

Despite the increasing sophistication of academic studies of Amish life, much of the best descriptive literature still focuses on specific themes or geographic locations, masking much of the diversity that appears only through the double vision that comes by way of comparative study. Four major questions shaped our approach and comparative research: (1) How have Amish migration history, church discipline, and ethnicity interacted in multiple and complex ways to shape distinct Amish cultures? (2) How have the foregoing factors combined in particular contexts—contexts that include non-Amish neighbors, influences, and authorities—to refine cultural identities, simultaneously embedding and distinguishing them? (3) Given the surprising degree of diversity in Amish life, what are the patterns, limits, and contours of that variety? (4) And finally, having explored the multivalent nature of Amish culture, how does it also make sense to speak of Amish culture in a singular sense? What, in fact, holds Amish people together, and how might we describe their unity in the absence of uniformity?

We explored these questions through comparative analysis of twenty distinct Amish settlements. While our work is grounded in a series of specific settlement studies, this book is not a community study. Instead, we have sought to identify factors that shape cultural identity and then have employed those variables in a theoretical framework that is applicable to other states and settlements and that we hope will stimulate further research and refinement.

A few notes on our choices of words and pictures. Seeking to avoid the temptation of pride or of being singled out from the group, Amish people typically ask to remain anonymous in published sources. As a result, we have not named Amish individuals whom we have quoted. However, in cases where names have previously appeared in print, as in newspaper stories or memoirs, we have included the names in our text. We have also attributed the quotes of informants who are no longer living. Sensitive to Old Order concerns about posing for pictures, we have used few close-up photographs of people. Amish typically refer to those outside their group as "English" because most outsiders with whom the Amish interact speak English instead of the Pennsylvania German or Swiss dialects the Amish use. For stylistic reasons, we have used the term *non-Amish* for those outside the Amish community.

This book is built on interviews, fieldwork, and archival research carried out over a period of five years under the auspices of the Amish and Old Order Groups of Indiana project, made possible by a grant from the Lilly Endowment, Inc. The project was conducted in conjunction with the Mennonite Historical Library at Goshen College. We are grateful to Lilly Endowment and to Mennonite Historical Library Director John D. Roth for their support. We received helpful guidance during our research from an advisory group that met annually and included John A. Hostetler (1918–2001), Beulah Stauffer Hostetler (1926–2005), Donald B. Kraybill, and four Amish individuals.

During the course of our research, we visited each of Indiana's twenty Amish settlements as well as selected settlements in Ohio, Michigan, Pennsylvania, and Ontario. We visited nearly all of the Indiana communities more than once, and in every place we interviewed Amish, and often non-Amish, residents. We are deeply grateful to the dozens of people who took time to visit with us on these occasions.

We thank departmental and administrative colleagues at Goshen College for their support in preparing this manuscript. In particular, we must mention Joe Springer and the staff of the Mennonite Historical Library, who were always most helpful. Sylva Keenan prepared the references, and Craig A. Mast assisted with proofreading and editing. Joel Fath, Dottie Kauffmann, and Dennis Hughes provided excellent photo illustrations, and Linda Eberly created all of the graphic art. We also express our appreciation to several Amish readers who critiqued the manuscript as we drafted it, to the two anonymous peer reviews arranged by the Johns Hopkins University Press, and to Donald B. Kraybill, editor of the press's Young

Center Books in Anabaptist and Pietist Studies. In every way, Kraybill provided helpful advice and counsel on the path to publication. At the press, editor Claire McCabe Tamberino generously assisted each step in the publication process. Copyeditor Elizabeth Yoder polished our prose. It has been a pleasure to work with all of these colleagues who have contributed to our efforts.

Plain Diversity

Introduction

Amish Images and Identities

Shipshewana, a village of just over five hundred permanent residents in La-Grange County, Indiana, swells each summer week by thirty thousand, as tourists from across the country roll into town. Local shopping venues, restaurants, and the Shipshewana Flea Market provide the primary draw, but Shipshewana's location in the midst of the world's third-largest Old Order Amish population plays a key role in the town's consumer attraction. Even visitors whose primary aims are commercial report that shopping in the midst of a living Amish community grants a humanizing air of authenticity to recreational retail, because visitors believe the Amish are a simple country folk, sharply separate from the rest of the world, whose presence guarantees honesty and old-fashioned integrity. Indeed, visitors believe they can feel a difference when they enter "Amish Country."[1]

This ability of modern Americans to identify the Amish—both geographically and as carriers of a distinct way of life—is remarkable. While rapidly losing interest in denominational differences of other sorts, Americans in recent years have identified and added the Amish to their collective sense of cultural literacy, moving Old Order people from the margins of obscurity to a place recognized by everyone from academics and journalists to comedians and marketing executives.[2] In July 2004, when the UPN Network began airing *Amish in the City*, a "reality TV" series that featured Amish-reared young adults, the press coverage of the show's premier assumed that readers and viewers knew who the Amish were and why the plot's upscale urban setting would offer dramatic juxtaposition of images. The "skein puts five Amish youth and six streetwise roommates into an ultramodern Hollywood Hills home and captures what happens when the two cultures come together," the release explained quite simply.[3]

Illustrations 1.1 and 1.2. Many Amish inhabit both modern and traditional worlds, creating complex cultural identities. Sources: Courtesy of the Mennonite Historical Library/Joel Fath and Dottie Kauffmann.

Images of small-scale dairy farmers who categorically reject technology, send their children to one-room schools, and all speak a German dialect called Pennsylvania Dutch lie near the center of popular positioning of Amish culture. Contemporary children's literature has begun to include the Amish in its panoply of multiculturalism, offering pictures of people curiously frozen in nineteenth-century time warps. Coffee table photography books offer pages of shocked wheat and simple windmills. Many academic studies unwittingly contribute to this homogenization by focusing on a single Pennsylvania Amish settlement, thereby conveying patterns of striking uniformity in everything from clothing styles to interaction with neighbors.

Lost in these images and interpretations, however, are Amish children who attend public schools with non-Amish classmates, or Amish adults who have trouble understanding a word of Pennsylvania German. Missing too are Amish household heads who punch daily time-clocks on the factory floor and turn out luxury motor homes for forty hours a week, or their wives who are more at home behind a Wal-Mart shopping cart than around a quilting frame.

For their part, traditional farmers, who are now a minority in almost all Amish churches and constitute as few as 10 percent of households in some large settlements, disagree among themselves over whether to use tractors, increase acreage, diversify, or go organic. Then, too, clothing styles, technology use, interaction with neighbors, and the practice of church discipline all vary across the Amish world, as do Amish appraisals of one another. "They're just stuck in tradition," an Amishman says of another Amish group, as he strokes his beard in an interview conducted by gas lamp light. While an Amish businessman in one community relies on his cell phone and cannot imagine work without it, other equally successful entrepreneurs conduct their business strictly by mail. Large brick homes with sundecks and landscaping house some Amish families, while others live in dowdy structures built from reused construction materials.

Seen in detail and considered in comparative perspective, the Amish emerge as anything but a singular people living out identical convictions in the face of modernity or adapting only when pressed to negotiate by outside forces. They are not suspended above the hurly-burly of neighborhood life, nor are they unaffected by the vagaries of local labor markets or regional demographic trends. Indeed, all of these factors shape Amish life in different and sometimes divergent ways, producing an array of distinct experiences.

Recognizing the diversity among the Amish, however, ultimately raises questions of commonality, since—different and deeply divided though they are—Amish people recognize in one another a shared identity. How does a group that values unity survive without uniformity? And how does a radically decentralized and geographically dispersed North American population of more than 170,000 maintain cohesion without centralized coordination or the glue of programs, budgets, and organizational flow charts that hold diverse modern individuals together? How might we make sense of identity in the absence of the bureaucratic tools that have come to dominate its modern construction? And what might this say to those seeking an understanding of community, culture, and diversity?

Remarkably, even those elements that at first blush seem to predict cookie-cutter conformity among the Amish actually nurture cultural diversity. A formative European religious legacy, small-scale social structure, and traditional understandings of order each militate against uniformity while providing important components of a coherent cultural identity. To each of these background elements we turn briefly before offering a model for understanding the complex, contextual construction of Amish cultural identity.

AMISH BEGINNINGS

In some ways, twenty-first-century Amish life exists in the shadow of the sixteenth century. Contemporary Amish conversation is never far removed from references to the "Old Country" or to Reformation-era martyrs. Firm convictions and fierce opposition are both part of that legacy, etching in Amish life a commitment to the centrality of the church in everyday life and a simmering suspicion of the wisdom of the world.

The Amish most often begin telling their story with the Protestant Reformation of the 1500s and its so-called radical wing. Alongside the better-known Continental actors such as Martin Luther, Huldrych Zwingli, and John Calvin, groups of more thorough-going reformers gathered in German-speaking central Europe and in the Netherlands. These radicals critiqued not only the teaching and structure of the late-medieval church but also broader social and political affairs, which they deemed hopelessly corrupt.

The antidote, they insisted, was a church composed only of those who made the voluntary decision to separate themselves from evil and follow the teaching of Jesus. Those teachings, they believed, pointed to the formation of a distinct people, a "little flock" scorned by "the world." They rejected the state-church system that linked Christianity and citizenship and that routinely baptized all infants. Instead, they argued that baptism was the sign of one's conscious decision to "take up the cross" of Jesus and live a disciplined life. After 1525, when they began to baptize one another as a mark of this new understanding of the church, they received the nickname *Anabaptists* (re-baptizers) and earned the condemnation of both Catholic and mainline Protestant leaders, who saw the Anabaptists as religious, social, and political revolutionaries.[4]

While most Anabaptists were orthodox Christians who pointed to the authority of the Bible and embraced traditional doctrines of the Trinity, sin, and the experience of God's grace as foundational to their faith, their ideas about the nature of the church and Christian life set them apart. The faithful church was an alternative community separate from surrounding society, they contended. Nor were its goals like those of the state, which strove to enforce a minimal morality on all people within the realm. Instead, the church was to be obedient to the teaching of Jesus Christ even to the extent of refusing violence in self-defense or bearing arms to protect the ruler.

These commitments often put the Anabaptists in conflict with leading political and religious leaders, who found the radicals subversive. Authorities used formal edicts, legal harassment, imprisonment, and even execution to oppose the spread of the movement, all of which confirmed the Anabaptists' sense of the hostility of the world. Between 1527 and 1614, some four thousand Anabaptists were killed, and the accounts of martyrdom are still a part of Amish consciousness today. A thousand-page collection of such stories, entitled *Martyrs Mirror*, remains in print from an Amish publisher and continues to enjoy steady sales.[5] Amish worship also draws on the martyr tradition, not only in sermon allusions but also through the hymns that comprise the Amish hymnal, the *Ausbund*, which includes martyr ballads and songs composed by imprisoned Anabaptists.[6]

The martyrdom of many early Anabaptist leaders contributed to the movement's lack of a singular spokesperson. By 1545, however, the influential writing of a Dutch Anabaptist named Menno Simons had resulted in some Anabaptists eventually receiving the nickname Mennists, or *Mennonites*.

Despite the dispersed and decentralized nature of the Anabaptist-Mennonite movement, adherents shared a conviction that what one believed must be closely reflected in how one lived. This attention to ethics garnered grudging respect and even quiet admiration from some non-Anabaptist neighbors. But it also proved to be a point of contention within Anabaptist circles as members debated the details of discipleship.

In a context of persecution, the line between the faithful dissenters and the violent world was fairly clear, but especially as religious toleration gained currency, Mennonites faced in more pointed ways the question of their relation to wider society. By 1693 the differences among the Anabaptists in Switzerland and their related communities to the north in the Palatinate and Alsace produced division. Jakob Ammann, a Swiss minister then living in a relatively tolerant Alsatian environment, rallied those who believed the church needed to redouble its effort to distinguish itself from the world. Ammann's supporters, eventually known as Amish Mennonites, or simply Amish, emphasized the importance of their baptismal vow and commitment to the church.[7]

An important issue for Ammann and the new Amish church was the exercise of church discipline. If a key Anabaptist concern had been the social dimension of faithfulness and the practical implications of church membership, then it followed, Ammann contended, that leaving the church also had social and practical consequences. Faithful church members needed to avoid social relationships with the willfully unrepentant. This avoidance—known as shunning—extended to matters such as not eating at the same table or entering into a business contract with those who broke their baptismal vows. In claiming that the spiritual ties of the church superseded those of the biological family, shunning applied even to relationships between marriage partners.

The disrupted interpersonal relationships that resulted from shunning reinforced the serious nature of one's commitment to the church and were intended to encourage repentance and restoration. Indeed, readmittance to the church was always possible.[8] Shunning was hardly the center of Amish identity, but it did express a conviction that religion always had concrete social implications. In time, shunning would emerge as a lightning rod in Amish history, attracting crackling attention in the storms of historical change. It also set the Amish apart from their spiritual cousins, the Mennonites.

Both the Amish and the Mennonites began immigrating to North America in the 1700s, drawn particularly to Pennsylvania and the promise of religious tolerance offered by that Quaker colony.[9] Some Amish families may have arrived before 1736, but most entered the port of Philadelphia between that year and the American Revolution. Another wave of Amish immigration crested between 1815 and 1850, taking many newcomers directly to the Midwest. The last European Amish congregation dissolved in 1937, and today the Amish live only in the United States and Canada, with two-thirds in Pennsylvania, Ohio, and Indiana, and the balance in Ontario and twenty-four states from Washington to Delaware and Maine to Texas.[10] As the Amish continue to fan out across the continent, a common memory of martyrdom and separation from the world remain important, but the legacy of a decentralized Anabaptist movement discerning discipleship in local contexts is also a historical taproot nourishing latter-day diversity.

SMALL-SCALE SOCIAL STRUCTURE

Another source of diversity is the social structure of Amish society, with its near absence of formal institutions that could impose uniformity beyond the local level. There are no national or regional offices, synods, conferences, or even written constitutions to ensure the proper function of abstract authority. In their stead are decidedly local sets of reciprocal relationships: church districts, settlements, and affiliations.

Amish church life is organized congregationally, with local churches known as *districts*. Hoping to keep church life focused on people and not property, the Amish do not worship in church buildings but meet in member's homes, rotating the hosting of Sunday services from one household to another. To better facilitate this rotation, church districts are defined geographically. When the membership of a district grows too large to meet comfortably in one place, the district divides—again, along geographic lines.[11] This pattern means that Amish church districts are all roughly the same size—there are no Amish "megachurches"—which helps maintain churchly equilibrium, even in places with large Amish populations. In the sizeable Elkhart-LaGrange Amish community in northern Indiana, for example, districts include on average only 139 people—65 adult members and 74 children and unbaptized teens. In other regions, where the typical house size is a bit larger or smaller, the average number of people per district varies accordingly.

Each district has its own leadership, almost always made up of a bishop, two ministers, and a deacon. The bishop oversees district religious life and guides congregational decision making and discipline in addition to carrying out the ritual responsibilities of preaching, baptizing, and conducting weddings and funerals. Ministers assist the bishop; deacons tend to the physical needs of members, coordinate mutual aid efforts, and also assist with matters of church discipline. Leaders are ordained for life and serve without salary or specialized higher education. A man's commitment to the church and to modeling a disciplined life—not his public speaking ability or individual sense of calling—are his most important credentials.[12] The specific ways in which district leadership and lay members work together to facilitate or forestall change, as well as leaders' interaction with the ministry in other districts, varies from place to place and receives more attention in later chapters.

Each Amish church district meets for worship only every other week, with half the churches meeting on any given Sunday. On the weeks when a given district is not meeting, its members spend the day at home with family or attending church in a neighboring district for which it is the regular Sunday to meet. These patterns of visiting are one of the ways the congregational Amish maintain contacts across a *settlement,* that is, a group of districts in a given geographic area that also share a common history in that place.[13] Some settlements may be large, such as the Elkhart-LaGrange settlement that in 2006 included 123 districts in three contiguous counties. Only the Holmes-Wayne counties, Ohio, settlement (210 districts) and the Lancaster, Pennsylvania, settlement (155 districts) are larger. Other settlements are small and comprise only a single district. Often these smaller settlements are of recent origin, begun by families moving to a new location, and will grow to include more districts or will disband.

While settlements describe spatial relationships among districts, *affiliation* describes their spiritual links. Church districts that recognize one another's discipline as valid constitute an affiliation and are said to be "in fellowship" with one another.[14] Districts of the same affiliation allow ministers to preach in one another's church services.[15] More conservative affiliations may strive for affiliation-wide standards on, say, the use of telephones, while other affiliations allow much more leeway for each district. In any case, an affiliation is hardly a structured organization. Rather, it is the informal but very practical result of local districts finding like-minded relationships within a wider Amish world. Considerable social interaction occurs between Amish of the same affiliation, whether they live in the same settlement or not. The choice of marriage partners is most often bounded by affiliation, for example. An affiliation is different from a settlement. In some cases all the districts in a given settlement also constitute a common affiliation, while in other places a settlement may include multiple affiliations. Nor are affiliations limited to a particular settlement; some affiliations have affiliated districts across a dozen or more settlements.

ORDERING AMISH LIFE

A third source of contemporary cultural diversity comes from the fundamental Amish understanding of social order, or *Ordnung.* A word without an exact English equivalent, *Ordnung* is the accumulated traditional wisdom about the proper ordering of life. Ultimately, Ordnung is rooted in a belief that God created an orderly natural world and that human life is best lived in harmony with that divinely revealed will. Ordnung also includes some practices that simply make for a commonly agreed-upon way of life and meaningful group cohesion and that do not pretend to have specific biblical mandates. Ordnung encompasses general principles, such as assuming a humble demeanor, as well as specific directives, such as the dimensions of a woman's bonnet.

Some prescriptions and prohibitions are common across North America, while other aspects vary considerably from place to place. For example, motor vehicle ownership is forbidden in all districts, but Ordnung surrounding the *use* of cars and trucks is far from uniform, with some progressive districts permitting their leasing and some conservatives restricting even the use of public transit. Meanwhile, Ordnung governing the entirely sanctioned mode of horse-drawn transportation has accumulated its own level of specificity and local conviction. For instance, the Daviess County, Indiana, Ordnung stipulates:

> Buggies can be made with plywood and covered with black vinyl. Doors can be snap or slide, for single seated buggies door on each side and on back, for two seated buggies two sets of doors on side and/or on back, plain rearview mirror for safety, head lights and tail lights on one or both sides. Triangle and reflector tape, not for luxury, but for safety. On [buggy] tops already made, all window frames must be painted black, lining must be black. All colored lining must be changed. Front window approximately width of top except for frame, side and rear window large enough for getting clear view of traffic, would encourage to build tops full length of box, especially new tops. Tape players, radios, CB's, etc. must be removed. No tinted windows.[16]

Although this set of Daviess County directives appeared in print, Ordnung rarely takes such written form. It is not a code that is taught so much as a rhythm of life that is caught. In fact, mothers and fathers are more important than bishops and ministers in its transmission, since children acquire an understanding of Ordnung in the process of growing up in an Amish home. Almost every aspect of life is governed in some way by Ordnung, and while the Amish know what its guidelines are, most would be hard-pressed to recite a detailed litany of Ordnung do's and don'ts. Ordnung is rarely ambiguous, but it is often intuitively grasped and understood. Ordnung is a way of life and a way of going about life.

Ordnung plays several roles in Amish self-understanding. On one level it is what sets their life apart, in practical ways, from "the world." It dictates everyday symbolic separators, such as driving a buggy when the rest of the world whizzes by in cars, trucks, and SUVs. It regulates in explicit ways the nature of interaction with the world, such as prohibiting college attendance or, in some communities, limiting the ability of fathers to take employment away from home. On another level, Ordnung locates Amish people in relation to other Amish. Even small differences in Ordnung concerning the size and shape of men's hats, for example, identify Amish groups as more or less traditional.

Ordnung changes slowly and often deliberately, sometimes after discernment within the church and sometimes as the result of coercive outside state or market

TABLE I.I
Relationship of Amish social structures and Ordnung

Church District	Defined geographically, often 1 square mile or less; typically thirty households, or approx. 150 people.	All members of a district conform to the district's Ordnung on all matters.
Settlement	Church districts in a geographic area that also share a common history in that place; settlements often cross county borders. A settlement may consist of a single district, and large settlements may have more than 100 districts.	Districts in a settlement might or might not share a common Ordnung. Often symbolic separators (e.g., buggy styles or clothing patterns) are the same, but the appropriation of technology or the practice of discipline is not.
Affiliation	Church districts that recognize one another's discipline. A settlement may include more than one affiliation; affiliations may exist across many settlements.	Districts in an affiliation share common Ordnung on ritual matters (e.g., prerequisites for baptism, implications for church discipline) but not necessarily on other matters.

forces. Most often the decision for or against change is lodged in local districts. District leaders, and especially bishops, play a major role in maintaining consensus and dealing with dissent. Cooperation in conforming to the Ordnung is a district matter, and all members are expected to be in agreement. To repeatedly flout communal understandings and place one's own wishes above the authority of the Ordnung is to exhibit arrogant self-centeredness and risk excommunication.

While Ordnung is determined at the district level and finds unified expression there, it is not necessarily shared across a settlement (see table 1.1). A few elements may be common settlement-wide, such as the Ordnung governing the style of buggies, but many other aspects of Ordnung vary from district to district within a settlement. Bicycles, for example, are permitted within the Ordnung of most districts in larger settlements, but not in all. Depending on the settlement, the same may be true regarding the use of bottled gas to fuel kitchen appliances or the acceptability of subscribing to secular newspapers.

Church districts within a given affiliation often share a similar Ordnung, but it is just as likely that they will also have some minor or even major differences in the way they order their lives. Instead of hinging on matters of technology or dress, affiliation revolves around observing the same Ordnung governing church rituals, such as the requirements for baptism or the implications of church discipline. Districts with relatively progressive appropriations of shop equipment—hydraulic power sources, for instance—may be in fellowship with Amish groups whose stance on technology is considerably more restrictive *if* they share a similar Ordnung re-

Illustration 1.3. Ordnung in more progressive church districts permit bicycles. Source: Courtesy of the Mennonite Historical Library/Joel Fath.

garding the administration of church discipline. Conversely, a shared outlook on mechanical innovation is not enough to ensure affiliation if the districts disagree on the details of church rituals.

In practice, Ordnung reinforces the small-scale structures of Amish society. Horse-and-buggy transportation minimizes distant travel, for example. While moderns celebrate technological advances that allow individuals more choices and increased control over their environment, Amish culture self-consciously avoids such possibilities and keeps many aspects of consumer gadgetry off-limits or at arm's length. From banning in-home telephones to prohibiting air-conditioning, the Amish have traditionally rejected the modern promise of achieving the sensation of individual control over one's surroundings. In many Amish communities certain power tools and other appliances that undercut the need for cooperative tasks are permitted only when their use is mediated through some sort of personal relationship. Renting space in a non-Amish neighbor's freezer or using a power saw at the job site of a non-Amish customer, for example, places a check on unbridled autonomy, since the Amish person is always bound, even in a small way, to the will and wishes of another in the process of accessing the technology. Self-taught Amish entrepreneurs may develop sizable businesses through attention to quality and customer satisfaction, but only rarely will they grow them larger than a dozen employees, intentionally staying small and even downsizing or choosing to reject new business to avoid being ruined by "bigness."[17] Yet while such limitations bolster a small-scale social structure, that structure, in turn, encourages the adoption, application, and negotiation of Ordnung in diverse ways.

IDENTITIES IN CONTEXT

Cultural identity is not an inherited disposition or essential set of sensibilities transmitted through time. Rather, the learned patterns of behaviors, mental habits, and folkways that comprise culture evolve and change, emerging from the interplay of specific social-historical factors.[18] Identity is relational and grows out of interaction between group members and outsiders in ways that mark boundaries while also recognizing those boundaries as porous and dynamic. Amish identity, in turn, is shaped by particular migration memories, churchly alignments, and ethnic cultures, all of which, in turn, are embedded in contexts marked by local politics, regional economies, and non-Amish neighbors.

Amish willingness or reluctance to work in industry illustrates these dynamics, which are shaped by both internal attention to Ordnung and external realities of labor markets. In churches with a more conservative Ordnung, working away from home in a factory is simply off-limits. Yet more progressive districts' openness to such jobs does not necessarily translate into industrial employment, since Ordnung also forbids membership in labor unions, which the Amish view as a coercive force for selfish gain. Thus, although factory jobs are plentiful around the Kokomo, Indiana, Amish settlement, the firms are unionized and have no Amish employees, even though the Old Orders there are not, in principle, opposed to factory work. In contrast, industry near Nappanee, in the northern edge of the same state is made up of open shops and has a heavy Amish employee base. Amish economic possibilities and employment profiles in these similarly progressive settlements are starkly different as a result of the interplay of Ordnung and local economic structures. Those opportunities and choices, in turn, help shape public perceptions of the Amish as either aloof or more socially integrated—coloring the context in which the *next* act of cultural identification will take place.

In this way, local contexts texture relations with outsiders and then affect the Amish community itself. In Allen County, Indiana, near Fort Wayne, the political weight of the area's influential Catholic and Lutheran parochial schools resulted in public bussing for school children enrolled in private schools. The Amish have been among those who benefited from the agreement, and their children are now bussed to what amount to modestly consolidated Amish schools. Four- or five-room buildings have multiple staff, with one teacher even designated as principal. In other places the Amish interest in private schools has expressed itself in the construction of small one- or two-room buildings within walking distance of students' homes. Conditions in Allen County produced a different outcome that in turn shapes the Amish private school experience there.

Recognizing the importance of local and regional context in shaping the Amish responses to the world—and even some aspects of Amish society and culture themselves—underscores the fact that Amish people are not isolated from surrounding society. Separation from the world is an important Amish value and social reality, but separation does not require withdrawal. The Amish cannot be understood simply in terms of their internal group values, for the expression of those values is very often shaped by a historically conditioned interaction between Amish culture and its social environment. Not only have local contexts shaped Amish economics, with implications for family life and notions of personal status, but even the tools of cultural separation and identity, such as Amish schools, have been shaped by non-Amish influences.

This book uses a four-part model, illustrated in figure 1.1, for moving toward an understanding of Amish identity. Three factors, largely internal to Amish culture, overlap in various combinations. The first is *migration history,* with its links to settlement development and the memory of non-Amish neighborly interaction. Understandings of *Ordnung,* cultural change, and affiliation form a second key cluster. The implications of *ethnicity* in the American environment has been a third component in the emergence of diverse Amish communities. All three elements intersect, yielding to one another in different times and places. Moreover, they interact with *contextual factors,* including local or regional demography, economy, geography, and civic life.

INDIANA AMISH WORLDS

The study that follows begins by examining the three internal factors and exploring how each unites and divides contemporary Amish life. Four community case studies then explore the interplay of these elements in specific local contexts that include differing landscapes, labor markets, tourist attractions, non-Amish neighbors and public officials, and other elements. Since the interaction of these elements in complex ways has been present to an unusual degree among the Amish

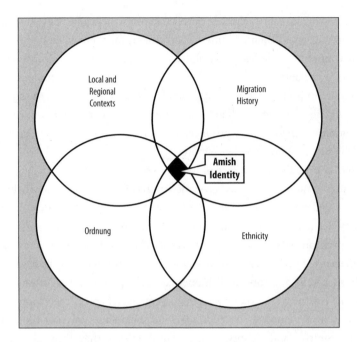

Figure 1.1. The Composition of Amish Identity

of Indiana, the Hoosier Amish world serves as a lens through which this study gains comparative clarity, even as it sketches the contours of Amish cultural identity across America.

With just over six million residents, Indiana ranks fourteenth in size among the fifty states, but it is home to the third-largest Amish population in the nation, following Ohio and Pennsylvania. In 2006 Indiana's 267 church districts included 37,000 people, with 40–45 percent of them baptized adult members. Today there are twenty Amish settlements in Indiana, several of which are more than 150 years old (see table 1.2). Yet nine of the settlements have begun since 1981, and in recent decades Indiana has drawn Amish settlers from Pennsylvania, New York, Ohio, and elsewhere. While Indiana's slower pace of population growth relative to the rest of the nation may be a bane to pro-growth Indianapolis officials, for the rural-minded Amish the lower population pressures and less expensive land are welcome.[19]

Amish settlements are spread around the state, but their weight is not evenly distributed. The two north central settlements, known as Nappanee and Elkhart-LaGrange, include 58 percent of the church districts. The northeastern settlements

TABLE I.2
Old Order Amish settlements in Indiana, 2006

Settlement and location	Origin	Size in 2006[a]
1. Berne (Adams-Jay-Wells Counties)	1840	40
2. Elkhart-LaGrange (Elkhart-LaGrange-Noble Counties)	1841	123
3. Nappanee (Marshall-Kosciusko-Elkhart-St. Joseph Counties)	1842	33
4. Allen County	1844	17
5. Kokomo (Howard-Miami Counties)	1848	2
6. Daviess-Martin Counties	1868	22
7. Paoli (Orange County)	1957	2
8. Steuben County, IN—Williams County, OH	1964	2
9. Milroy (Rush-Decatur Counties)	1970	4
10. South Whitley (Whitley-Wabash Counties)	1971	1
11. Salem (Washington County)	1972	1
12. Salem (Washington County)	1981	2
13. Vevay (Switzerland-Jefferson Counties)	1986	2
14. Parke County	1991	5
15. Worthington (Owen-Greene Counties)	1992	2
16. Wayne-Randolph-Henry Counties	1994	4
17. Paoli (Orange-Lawrence Counties)	1994	2
18. Rochester (Fulton-Miami Counties)	1996	1
19. Vallonia (Washington-Jackson Counties)	1996	1
20. Vevay (Switzerland County)	2003	1

SOURCE: Origin dates from interviews and archival work; size in 2006 from Stephen E. Scott, Young Center for Anabaptist and Pietist Studies; *The Diary;* and Raber's *Almanac.*
   [a]Number of church districts.

in Allen County and in Adams County comprise another 21 percent. Many of the remaining sixteen settlements—including most of the newly established ones—are located in the state's less-populated southern tiers. Indiana's economy is weighted toward manufacturing and agriculture, with service and high-tech sectors relatively less developed. This general profile matches Amish interests and employment credentials. Although there were some conflicts between the Amish and state officials over issues of compulsory secondary schooling, beginning in LaGrange County in the 1920s and peaking in Jay and Allen Counties in the 1940s-1960s, public officials and the church have arranged amiable relationships, which have generally come to characterize Amish interaction with government.

If none of these particular elements are unique to Indiana, their combination—in conjunction with the unusual composition of the state's Amish population—make it arguably the most varied and diverse slice of the Amish world. Demographically, Indiana is home not only to descendants of Amish immigrants who came to North America in the 1700s but also to the largest concentration of the so-called "Swiss Amish," who arrived in North America a hundred years later. Nearly a third of Hoosier Amish stem from this second, nineteenth-century cohort, a

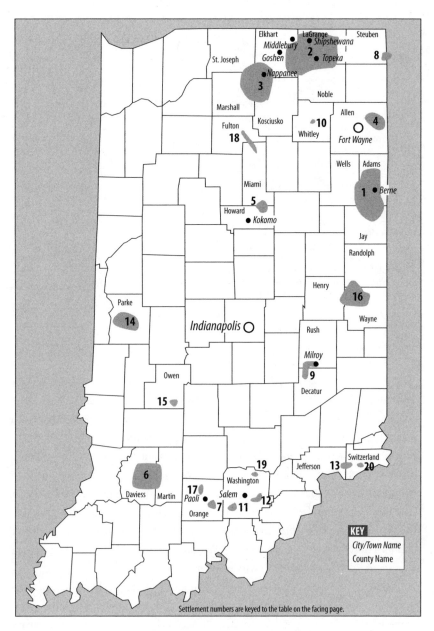

Settlement numbers are keyed to the table on the facing page.

Map 1.1. Old Order Amish Settlements

ratio exceeding that in any other Amish-populated state. These two immigrant streams also represent two different Amish ethnicities, with different folkways and even decidedly different German dialects.

Indiana is also home to a variety of affiliations and a wide range of Ordnung expressions, from ultra-conservative Swartzentruber Amish, to several mainline Old Order groups, to two so-called New Order Amish settlements, whose horse-and-buggy-driving members have combined theological innovation with a more open stance toward technological change. The arrival in the 1990s of transplanted Lancaster, Pennsylvania, families added another piece to the state's Amish mosaic. Part of the larger Lancaster-based affiliation, these newcomers are distinct in appearance, tradition, and Ordnung.

Although the Lancaster Amish moved to Indiana in search of less-crowded spaces—and found them in sparsely populated parts of the state—other Hoosier Amish live in the midst of growing urbanization. This is true in places such as the Elkhart-LaGrange settlement in the north central region, as well as in Allen County, where the Amish live on the edge of Fort Wayne's quarter-million residents. Indeed, the Allen County Amish exist in closer proximity to a major metropolitan area than does any other settlement in the United States.[20]

Occupations also run a wide gamut in Indiana. Nearly everywhere farming as the primary means of earning a living is on the decline. In place of tilling the land, three alternatives have emerged among Amish Hoosiers. In north central Indiana, employment in industry is the most common occupation, with 59 percent of Nappanee settlement working-age men in factories, and nearly that many in the nearby Elkhart-LaGrange community. In contrast, work in mobile construction crews is the norm for Amishmen in places such as Allen and Adams counties or in Milroy, southeast of Indianapolis. Meanwhile, small businesses and at-home shops, engaged in everything from producing hardwood furniture to selling fabrics, flourish in most of the smaller southern settlements and in communities composed of recent arrivals from other states. That each of these alternatives to agriculture carries its own set of challenges to Amish life and social position becomes especially clear when viewed comparatively.

The complex picture of Amish diversity that emerges from a comparison of life in these places opens the possibility of assessing the meaning of that variety, asking how the Amish situate themselves in relation to it and how cultural identity is composed and sustained. The two final chapters of this book explore the nature of that diversity, sketching its contours and exploring the commonality that emerges in the midst of difference. Having documented diversity, we ask: What holds these people together? What allows them to draw sharp boundaries among themselves and still recognize one another as Amish? What undergirds community for a decentralized and dissenting people in the midst of the modern world? The clues lie in the cultural conversations that produced the diversity itself and hold implications for understanding identity and community for many people, well beyond "Amish country."

PART ONE

Patterns of Peoplehood

CHAPTER TWO

Migration

The Amish are a people of history. One of the remarkable characteristics of Amish society is its refusal to play by the rules of progress, to accept as inevitable the modern conviction that *new* and *improved* are synonyms, or to believe that change always carries the seeds of success. While the Amish are neither principled reactionaries nor fossilized fragments of a lost world, they do defer to the wisdom of the past in notable ways.

Unlike the dominant culture that invests power in the promises of a technology-filled tomorrow, the Amish grant authority to tradition. While moderns "face the future" and eagerly "look ahead," the Amish are as likely to use aphorisms that cast a backward glance. "The church that remembers its past has a future," proclaims the cover of the 2002 *Indiana Amish Directory*. While mainstream Americans try to "get ahead" in life, the Amish express concern about "running ahead" and shrink from "a faster way of life" that leaves the familiar behind. They are more apt to employ metaphors of stability than innovation, of roots than quick growth.

For the Amish the authority of tradition is external to the individual and is best interpreted by the community. Through Reformation-era hymns and sermons filled with allusions to past events, Amish religious ritual is drenched in self-consciously historical references. The slowly evolving Ordnung finds relevance in the experience of "our forefathers" as much as in contemporary contexts.

This is not to say that the Amish are scholars of history in the academic sense; in fact, few are versed in the details of world history. Even the specifics of Jakob Amman's life and his debate with other Anabaptists in 1693 are not common knowledge in Amish circles.[1] Nor do many Amish schools teach their own church's history in any systematic way. Yet the presence of the past and the way it informs Amish life percolate through the culture. If all societies are shaped to some degree by history, the Amish are often more conscious and welcoming of that influence. Anabaptist history is a key element of their identity, shaping the church's understanding of being a set-apart people and confirming their notion that faithfulness does not produce popularity or social acceptance.

But the sixteenth century is not the only source of history that bears on Amish sensibilities. Today's Amish communities are products of specific North American histories and local historical contexts. Patterns of migration and interactions with neighbors have shaped settlement memories and help determine what it means to be Amish in a particular place. One way to make sense of diversity in contemporary Amish life is to uncover these multiple memories and dynamic histories.

FOUR SOURCES OF MIGRATION

The twenty Amish settlements that mark the twenty-first-century Indiana Amish landscape are the product of four distinct migration streams. First, during the 1840s Amish families whose ancestors had come to North America in the 1700s began moving to Indiana from the eastern United States. At about the same time, a second immigrant cohort started arriving in the American Midwest directly from Europe. Members of both groups formed communities that have persisted to the present. These original nineteenth-century Hoosier settlements, in turn, have spawned new "offshoot" or "daughter" communities (to use Amish descriptive terminology) in other parts of the state, providing a third source of new settlements. Finally, in very recent decades, Amish households facing rising land prices and demographic pressures in Pennsylvania, Ohio, New York, and elsewhere have relocated to Indiana, adding new layers to Indiana's Amish diversity. Settlement genesis is a significant factor in sorting out how communities understand themselves and relate to one another as well as to their non-Amish neighbors and to civic institutions such as public schools.

NINETEENTH-CENTURY NEWCOMERS

The Amish were not among the first white settlers to people Indiana. By the time they arrived in the 1840s, the state had largely passed through its "frontier" era; white settlers were by then leaving Indiana to move further westward.[2] In fact, many early Hoosier Amish bought land from prior deed-holders—residents or absentee speculators—in addition to the government, even though the Amish were

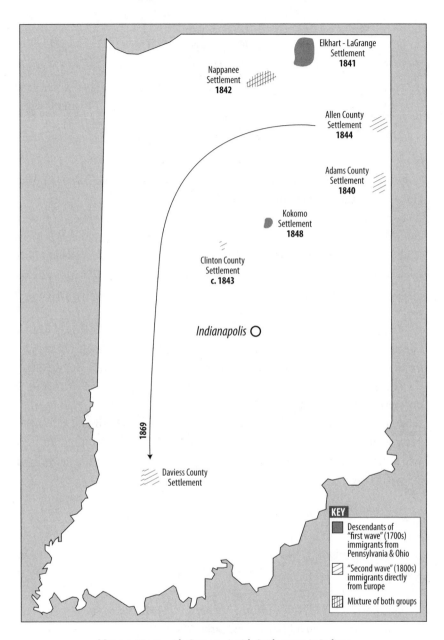

Elkhart - LaGrange
Settlement
1841

Nappanee
Settlement
1842

Allen County
Settlement
1844

Adams County
Settlement
1840

Kokomo
Settlement
1848

Clinton County
Settlement
c. 1843

Indianapolis ○

1869

Daviess County
Settlement

KEY

Descendants of
"first wave" (1700s)
immigrants from
Pennsylvania & Ohio

"Second wave" (1800s)
immigrants directly
from Europe

Mixture of both groups

Map 2.1. Nineteenth-Century Amish Settlements in Indiana

TABLE 2.1
Early Indiana settlements (1840–1848)

18th-century European immigrants to Pennsylvania	19th-century European immigrants directly to the Midwest	Mixture of both streams
Elkhart-LaGrange, 1841	Adams County, 1840	Nappanee, 1842
Kokomo, 1848	Allen County, 1844	
	Clinton County, c. 1843	

moving into northern and northeastern parts of the state that were less populated at that time than its southern tier.

Initial Amish settlements in Indiana all began in the 1840s (see table 2.1). In some cases, organized religious life and regular church meetings lagged behind the arrival of the earliest households by a few years, but between 1840 and 1848, families established what would become the Adams County, Allen County, Elkhart-LaGrange, Nappanee, and Kokomo settlements.[3] In about 1843, a small Amish group also established itself in Clinton County, though this settlement did not endure.

These first settlements were far from static, and the ongoing arrival of families bolstered the communities' growth and evolution. The Allen County settlement, for example, remained small until the coming of a group of twelve households in the spring of 1853. Nevertheless, the 1840s germination of six settlements in the northern half of the state illustrates the way in which Amish migration was not random. It followed established patterns that directed Amish and non-Amish newcomers alike to available acres. Nevertheless, these first communities had two distinctly different origins: heirs of "first-wave" immigrants from the 1770s, and "second-wave" settlers direct from Europe.[4]

Heirs of First-Wave (1700s) Immigrants Moving West

One stream of early Amish arrivals were descendants of the first wave of transatlantic Amish immigration in the 1730s to 1770s, families who had been in North America for generations. The ancestors of these Indiana settlers had arrived through the port of Philadelphia and established themselves in southern and central Pennsylvania, including Lancaster, Berks, Mifflin, and Somerset counties. Here they often lived as part of a larger German-speaking immigrant population, often with Mennonite neighbors, and forged ties of common community interest that in some cases led them to participate in local government and eventually in public school creation.

By the early 1800s, some of these Pennsylvania Amish—especially those in the

Somerset County area—also shared their neighbors' interest in western migration, and after 1809 they began moving into eastern Ohio. By 1840 some Somerset residents were looking beyond Ohio. That year four men left southwestern Pennsylvania to scout for land in Iowa, but on the way home, they stopped in northern Indiana and visited Elkhart County. "After inspecting this country which suited them very well," one of the men's sons later recounted, "they agreed to make this region the future home for their church." When those in Pennsylvania "heard the good news from the land seekers, that they had seen . . . a good and flourishing region and well-contented settlers, many of them became interested in emigrating westward."[5]

The next year four households bearing the surnames Miller and Borntrager took up farms east of the town of Goshen: two in Elkhart County and two in LaGrange County. Their cross-country journey to Indiana had included a one-week stopover in the young Holmes County, Ohio, Amish settlement, and that fall five families from that community moved to northern Indiana as well. The fledgling Elkhart-LaGrange group included two ministers and a deacon, and the families gathered for a first church service in a home in LaGrange County in the fall of 1841. Beginning on Easter Sunday 1842, they began meeting biweekly for worship.[6] The settlement continued to grow as an additional nineteen households, including several older couples and a widow, followed from western Pennsylvania and eastern Ohio. But whatever their immediate past home, they all hailed from colonial-era, first-wave immigrant stock.

A similar path of westward migration took other heirs of eighteenth-century Amish immigrants from Pennsylvania to Miami County, Indiana. In the early 1840s, several households bought land in the northern part of that county, but they never formed a stable church. In 1848, however, Pennsylvania-rooted Amish families bearing the names Hostetler, Gerber, and Stineman moved from eastern Ohio to southern Miami County, north and east of where the city of Kokomo would later emerge. Some twenty additional households arrived during the next few years from Holmes and Tuscarawas counties in Ohio, expanding the settlement south into Howard County. In the spring of 1851, what would come to be called the Kokomo settlement ordained two resident ministers.[7]

Second-Wave Immigrants (1800s) Directly to the Midwest

By the time first-wave immigrants had made their way through Pennsylvania and Ohio to Indiana in the 1840s, a distinctly different course of transatlantic immigration had begun channeling European Amish directly to the American Midwest. In the wake of the Napoleonic wars and the institution of military conscription in much of Western Europe, a growing number of European Amish were considering North America.

A second Amish immigration wave crested between 1817 and 1860 and took its participants to a different America than that which had greeted colonial arrivals a century earlier. For one thing, many of these new arrivals now bypassed Pennsylvania and landed in the bustling ports of New York, Baltimore, or New Orleans and then headed for land offices in Ohio, Indiana, Illinois, or Iowa. Some who sailed to New York, for example, traveled by way of the Erie Canal and Lake Erie transport boats to northeastern Ohio. Some remained in Ohio's Stark, Wayne, or Butler counties; but for other newcomers, an Ohio sojourn of a few months or a few years was only the staging ground for a journey further west. A subsequent trek to Indiana, for example, might be an overland trip or a combination of road and water. The new Wabash and Erie Canal connected Toledo, Ohio, and the rapidly growing town of Fort Wayne, Indiana, and some Amish immigrants made use of this new conveyance. Indeed, some of the new 1800s immigrants skipped eastern Ohio entirely and headed directly across Lake Erie from Buffalo for Toledo and the canal. Even for those uninterested in living around Fort Wayne, the government land office there meant that some people destined for Indiana had to visit there sometime, either at the point of migration or as part of a preliminary trip to explore settlement options.

The two primary Indiana destinations of these second-wave newcomers were Adams and Allen Counties in the northeast part of the state.[8] Christian Schwartzentruber, a single man who moved by 1840 from Ohio to Adams County was likely the first Amish person in the area, but he was soon joined by others, such as the family of Jacob and Katharina (Wenger) Liechti. An immigrant of 1832, Liechti had purchased Adams County acreage in 1837, but moved there only in 1841. European arrivals John and Elisabeth (Schwartz) Richer had also purchased land in Adams County in 1837, but did not settle on it until 1843.[9] Richer was a minister, ordained in France by Amish elder Peter Graber, who gave Richer a sixteenth-century Bible to take to America. Other immigrants whose surnames would become prominent in the settlement soon followed, including John and Barbara Eicher about 1844, and Johannes Schwartz in 1853.[10]

To the north, in Allen County, Amish settlement began about 1844 with the arrival of Peter and Anna (Sauder) Witmer. Though a few households joined them, apparently a fully functioning church did not develop until 1852. The next year, the community achieved a more secure footing with the arrival of twelve immigrant

Illustration 2.1. The Allen County Amish are heirs of nineteenth-century immigrants. Amish in most settlements stemming from second-wave arrivals drive only unenclosed buggies. Source: Courtesy of Thomas J. Meyers.

families originally from the French Amish enclave around Montbéliard. Their journey had taken them first to Canton, Ohio, and then to northeast Indiana. The Allen County Amish clustered around what would later be the towns of Grabill, Leo, Harlan, and Woodburn, and attracted additional Amish in the years that followed.[11]

Immigrant Interaction

The two immigration streams brought to Indiana both Amish who were fresh from Europe and adjusting to life in North America, and those whose ancestors' arrival had pre-dated the independence of the United States. Given these two distinct histories, it is perhaps not surprising that in many ways the ties of family and kinship forged through the process of migration were more prominent than any shared sense of religious affinity between the two groups. Choices regarding moving and securing land, for example, were often dominated by advice and aid from family and acquaintances from the same immigrant cohort. Settling in distinct geographic lo-cales was both a product of these differing migration experiences and a character-istic that reinforced the differences between them.[12]

Even churchly discussion and debate could end up channeled in ways that had as much to do with migration networks as with the theological issues involved. For example, in the 1850s and 1860s the Apostolic Christian Church—a Swiss-originated restorationist movement—drew converts from a variety of North American Amish communities, but all of these were of nineteenth-century immigrant stock. Stories of conversion and condemnation, while expressed in Amish religious rhetoric, passed among relatives and immigrant acquaintances in a particular circle of Amish settlements.[13] Likewise, the message of the revivalist-inclined immigrant Amish minister Henry Egly (1824–1890), who in 1850 had moved from Butler County, Ohio, to Adams County, Indiana, drew his following from family networks that kept the debate centered in settlements composed of more recently arrived Europeans. Egly organized supporters in Adams and Allen counties in 1866, as well as in related communities in other states.[14] The entire Clinton County, Indiana, settlement of nineteenth-century newcomers adopted Egly's approach.[15]

Occasionally, Amish from both waves of immigration populated the same space. The settlement spanning southwestern Elkhart County and northeastern Marshall counties—later dubbed the Nappanee settlement—was one such place and illus-trates the complex interplay of immigration, migration, and family networks in Amish history. In the 1830s, several formerly Amish families named Mishler moved to the future Nappanee area from Canada. Descendants of first-wave immigrants, the Mishlers had left Somerset County, Pennsylvania, and gone to Ontario, where they dropped their Amish religious affiliation but apparently kept up personal ties with Amish relatives in Pennsylvania and Ohio.[16] Then, in 1842, an extended fam-ily of recently arrived European Amish immigrants bearing the surname Stahly ar-rived in the Mishlers' Indiana neighborhood. Now there were two Amish-linked family groups in the area: a Stahly clan of recent, second-wave Amish immigrants, and the formerly Amish Mishlers, who represented first-wave Pennsylvania stock.

Soon, more Amish descended from first-wave immigrants—Yoder, Hostetler, and Miller households from Ohio—arrived on the scene. Kinship ties linked them to the Mishlers and had drawn them to the area; yet when it came to church affili-ation, they joined the second-wave immigrant Stahlys in Amish worship. Then more second-wave European Amish arrivals—the Ringenbergs and the Berlin-courts—showed up, as did more heirs of first-wave families making their way west from Ohio and linked to local family systems.

Over time, the evolving Nappanee settlement drew more first-wave than second-

wave families, but its origins clearly lay in a mixture of both streams—a cir-
cumstance that helped ensure that its identity would be distinct from that of the
nearby Elkhart-LaGrange settlement. Elkhart-LaGrange—although located just a
few miles to the east—was wholly made up of first-wave, eighteenth-century-era
immigrant stock, giving it, from the start, a history and composition different from
Nappanee's mixed heritage.

SPAWNING NEW SETTLEMENTS

The establishment of permanent Amish communities hardly ended the saga of
Amish movement. In fact, a story of static Amish settlement would be more exceptional than typical. The North American Amish population has remained in mo-
tion, in search of land, economic opportunity, a different church community, or simply from wanderlust and a craving for adventure. In some cases individuals or
families have come full circle, moving away from a location only to return there
again after sojourns in one or more places in between. Well-known bishop and mid-
twentieth-century leader Eli J. Bontrager (1868–1958) is one example. Reared in La-
Grange County, Bontrager and his wife Mattie Miller moved in 1895 to North
Dakota, where a number of Indiana Amish families had begun a new farming community in Rolette and Pierce counties. Fifteen years later, the Bontragers left North
Dakota for Exeland, Wisconsin, where they remained until 1916. That year they
moved back to Indiana, where Eli took over his father's farm.[17]

The communities in which the Bontragers lived in North Dakota and Wisconsin no longer exist as Amish settlements. The process of migration was never free
of risk, and many Amish communities failed. A few failed to remain Amish, or their
members drifted into Mennonite affiliation. Some broke up as a result of internal
church disagreements. But most succumbed to simple but stark realities: bad
weather, poor soil, limited access to markets, or wider patterns of falling prices and
rising costs that made marginally productive regions untenable. The Amish communities never strove for economic self-sufficiency, and they were always tied to
wider economic forces.[18]

If the rise and fall of Amish settlements was part of a much broader pattern of
rural life experienced by other hopeful homesteaders, a notable feature of Amish
migration was its corporate nature. Amish settlement efforts combined at least several families in an area's fortunes. To be sure, each household had its own land and
was financially responsible for itself; the Amish did not live in communes or maintain a "common purse." But the collective nature of Amish migration and a commitment to mutual aid meant that some of the weight was shared. Even in recent

years, Amish settlement efforts are the result of group decisions on the part of at least several households, and even if one family moves alone, it is with the hope that others will follow. Settlements of single families do not exist—or do not exist for long.

Some Amish observers use the label "daughter settlement" to refer to communities begun with the blessing of the community from which the pioneers left. While Amish church districts as such do not organize or promote particular new settlements, they can offer a sort of endorsement by supplying church leadership until resident leaders are ordained. Such spiritual links suggests a special relationship between old and new communities. Typically, a daughter settlement will defer to the home community's Ordnung and live within its understandings or deviate only with permission from the parent settlement. Daughter settlements in this sense are fairly rare, largely because the congregational nature of the Amish church makes settlement-wide discussion and endorsement of a new community difficult, even if everyone thinks it is a good idea and no one opposes the effort. The two recent settlements of Lancaster, Pennsylvania, Amish—those of Indiana's Parke and Wayne counties, established in 1991 and 1994—might be termed daughter settlements because of their especially close connection to their Lancaster parent.[19]

Most other new settlements fall into a category often tagged "offshoot settlements," meaning that they are clearly outgrowths of particular communities and may even be connected through frequent visits and personal interchange, but they are not viewed as extensions of the original settlement itself. The Vallonia settlement established in southern Indiana in 1996 by Elkhart-LaGrange members is an offshoot of that longstanding Amish community. Much of the Vallonia Ordnung is patterned after the latter's, and until Vallonia had resident ministers, its young people boarded with relatives in the north to attend catechism and be baptized by Elkhart-LaGrange bishops. Still, no one thought of the Vallonia settlement as having been started by the Elkhart-LaGrange settlement. Instead, Vallonia was begun by individual households who shared a common interest in a more rural way of life than was possible in the suburbanizing north.

Finally, some new settlements involve families coming from several different parent settlements (table 2.2). However, in such situations all the newcomers typically are members of the same affiliation. For example, beginning in 2003, households from the Elkhart-LaGrange and Milroy settlements, as well as settlements in Somerset County, Pennsylvania; Dover, Delaware; Wayne County, Ohio; Glasgow, Kentucky; and Rexford, Montana, began a new settlement near Vevay, Indiana, close to but distinct from an already existing Vevay Amish community.

Illustration 2.2. Many members of the Vallonia settlement, begun in 1996, live in new log homes in the wooded hollows of this very rural part of southern Indiana. Source: Courtesy of Thomas J. Meyers.

TABLE 2.2
Later Indiana settlements (1869–2003)

"Offshoots" of established Indiana settlements
  Daviess County (1869) from Allen County
  South Whitley (1971) from Allen County
  Salem-Swiss (1981) from Adams County
  Steuben County (1964) from Adams and Allen Counties
  Vevay-Swiss (1986) from Salem-Swiss settlement
  Rochester (1996) initially from Nappanee settlement
  Vallonia (1996) from Elkhart-LaGrange settlement

Arrivals from other states
  Parke County (1991) from Pennsylvania
  Worthington (1992) from Ohio
  Wayne County (1994) from Pennsylvania
  Paoli-Swartzentruber (1994) from New York and Ohio

Multi-state, multi-settlement roots
  Paoli (1957)
  Milroy (1970)
  Salem (1972)
  Vevay (2003)

MIGRATION MOTIVATIONS

The motivations behind launching a new community are often mixed. Traditionally, the desire for more land has ranked high on the list. From Allen County families who moved to Daviess County in 1869 to Nappanee households who moved south to Rochester in 1996, the desire for available and affordable land has been key. A related goal is what one informant termed "elbow room," a desire for more space and a more rural location.

Not all of those drawn to the possibility of available land are looking to farm. In fact, a number of new rural settlements have sprung up in areas not particularly well suited to agriculture. The Amish living in the hilly and wooded Worthington or Vevay communities, for example, are mostly engaged in lumber, woodcraft, and carpentry trades. Few of them farm, and indeed, few ever tried to farm. When these Amish talk about the land prices and population pressures they fled in other parts of Indiana or Ohio, they paint a picture of vanishing rural landscapes, but not necessarily an agricultural future. To be sure, such settlers buy multiple acres and establish horse pastures, and their homes are often secluded down long lanes. But few actually till the soil for a living, and few ever intended to do so. Several new settlements were begun by people hoping to farm, including those of Rochester and Steuben, Parke, and Wayne counties, though the number of nonfarm jobs is rising in all of these settlements. Nevertheless, residents believe they have succeeded in their search for land.

Family connections and commitments serve as another motivation for movement. Several offshoot settlements have begun as the brainchild of a particular person who has rallied relatives to join the project. Sometimes the settlement remains dominated by a particular clan for some time, while in other cases only the initial group was family-focused. The South Whitley settlement, begun in 1971 by Allen County Amish, attracted a heavy contingent of Schwartz kin. As late as 2000, twenty-five of the settlement's thirty-seven households were adult children or grandchildren of the founding family.[20] Two Miller households—parents and their married son—from Nappanee launched the Rochester community in 1996, which within five years had grown to twenty-five households. While the Millers did not dominate the demography there, kin connections were not unrelated to settlers' migration decisions. In 2001 all but one household included an adult related as a sibling, parent, or child to another adult in the settlement. Thirty-six of the forty-nine adults in the community had an immediate family member living there.[21]

A third factor motivating Amish migration has been searching for church affiliation of a particular sort or avoiding church controversy elsewhere. Beginning in 1957, for example, self-consciously conservative Amish from a number of states, but including some from Indiana's Elkhart-LaGrange settlement, moved to Paoli, Indiana, to create a community committed to an especially traditional Ordnung. The remote and sparsely populated location dampened economic opportunity, the accumulation of wealth, and easy access to consumer goods and commercial influences. The 1970 origins of the Milroy, Indiana, settlement reflect somewhat similar dynamics. Families from Missouri, Wisconsin, and Ohio who all shared a sense of unease with the pace of change in their respective districts moved to Milroy to form a more tradition-minded church, though the stress of forging unity among people of different backgrounds and expectations led some of the original families to leave, and Milroy has since taken on a much more progressive cast.

Often migration motives include a mix of factors. For example, the Daviess County settlement in southwestern Indiana that began in 1869 and 1870 drew families from Allen County, Indiana, as well as from Ohio, Ontario, and Missouri.[22] The quest for land was a clearly stated goal of the migrating households, to be sure, but family ties and desires to live together also played roles in the settlement's genesis. The nineteen Allen County households were almost all close Graber family relatives. But here too, churchly issues were at play. Bishop Peter Graber (1811–96) remained in Allen County, while his brothers, John (1816–77) and Jacob (1821–1904), and their children formed the Daviess settlement. All three brothers were ordained church leaders, and family lore has suggested they parted ways over disagreements involving discipline.

CONTINUING ATTRACTION TO INDIANA

While migration continues in the twenty-first century, sending Hoosier natives from one settlement to another, recent decades have also seen the birth of a new set of settlements begun by Amish arriving from other states. Again, the motivation that spurs families to leave their old homes is typically the desire for land—or the possibility of affordable land for the next generation—coupled with the ties of kinship. Settlements peopled by households from Pennsylvania, Ohio, and New York all began in the 1990s.

Population pressures and land prices in Lancaster, Pennsylvania, prompted the launching of daughter settlements in Parke and Wayne counties. Migration into these new settlements has not abated; by 2006, Parke counted five church districts;

and Wayne, four. Each had a full complement of ordained leaders. Similar pressures in New York and Ohio prompted a group of Amish from the ultra-conservative Swartzentruber affiliation to locate near Paoli, Indiana, in 1994.

The establishment in 1992 of a so-called New Order Amish community near Worthington followed a somewhat different course.[23] One mark of the New Order affiliation is an active concern for seekers interested in Amish faith. When a serious inquiry about joining the Amish came from a non-Amish family in Worthington, some Ohio New Orders decided to relocate there and spread their message by way of a living example. If the initiative in this case was less than typical, the resulting settlement illustrated a common pattern. Half the resulting population was a single extended family; kin connections had dictated the Ohio-to-Indiana relocation.

If the offshoot settlements that emerge within a state (or across the border in southern Michigan or western Ohio) help create a denser Indiana network of community visiting and communication, the arrival of folk from further afield points to the continuing importance of migration trails in the twenty-first century. The recent Ohio and Pennsylvania daughter settlements, for example, have more frequent and more significant contact with their parent communities hundreds of miles to the east than they do with other Indiana settlements that are geographically much closer. As in the 1840s and 1850s when immigration streams created circles of communication and networks of discussion, today's settlements often identify themselves in terms of migration memories—whether "offshoot" backgrounds or "daughter settlement" relationships—that tie them to some people while estranging them from others. Such patterns remain critical in making sense of the Amish social landscape.

COMPETING MEMORIES: THE EXAMPLE OF AMISH SCHOOLS

The relationship between settlement histories and Amish memory offers clues to the dynamics of contemporary Amish life. The current state of Amish private schooling provides one such example. Though the Amish are today widely known for enrolling their children in Amish-run one- and two-room schools, this pattern is a fairly recent phenomenon. Families living in older settlements with longstanding non-Amish neighborly networks participated for years in rural public schools with few misgivings. In the Elkhart-LaGrange settlement, state efforts to compel high school attendance in the early 1920s left some resistant Amish fathers with brief jail stints, but the controversy was soon resolved.[24]

Even in 1948, when an Amish school was begun in the Elkhart-LaGrange settlement, it was not followed by a crush of others. The Amish dissatisfaction with pub-

Illustration 2.3. Today about sixty percent of children in the Elkhart-LaGrange settlement attend Amish schools. Source: Courtesy of the Mennonite Historical Library/Dottie Kauffmann.

lic schools stemmed more from the school consolidation of the 1960s that began to wipe away the shared memory of local schools. For the non-Amish population, the focus was on updating schools in a way that set them apart from their past. For the Amish, in contrast, it was past patterns that validated the schools' worth. During the early 1960s, the slow beginnings of school consolidation in the older Amish settlements prompted the creation of more Amish schools as parents watched local, trusted institutions close in favor of distant unknown ones.[25]

In 1967 plans to consolidate the western portion of LaGrange County into the Westview School Corporation, close rural elementary schools, and bus students to larger elementary schools prompted a spike in private Amish schools. During the two years that followed, thirteen Amish schools opened in the new Westview territory. Since then the number of schools has continued to rise, as has the percentage of Amish children enrolled in them. The old understandings forged in local tradition were changing, and many Amish opted out when the memory of public schooling no longer matched the contemporary reality.

Nevertheless, 20–40 percent of Amish children continue to attend public schools in the older settlements.[26] In almost every case, these students are children of families who for generations have attended one of the local public schools that were not closed as a result of consolidation, such as Shipshewana-Scott in LaGrange County, Millersburg in Elkhart County, or Berne in Adams County.[27] Westview's

Honeyville Elementary School presented a somewhat different story. A rural public school, its location ensured that it would have virtually an entirely Amish student body, although its teachers followed the district-wide public curriculum. After officials closed Honeyville in 2001, some of its Amish students transferred to the new, larger school that replaced it—a facility that was only a few miles away but that had a mixed student body. Others enrolled instead in a new Amish private school that sprang up in Honeyville's wake. In any case, families in Indiana's older settlements with generational ties to particular public schools will likely continue to send their children to those places, committed to the compact those local public schools forged with their ancestors. For example, as computers and television monitors become ubiquitous in public school classrooms, teachers have modified assignments for Amish students, allowing them to avoid the Internet, for example, but often assuming that they will watch instructional videos.[28]

In the more recently established Amish settlements, by contrast, all Amish children attend private schools. Even though many of these newer settlements are in rural locations with public schools that are much smaller and have more modest facilities than those in the suburbanizing older settlements, there is no shared history—no common memory—that united the Amish newcomers to these rural public districts. Although an occasional special education student might be placed in a publicly funded classroom (and often only temporarily), they are the exceptions that illustrate the rule. Without local memory, Amish migrants to new locations assume that they will build, staff, and fund their own schools.

One memory that remains keen in Amish communities but has receded into the mists of time for many non-Amish Hoosiers, is the 1967 agreement between Old Orders and the state that legitimated Amish schools and obligated parents to maintain student attendance rates of at least 97 percent. For their part, Amish school board members continue to take the agreement quite seriously and still praise the cooperative spirit of then-Superintendent of Public Instruction Richard Wells for brokering the deal in Indianapolis. "We feel that God, through the hands of Richard Wells, gave us the right to have our own schools," the school directors said enthusiastically as recently as 2001.[29] For most contemporary Hoosiers, however, Wells's name rings no bells, and in an age of home-schooling that has redefined the enforcement of truancy laws, few care that Amish students are in the classroom almost every school day. Indeed, Amish in recently established settlements report that they have had virtually no conversation—not to mention conflict—with public school administrators in their new locations. When the Amish have initiated such contact with school officials, the administrators register little interest and even communicate surprise when Amish parents try to submit their annual attendance figures to the local superintendent as per the 1967 agreement. Asked one southern Indiana school official upon receiving the enrollment and attendance register, "What am I supposed to do with this?" For the Amish, this turn of events—from jailing at the hands of truant officers in the 1920s and 1940s to benign neglect in the twenty-first century—is remarkable, and they express bemused gratitude.

Symbolic of this evolution was the experience of the Rochester settlement. The settlements' first children attended an Amish school held in a private home until their families could secure funds to build a schoolhouse. While most of the money came from the parents, some families decided to begin weekly benefit sales as a means of raising funds from the general public. Happily, non-Amish neighbors offered a venue at the Fulton County Historical Museum and then purchased many of the baked items benefiting the school fund. In late 1998 the Mount Zion School opened, paid for in part by supportive neighbors. In such experiences, new memories are forged.[30]

At the same time, private school education—to the degree that it has become an assumed norm for Amish children and parents—is itself providing a new common memory for rising generations. Amish education, while differing in certain ways from settlement to settlement, has become a new sort of Amish common experience across the state and beyond, and in one sense leveling some of the inherited differences that history has left among various migrating groups. Indeed, the work to secure state recognition in the 1960s united Indiana leaders from second-wave immigrant settlements such as Allen County with settlements from other backgrounds.

Clearly, migration memories and local histories, critical as they may be, are not the only components of Amish identity and potential diversity. Differences in church Ordnung and understandings of ethnicity also play key roles in the Amish world—roles explored in the chapters that follow.

CHAPTER THREE

Ordnung

The sources of Amish cohesion puzzle observers accustomed to locating group identity in formal institutions, professional job titles, and program affiliations. Ready to place people on organizational flow charts, outsiders search in vain for Amish denominational headquarters, public spokespeople, position papers, or published budget priorities.

In contrast to these modern bureaucratic markers, radically decentralized Amish society embraces as its social glue something it calls *Ordnung*. Translated incompletely as "order," *Ordnung* is the collected wisdom of past generations, combined with the commands of Scripture and insights into human nature and the workings of the natural world. Ordnung prescribes and proscribes, directing and limiting activity. Ordnung governs the particular style of clothes one puts on the morning and how one travels to work. It mandates certain activities on Sunday and labels others taboo. It counsels general virtues like humility and submission to authority, while also requiring a stubborn allegiance to God rather than to the state if the two should come into conflict.

Ordnung is passed on orally and rarely written down; it is absorbed more than dictated, but it is a real presence in everyday Amish life.[1] Church discipline enforces adherence to Ordnung, but Ordnung governs the manner in which church discipline itself can be carried out. As a traditional way of ordering life, Ordnung is also local in its orientation and reflects immediate and traditional sensibilities rather than generalized mandates from afar (see table 3.1). Submitting to life monitored by Ordnung becomes a way of situating oneself in the world and in relation to others.[2]

TABLE 3.1
Sample Ordnung similarities and differences across Indiana settlements

Proscribed in all settlements
  Automobile ownershp
  Televisions
  Conducting business on Sunday
  Men wearing neckties
  Attending high school

Prescribed in all settlements, but differing in specifics
  Buggy style
  Women's head coverings

Proscribed or prescribed in certain settlements or districts
  Church services in homes: prescribed everywhere but the Salem settlement, which has a
    meetinghouse
  Married men working away from home: prohibited in Steuben County and Paoli settlements,
    but permitted elsewhere
  Access to telephone: varies by settlement and sometimes by district
  Farming with tractors: permitted in Kokomo for field work; permitted in Salem for moving
    wagons around the barn but not for field work; prohibited everywhere else

It was a commitment to traditional Ordnung that gave rise to the designation *Old Order* Amish. Yet Ordnung is more an approach to life than a singular set of rules. If to the casual observer, Old Order people appear to be frozen relics that time forgot, closer inspection reveals a host of evolving interpretations, understandings, and developments across the Amish world. On one level, Ordnung unifies the Amish, yet in sanctioning localized tradition, Ordnung is also a source of diversity.

Alongside migration and memory, approaches to Ordnung provide another way of making sense of the Amish mosaic. But Ordnung itself has a history, and understanding its evolution sheds light on today's Amish world. Developments of the 1850s and 60s and of the 1950s and 60s were especially critical. In the mid-nineteenth century, Ordnung emerged as an alternative social regulator in a society bemused by individual progress and social refinement. A hundred years later, events in most Amish settlements triggered increasing Ordnung rigidity around religious matters while allowing more flexibility on technological and occupational innovation—simultaneously opening and closing possibilities for change and sparking the formation of new subgroups committed to different interpretations. These legacies all contribute to the Amish mosaic.

FORMULATING THE OLD ORDER, 1850S AND 60S

The distinctive approach to life and faith that came to be known as the "Old Order" emerged in the mid-1800s as a decided protest against social refinement and religious rationalization.[3] In the nineteenth century, Amish heirs of first-wave immigrants and more recent second-wave arrivals found themselves in an America that was wrestling with the implications of political democratization, a new social mobility, and an emerging consumer economy—all of which conspired to unsettle established norms and traditional hierarchies that had long governed public life.

This yeasty social mix produced a popular celebration of equality, on the one hand, and a new set of class distinctions, on the other. No longer bound by their station of birth, individuals sought to cast off tradition and create their own personas by adapting new tastes and purchasing the tools and symbols of social refinement.[4] New guidebooks based on Renaissance-era Italian nobility manuals instructed readers on how to talk, walk, eat, laugh, and dress like a gentleman or a lady. Since genteel activities demanded genteel surroundings, even common folk now fitted their houses with carpets, mirrors, and display objects such as dishes that one had only "for show." Ordinary people worked long and hard to give the appearance of not working at all. Refined people read novels, had more clothes than they could wear, and found creative ways to demonstrate that they possessed discretionary wealth. By 1850, for the new middle class—rural and urban—being respectable had come to mean something other than plain and simple.

Simultaneously, Protestant churches were rethinking their relevance in an expansive society that claimed to distain tradition and celebrate growth and change. Religious renewal, influential voices claimed, demanded efficiency and rationalization. Denominational leaders hastily constructed a host of bureaucratic institutions and built benevolent enterprises that merged churchly goals and national well-being into plans to reform society. By pouring their energies into special-purpose organizations championing education, publication, and social uplift, Christians could prove their worth in a pluralistic society and find their identity in denominational causes more than in local relationships and peculiar practices.[5]

By the mid-1800s some Amish voiced alarm over the popular pull of consumer gentility and the restructuring of religious life. Could a traditional bias against ostentation endure in the midst of market logic? Would individuals find their value in communities that looked to the past for their sources of authority, or in contemporary and self-determined quests for gentility? Might religious rationalization and denominationalism displace the discernment of local congregations and cater to values of personal choice, organizational achievement, and bland patriotism?[6]

Already in the 1850s, several Amish leaders had proffered the possibility of a national ministers' meeting (*Dienerversammlung*) to discuss such questions and bolster a commitment to locally oriented, tradition-guided ways of life and faith. Gathering annually from 1862 to 1878 (except 1877), these *Dienerversammlungen* brought together Amish leaders from across the United States and Ontario. But the meet-ings—two of which were held in Indiana—soon took on a sort of denomination-alist cast themselves, as participants appeared to legislate on matters in a manner that was at times disconnected from local contexts.[7] Then too, the conferences seemed to attract change-minded Amish who were less averse to the promise of refinement and who promoted church renewal in programmatic terms. For exam-ple, many endorsed Sunday schools, a novel program that rationalized and segre-gated Christian education into age-defined classes and used distantly produced cur-riculum that focused on individual conversion rather than on the centrality of the corporate church.

Although tradition-minded Amish participated in the *Dienerversammlungen* at first, few attended after 1865. Instead, these conservatives sought renewal through more careful attention to traditional Ordnung—the old order—that was locally ori-ented, communally constructed, and guided by deference to past precedent. These Old Order advocates did not precipitate a formal schism in Amish ranks as much as quietly establishing new networks of fellowship with like-minded conservatives. In some places—such as Iowa and Ontario—this realignment was not complete until the 1890s, but in Indiana the lines were clear by the 1860s.[8] In the Elkhart-LaGrange settlement, two of seven Amish churches sided with the Old Order movement; in Nappanee, Kokomo, and Allen and Adams counties, approximately half the Amish chose the Old Order path. Two small settlements in Clinton and Starke counties produced no Old Orders, while the just-established Daviess County settlement was made up entirely of Old Order sympathizers.[9]

In time, the change-minded (non-Old Order) Amish followed their denomina-tionally oriented logic to its conclusion and merged with one of several Mennonite groups that had even more eagerly embarked on a program of institution building and had embraced cultural refinement so as to render plainness passé. In the wake of the progressives' merger with the Mennonites, the traditionalists came all but to define the Amish way. In broad strokes, that Old Order tradition emerged from its mid-nineteenth century context as a cluster of related commitments that would continue to shape the contours of Ordnung into the twenty-first century:

— plainness, simplicity, and a skepticism of genteel refinement and consumer culture, resulting in Ordnung prescribing and proscribing such things as clothing and home furnishings.

— church defined in small-scale, local terms, resulting in a rejection of church buildings, denominational structures, and salaried clergy.

— Ordnung as the best way to maintain unity and social balance, resulting in a

Illustration 3.1. Old Order Amish meet in private homes (or barns or shops) for biweekly Sunday worship. Each district has a "bench wagon," like the one parked outside this Nappanee settlement home, which carries the church benches and hymnals from house to house. Source: Courtesy of the Mennonite Historical Library/Dottie Kauffmann.

skepticism of the machinery of modern authority such as written constitutions or professional expertise.

These initial convictions and dispositions foreshadowed later Old Order decisions such as those after 1910 in favor of horse-drawn transportation instead of automobiles. Cars were status symbols, and buggy travel kept family and community life local and face-to-face. Similarly, the twentieth-century Old Orders' critique of public education often centered on the size and scale of consolidating schools and the individualistic assumptions behind progressive curricula that championed competitive achievement, critical thinking, and specialization. In contrast, small Amish schools, established as alternatives in most settlements, operate on a human scale, stop with eighth grade, employ Amish teachers valued for their loyalty to the church, and promote values of cooperation, submission, and humility.

REFORMULATING THE OLD ORDER, 1950S AND 60S

Ordnung's durable yet dynamic character meant that Old Order life was always evolving—often in measured and predictable ways, to be sure—and never static. Even so, events of the mid-twentieth century marked a rather dramatic episode in

Old Order experience, producing a reformulation of Old Order sentiments that sparked some of the variety that still colors the Amish world. The 1950s were tumultuous times in many settlements and witnessed the emergence of a controversial so-called Amish mission movement.[10] For a decade or more, soon after the end of the Second World War, a significant number of Old Orders—including many in Indiana—promoted a kind of Amish church activism that sought to reform aspects of Amish life and serve those beyond Amish circles in fairly formal ways. Amish mission movement activists challenged longstanding patterns of rowdiness by unbaptized Amish teens, condemned smoking among adult men, and encouraged a more introspective devotional life. They also held mission conferences, participated in Mennonite voluntary service programs, distributed mission-oriented literature to thousands of Amish homes, and funded full-time Old Order mission workers in Mississippi, Arkansas, and Ontario. Several dozen attended college to obtain credentials they saw as important for their success in such work—all the while remaining Old Order Amish church members. By the mid-1960s all this would become unthinkable in an Old Order context, but that fact itself points to the influence of these events on the subsequent reformulation of Ordnung boundaries in many communities.

The story of the Amish mission movement is complex and involved the interplay of new influences and old relationships. Despite their parting ways with Amish progressives after the 1860s, the Old Orders had not severed all relationships with their change-minded neighbors and kin. In Indiana's Elkhart-LaGrange, Nappanee, and Kokomo settlements, for example, Old Order Amish subscribed to progressive Mennonite periodicals, supported Mennonite charitable work, and even attended Sunday evening church services at area Mennonite meetinghouses. The implications of these contacts may have lain dormant, but the impact of World War II and the placement of hundreds of drafted Amish conscientious objectors (COs) from across the country into public service assignments, under Mennonite auspices, helped prompt these older mediated contacts with the wider world to take on an Amish life of their own. Some COs returned home hoping to engender interest in organized service activities in their own Old Order church districts. Young adults in several communities organized Bible study groups that soon became forums for acting apart from the district leadership.

Significantly, however, mission movement proponents began with an understanding of and respect for traditional Ordnung assumptions. For example, when Old Order church members from around the Midwest went to Arkansas in 1953 to staff a home for indigent non-Amish elderly, they were careful *not* to organize an Amish church there, but instead self-consciously construed the "rest home" as alien turf, formally outside of any local Ordnung.[11] Amish staff might then make provisional practical use of normally forbidden things like automobiles while away from home, without implying any challenge to the discipline of their home congregations.[12] The arrangement was purposeful and pointed to respect for their local Ordnung in the process of undertaking innovative work elsewhere. In many ways it paralleled the distinction Old Order carpenters observed in avoiding certain tools and technologies at home while using them freely at non-Amish customers' work sites.

Yet the very nature of the mission movement's activities—from establishing formal institutions such as the Arkansas "rest home" that required articles of incorporation and boards of directors, to engaging in social service activities such as schools for indigenous people in Ontario that were accountable to the government more than to the church—pressed the limits of the Old Order. As well, mission movement activists were, in the end, committed to an assertive, organizationally oriented, and reformist view of the world that was difficult to interpret through the lens of Ordnung, no matter how hard they tried.

By 1960 most mission movement advocates had come to believe that their interests were incompatible with the strictures of Old Order life and left the fold; others were forced out by unsympathetic home churches. The tumultuous exodus of this block of families out of Old Order circles—often to neighboring Mennonite congregations or to the progressive, car-driving Beachy Amish (a group formed in the 1920s)—had a profound impact on those they left behind. In the mission movement's aftermath, the meaning and limitations of the Old Order were reformulated in critical ways, including a reshuffling of proscribed activities and the formation of new affiliations.[13]

A PANORAMA OF PRACTICE

For those who remained in the Old Order orbit, the mission movement's rise and fall buried future possibilities of joining in individually focused mission work, attending college, or establishing autonomous special interest religious groups within the church. In the decades since 1960, Old Orders have in many ways become more religiously sectarian. Subscribing to periodicals from other denominations or attending religious services elsewhere is now very rare. Meanwhile, the rise of Amish schools and the appearance of devotional publications from Amish-affiliated Pathway Publishers has further insulated them from religious interaction with outsiders.[14]

Yet this intensified religious sectarianism took place alongside greater Old Order openness to technological change that paralleled a shift away from farming and a rise in disposable income. As a result, in many places *technological and religious conservatism were decoupled,* with the Ordnung surrounding religious life becoming more fixed even as occupational innovation became more likely. This expression of the Old Order—while a relatively recent reformulation—is now common in Indiana and many other settlements across North America.

However, the legacy of these mid-twentieth-century events was not singular, and those years birthed other combinations of Amish values, adding to the range of Old Order expressions. For example, a few Amish leaders had shared the mission movement advocates' concern to bolster Amish devotional life and curb the excesses of rowdy youth, but they sought to achieve these ends through very different means. Rather that rallying interest in externally focused activism, they harnessed the power of Ordnung itself and incorporated into church discipline things that previously had been considered the prerogative of parents. For example, they enforced prohibitions on tobacco and unsupervised teenage socialization and courtship, and further limited members' interaction with the world. Coupled with a principled commitment to staving off technological innovation, many moved to more isolated Midwestern areas, such as Paoli, Indiana, in 1957, and formed a loose network of settlements construing Old Order identity in terms of rigorous moral discipline and especially conservative attitudes toward cultural changes.[15]

Yet another expression of Amish understandings to emerge from the tumult of the 1950s was the so-called New Order Amish—a somewhat confusing label for this Old Order subgroup. In Ohio and Pennsylvania some members who had sympathized with the mission movement remained in the old church, but as a more sectarian environment settled in the post-1960 years, they found themselves increasingly uncomfortable within the new strictures. Like the mission movement advocates of the previous decade, the New Orders promoted activities like youth Bible study meetings, forbade tobacco and otherwise insisted on "clean" living, and employed a more subjective language of personal faith. However, they also nurtured localist sensibilities, did not participate in distant mission work, and banned higher education. Moreover, they maintained many technological limits, for example, remaining committed to horse-and-buggy transportation.[16] By the mid-1970s the first of two New Order settlements had taken root in southern Indiana.

Finally, there were several segments of the Amish world that were hardly touched by the turbulence of the mid-twentieth century—an absence that in itself set them apart after 1960. For example, the understanding of the Old Order among the Amish in Allen and Adams counties continued to develop throughout the twentieth century but without much reference to the mission movement currents, which left few ripples in these settlements. Similarly, the movement did not shake the ultra-conservative Swartzentruber Amish affiliation that had coalesced in Ohio after 1913 (and whose members moved to southern Indiana in the 1990s). The Swartzentrubers were committed to maintaining an Ordnung that prized highly traditional ways of life, yet they did so without having embraced or reacted against the mid-century mission movement idiom or agenda, thus construing their conservatism in a different way than, say, the highly tradition-minded Old Orders who moved to Paoli after 1957.

ORDNUNG AND THE AMISH HIERARCHY OF VALUES

As the story of the nineteenth-century formulation and twentieth-century reformulation of Old Order sensibilities suggests, Ordnung is as dynamic as it is durable. In the different ways it changes and resists change, Ordnung reveals an Amish hierarchy of values that both reflects and creates Amish culture. The role of Ordnung in four particular areas—religious ritual, an agricultural ideal, domestic life, and relationships among Amish groups—suggests a hierarchy of values that both define core commitments and predict diverse practice among today's Amish.

Religious ritual is perhaps the most symbolically significant sector of Amish life and consequently the area most resistant to change. The format of biweekly worship services is established and is not open to tinkering. Universally, Amish churches sing the "Loblied" (O Father God We Praise Your Name) as the second hymn in every worship service, although the tempo of this song might vary, depending on who is doing the singing. (Progressive-leaning churches may get through four verses in twelve minutes, while conservatives savor the same set of stanzas for eighteen.) Similarly, scripture readings follow a prescribed lectionary of New Testament texts from which districts do not deviate.[17] Local Ordnung stubbornly upholds the details of such practice, including the ministers' role in the public reading of the Scriptures on a Sunday morning—except among Amish from Lancaster, Pennsylvania, where Ordnung assigns that task to deacons. In some settlements Ordnung dictates that the congregation remain seated during the scripture reading; in others, all stand and face away from the reader. In Indiana's Elkhart-LaGrange and Nappanee communities, men stand facing the reader, while women stand with their backs to the reader. The origin of Ordnung surrounding such church ritual is obscure, but is never challenged.[18]

Ordnung also closely regulates the practice of church discipline and testifies to the place of that ritual in the hierarchy of Amish values, since districts that do not observe the same Ordnung on shunning cannot be in fellowship with one another no matter how similar they are in other ways. The Ordnung of some Old Orders

TABLE 3.2
Ordnung surrounding church discipline, by settlement

Non–*Streng Meidung* settlements[a]	*Streng Meidung* settlements[b]
Adams County (some affiliations)	Adams County (some affiliations)
Elkhart-LaGrange	Allen County
Nappanee	Daviess County
Kokomo	South Whitley
Milroy	Paoli
Salem	Paoli-Swartzentruber
Worthington	Salem Swiss
Rochester	Steuben County
Vallonia	Vevay Swiss
Vevay	Park County
	Wayne County

[a]Represents approx. 70% of population
[b]Represents approx. 30% of population

calls for *streng Meidung* (strict shunning), which regards the ban as lifelong unless the offender repents. In contrast, many other Amish do not view shunning as necessarily indefinite. They draw a distinction between excommunication for moral offenses and that incurred when one leaves the church to join a somewhat more liberal group. In the latter cases, the ban serves as a public but temporary reprimand of the broken baptismal vow and can be "lifted" if the offender subsequently affiliates with another "plain," albeit more progressive, Anabaptist group and becomes a sincere and submissive member there.[19]

Ordnung surrounding shunning divides Indiana's settlements almost evenly in number, though not in terms of population; only a minority of Indiana Amish observes *streng Meidung* (see table 3.2). This disciplinary distinction is crucial, since Amish churches that practice *streng Meidung* refrain from full fellowship with those that do not. Especially in a settlement where both practices prevail—such as Adams County—keeping the distinction clear is crucial. For example, Lancaster County, Pennsylvania, Amish transplants to Wayne County, Indiana, whose Ordnung calls for *streng Meidung,* know that they are in fellowship with the so-called "Joe L." affiliation in the Adams County settlement to the north because that subgroup shares this disciplinary practice—even though the Lancaster Ordnung as a whole has much more in common with Adams County's more technologically progressive "Shetler" affiliation. The Shetler group does not observe *streng Meidung.* Agreement on any number of details of daily practice is not enough to overcome differences in discipline; Ordnung around shunning trumps other potential points of commonality or difference.

ORDNUNG AND THE AGRICULTURAL IDEAL

If Ordnung surrounding church ritual and discipline reveals Amish values through its resistance to adaptation, Ordnung regulating the world of work illustrates its selectively flexible nature. Virtually all Amish people insist that farming is the best way of life, the best place to raise a family, and the traditional context for living Amish life. This sentiment is shared even by—indeed, often especially by— those not employed in agriculture. Yet those who make such claims quickly follow them with observations on growing populations, shrinking land availability, and the economic realities of farming on the small scale that the Amish prefer. Milking cows by hand and shocking grain without the aid of machinery limits the viability of Amish farming even as other opportunities—from carpentry to small businesses to industrial work—offer steady paychecks.

As a result, in many places there is a paradoxical relationship between the farming ideal and the practical possibility of farming. Because farming has long been central to Amish identity, it is among the areas most specifically governed by Ordnung and most resistant to change. Farming has been slower to modernize in many Amish settlements even where highly mechanized nonfarm jobs are endorsed. Un-

Illustration 3.2. Ordnung governing farming is more resistant to change than Ordnung surrounding most other occupations. Source: Courtesy of the Mennonite Historical Library/Joel Fath.

til the early 1990s, for example, Amish farmers in Allen County did not use bulk milk tanks or automatic milkers, typically keeping herd sizes to a dozen animals and forcing their milk into the lower-paying Grade B classification. Meanwhile, Amish shops in the same settlement were producing state-of-the-art hydraulic valves and other metal machining parts with sophisticated equipment. By the time the Ordnung changed to permit milking technology necessary for Grade A production and the expansion of herds to thirty or more cows, few farmers were left. Similar stories are traceable in portions of the Elkhart-LaGrange, Nappanee, and Adams County settlements.[20]

To outside observers, the choice may seem puzzling: If farming is so important, why not modify farming Ordnung more quickly to save this esteemed way of life? Yet for many Amish it is the traditional component of farming practices that makes them so significant, and modifying them hastily would eviscerate the very value in farming as an ideal way of life. Accepting changes and adaptations in nonfarm jobs is not nearly so threatening to Amish identity as are even modest alterations in farming, since these other occupations—be they home-based or industrial—are not closely associated with what it means to be Amish. Simply put, being a tax accountant or a forklift driver is so marginal to the history and meaning of being Amish that such jobs can absorb much more innovation and flexibility than can farming, without challenging Amish sensibilities. In the end, the relative inflexibility of the Ordnung around farming has in many cases practically pushed Amish people off the farm and into occupations more peripheral to Amish identity, where change is more acceptable and less threatening to the Ordnung. In order to maintain the integrity of the center of the Amish ideal world, fewer people can actually function there in today's economic market.

PROTECTING HOME AND FAMILY

As with farming, Ordnung surrounding home life is less open to modification than that informing many other aspects of Amish society. From birth to death, the home is the real and symbolic center of Amish life; church services, weddings, and funerals typically take place in the home. Shielding the family, and especially children, is a common Ordnung thread. Divorce is forbidden everywhere. Horse-drawn transportation keeps people closer to home. Telephones are more problematic when they invade the home than when they appear in a business or on a work site removed from the household hearth.[21] And Amish schools, which inculcate Amish values in the next generation, are decidedly low-tech and devoid of any mass media. Conversely, Ordnung typically is more flexible when one is on alien soil, work-

Illustration 3.3. Home-based businesses among the Swartzentrubers typically involve low-tech handcrafts such as basket making because of the especially restrictive Ordnung observed by this ultra-conservative affiliation. Source: Courtesy of Thomas J. Meyers.

ing at a non-Amish job site, traveling away from home, or not directly influencing children.

Yet even a common commitment to the priority and protection of the home is expressed in sharply different ways depending on the choices of church districts, as Ordnung surrounding permissible occupations illustrates. Some Amish encourage fathers to work at home even if this means introducing novel production and sales technology into the heart of family life, while others strive to keep any domestic disruption at arm's length even if that means household heads have to work away from home.[22] For example, Amish in Kokomo, Parke County, and portions of the Elkhart-LaGrange settlement, among others, have embraced home-based shops and small businesses that mimic farm-life rhythms, keep work centered in the household, and include the skills of several generations. At the same time, the practical demands of retail or wholesale customer service and the need to improve product lines can, in the end, introduce an innovative impulse—from telephone use, to electric cash registers, to daily contact with the UPS driver—into the very center of the homestead itself. Alternately, more restrictive church rules on such interaction and technology can have the effect of encouraging employment away from home, where a non-Amish firm or client can provide tools in an admittedly worldly environment. Many Amish in Adams County, among other settlements, have adopted this approach, successfully staving off change around home but also pushing up to 80 percent of adult men into work at distant construction sites and away from their homes for long periods of time each day.

A few settlements—including those in Steuben County and at Paoli—have tried to have it both ways by adhering to a restrictive Ordnung that bars married men from working away from home *and* tightly limits the technology available for use in home-based small businesses. The combination leaves business owners with a limited labor pool and low-tech operations, and it has resulted in economies stocked with a narrow range of small, unskilled firms, such as rough lumber work or pallet-building shops.

ORDNUNG AND AFFILIATION

Ordnung is informed not only by common commitments to church practices and home-centered ideals but also by the presence of related and even competing Ordnung standards in other churches. Districts that wish to remain in fellowship with those of more tradition-minded predilections might consciously temper their boundary testing to signal such interests. Likewise, a new settlement affiliating with the network of New Order districts would need to adopt an Ordnung that included certain prohibitions, such as a ban on tobacco, if it wished to indicate its adherence to the convictions that those districts consider marks of fidelity. In southern Indiana around the towns of Paoli and Salem, there are four distinct, yet all-but-contiguous settlements, each with its own Ordnung. As described in chapter 8, the proximity of these groups means that the self-identity of each is defined as much by how its Ordnung differs from the other three Amish groups as it is by interaction with the non-Amish world.

Yet even the relationship between Ordnung and affiliation is not uniform from settlement to settlement. At a basic level, Ordnung binds a local Amish church district together, but the degree to which it is shared more broadly, beyond the bounds of the local district, varies considerably. If Ordnung is the glue that cements a church district, it is sometimes an affiliation adhesive too, since an affiliation is made up of Amish church districts that are "in fellowship" with one another, symbolized by welcoming one another's ministers to preach on a reciprocal basis.

The relationship between Ordnung and affiliation is complex. While the absence of affiliation between churches typically suggests that each observes a different Ordnung, the opposite is not necessarily the case. In other words, differences in Ordnung do not necessarily imply a lack of affiliation; some churches that are in fel-

	Single Affiliation Settlement	Multiple Affiliations in Settlement
No Common Ordnung	Elkhart-LaGrange (IN) Settlement	Holmes-Wayne (OH) Settlement Adams County (IN) Settlement
Commonly Shared Ordnung	Lancaster (PA) Settlement Parke and Wayne (IN) Settlements	

Figure 3.1. Relationship between Ordnung and Affiliation, selected settlements

lowship with one another do not share a common Ordnung. In fact, there are three distinct patterns of Ordnung and affiliation relationships, and each of the largest Amish settlements in the United States illustrates one of these, as do Indiana's smaller communities (see figure 3.1).

The Lancaster, Pennsylvania, settlement contains only one major affiliation, and all of the community's 154 Old Order church districts work to maintain a common Ordnung. While minor differences have surfaced and certain sections of the settlement have gained reputations as being more or less conservative than the settlement as a whole, to a remarkable degree districts there have maintained a similar Ordnung. A feature unique to the Lancaster community is a settlement-wide gathering of bishops that reviews, reaffirms, and considers adjusting the Ordnung.[23] This practice has not only helped this large settlement maintain a common affiliation and a common Ordnung, but it has extended its reach to the daughter settlements established by Lancaster Amish migrants elsewhere—including recent transplants to Indiana's Parke and Wayne counties.

The close link between affiliation and Ordnung in the Lancaster community may seem natural to observers who predict such organizational and practical coincidence, but it is rare. More common nationally—including parts of Indiana—are the patterns that involve notably different expressions of Ordnung within a given settlement. In the world's largest Amish settlement, in eastern Ohio's Holmes, Wayne, and adjacent counties, Ordnung and affiliation are closely tied, but the settlement includes at least four major affiliations.[24] Each affiliation maintains a common Ordnung, but the presence of several affiliations within the same settlement results in a range of practice within the settlement as a whole. This pattern also prevails in

Indiana's Adams County settlement, where five affiliations exist, each with a distinct Ordnung.

A third possibility is that found in northern Indiana's Elkhart-LaGrange counties—and many other Midwestern Old Order Amish settlements—where there is no common settlement-wide Ordnung, but neither are there multiple affiliations. Here the details of the Ordnung are a distinctly district concern, and a range of practice marks the settlement. Yet churches within the settlement have maintained affiliation in spite of their differences. For outsiders seeking to use affiliation as a measure of Ordnung—and vice versa—patterns of practice here are much harder to delineate.

Taking account of the complex function of Ordnung—from its historical formulations to its contemporary reflecting and refracting of Old Order values in different combinations—helps make sense of some of the diversity that marks contemporary Amish life. There remains yet another major aspect of Amish identity to examine. Indebted to the currents of history and the influence of Ordnung, ethnicity is a third significant factor in sorting the Amish story, a factor to which we turn before exploring how these elements combine in particular contexts to shape specific communities.

CHAPTER FOUR

Ethnicity

When asked to describe themselves, Amish people rarely launch into autobiographical description peppered with first person singular pronouns. They talk instead in collective terms of family, church, or simply "our people." Frequently, these categories overlap and even blend together. While the Amish are quick to note personality characteristics, temperaments, and dispositions that mark individuals, they are not steeped in the language or logic of individualism that pervades modern life. Neither is their sense of belonging something that emerges only for scheduled ethnic festivals. They do not pull out folk costumes on certain holidays or carry on their way of life for the benefit of a seasonal tourist cycle or to serve as a sort of living history museum.

There are religious foundations to Amish peoplehood, and their Christian commitments are daily and all-encompassing. Questions about whether one might "live Amish" but not "practice the religion" make no sense to them. The sort of fluid and self-selective identities that allow moderns to talk about "practicing Catholics" or "observant Jews"—with the implication that devotional practice or religious observation may not be essential to spiritual identity—do not have Amish analogues. A person cannot be a member of the Amish church without submitting to the Ordnung of the church, nor can one become Amish simply by buying a buggy or disconnecting from public utility service.

This connection between church membership and identity is expressed in the practice of adult baptism with its possibility that children raised in Amish homes might not join the Amish church. Although the percentage of those who do not join has dropped during the past sixty years, about one in ten Amish-born children leave the tradition.[1] The voluntary component of church membership means that being Amish is not the same thing as being part of an ethnic group in the way that terminology is commonly used by North Americans. Amish identity is not necessarily inherited by children or limited by parentage, since those raised in non-Amish homes can also join the church (though very few do).

Yet it is also clear that the Amish posses a strong system of family ties and kinship networks, a distinctive dialect, durable folkways, and a clearly identifiable culture that creates a sense of peoplehood that many observers would call *ethnic*.[2]

ETHNIC AMISH

Ethnicity is, most basically, a shared sense of peoplehood. In North America it is often based on some specific mix of genealogy, national origins, or language.[3] This shared sense is cultivated and sustained through patterns of relationship within the group, such as marriage or residency, that bolster rather than dilute cultural convictions, and through the sort of ethnic education one receives in parochial schools or informal networks of visiting, worshiping, and finding employment with fellow group members.

Amish society is a densely structured web of overlapping connections that tie people together in multiple ways. Church members live within a locally defined district where one's neighbors are often also extended family. With an average of seven to eight children per household, the typical married person has kin ties to fourteen other family units of ten people each (two parents and eight children), simply through in-law relations. Children often attend school with other youngsters from their church, including siblings and cousins, and often are taught by a young woman who is a member of the district and perhaps even a relative. Household heads may work in small shops owned by an Amish entrepreneur, and even those employed in factories spend their breaks and lunch hours with fellow church members in dialect conversation.

Amish society thrives as a high-context culture, where members know one another in multiple ways—as relatives, neighbors, church members, and co-workers.[4] Modern society, in contrast, is segmented and stratified so that people typically interact with one another only in singular and carefully prescribed occupational or age-defined roles. As a high-context, densely structured society, the Amish community is better able to maintain a sense of group identity that is durable and definable.

But ethnicity is not a static "thing" that exists continuously across time and place. Instead, it takes shape around the interplay of insider assumptions and outsider

Illustration 4.1. Family is one of the primary means by which ethnicity is cultivated and transmitted from generation to generation. Source: Courtesy of the Mennonite Historical Library/Dottie Kauffmann.

opinions. The assumed values and convictions of group members are important in defining ethnic group boundaries, but so are the categories and stereotypes of non-members. For example, the ethnic labels "Hispanic" and "Latino" have as much to do with outsider perceptions of linguistic and geographic commonalities as they do with any culture shared by the diverse people placed into those categories.[5]

The Amish also find that the boundaries they construct to define themselves are often matched by parameters erected by others. When states exempt "the Amish" from high school attendance, or when the federal government outlines provisions for "the Amish" to opt out of Social Security, the lines that delimit the church are at least partly the creation of others. Amish groups that otherwise may have few natural connections to one another geographically or historically have found themselves fused together in popular perception created for tourist consumption. In fact, a commitment to separation from the world actually grants the world influence in defining who the Amish are.

SYMBOLIC SEPARATORS

The most common marks of ethnicity are practices or artifacts that function as *symbolic separators* in Amish life. Symbolic separators publicly draw the boundaries between the Amish church and the world. While they hold meaning in themselves, their larger significance comes from the way they establish a sense of belonging among group members and provide marks of identification for outsiders.

The Amish use of horse-drawn transportation is a prime example of a symbolic separator that defines Amish ethnicity. Outsiders recognize the Amish as people who drive buggies. While the Amish may ride in cars, driving an automobile is a sure indication that one is not Amish.[6] For the Amish themselves, buggy travel demonstrates one's willingness to live within the Ordnung and to be identified publicly as Old Order.

But horse-and-buggy travel is not simply an alternative to motor travel; it is the basis for an entirely different travel culture. Living within a "horse culture" means that Amish families do not frequent gas stations, auto repair garages, or used car lots. Instead, they are closely tied to buggy, tack, and harness shops. With rare exceptions, each home must have provision for at least a small horse barn and pasture. One's sense of time and planning are shifted in the world of horse culture. Minor errands take more forethought, as do trips for which one might hire a non-Amish driver. Travel is less likely to be alone and is more often coordinated with others or with multiple tasks. Yet while horse-drawn transportation supports Amish cultural values, the Amish do not assume that automobiles are evil. In that sense, the issue at stake is not so much the automobile itself or the horse per se, as it is what each represents. The car symbolizes the world, while the horse is a symbolic separator from the world.

Although symbolic separators constitute boundaries that are not open to tampering, the Amish rarely invest *ultimate* value in these particular practices. In some ways the rationale is familiar to any modern person who participates in an organized sports team. While athletes would never claim that the specific colors of their uniform make them better players or that possessing the uniform is a substitute for skillful play, it is absolutely necessary that team members wear their assigned uniforms and not those of the opposing team in order to maintain the integrity of the game. What is important for the game to function smoothly is that all sides respect the distinctions that the uniforms represent.

Other elements of ethnicity, such as prescribed Amish clothes, the refusal to have one's home wired for public utility electricity, or ending formal education with eighth grade, are also symbolic separators. So are speaking a German dialect and maintaining a ritual calendar different from surrounding society. All of these elements also carry some theological freight and are related to Amish faith and values such as simplicity, modesty, and community. In its own way, each bolsters Amish cultural values and shapes Amish life. But taken together, they serve as symbolic separators that let Amish and non-Amish alike know where peoplehood starts and stops, where the church and world divide.

TWO STREAMS OF PEOPLEHOOD: PENNSYLVANIA GERMAN AND SWISS

Although compact social and kin networks, along with symbolic separators, function as ethnic markers that define Amish society and reinforce group values, those networks and separators can also vary significantly. In fact, while casual on-lookers may categorize the Amish as a singular ethnic group, the Amish population actually includes two distinct ethnic groups—two cultural traditions, each bearing their own customs, history, conflicts, and social networks and each marked by particular sets of symbolic separators that have emerged out of a social dialogue between context and conviction.[7]

These two Amish ethnic streams are designated as *Pennsylvania German* and *Swiss*, though those names are imprecise and can be misleading. Nationally, the Swiss group is the smaller of the two, but in Indiana both populations are well-represented (see table 4.1). Those inside and outside Swiss Amish circles use the label "Swiss" to identify that Amish ethnic group, while the term "Pennsylvania German" is rarely used in common conversation to label the other ethnic stream.[8] Asked to name Amish ethnicities, a non-Swiss Amish person is apt to reply as one man in LaGrange County did: "There's the Swiss, and then there's . . . well, the rest of us regular Amish"—a response that betrays a sense of his ethnic majority status. For their part, the Swiss sometimes call other Amish "High Germans."

The ethnic labels point to differing language dialects that are a primary means by which the Amish differentiate the two ethnic groups. The Swiss Amish speak a

TABLE 4.1
Dominant ethnicity by settlement

Pennsylvania German	Swiss	Some ethnic transition
Elkhart-LaGrange	Adams County	Daviess County
Nappanee	Allen County	Milroy
Kokomo	Steuben County	
Paoli	Salem Swiss	
Salem	South Whitley	
Worthington	Vevay Swiss	
Parke County		
Paoli-Swartzentruber		
Wayne County		
Rochester		
Vallonia		
Vevay		

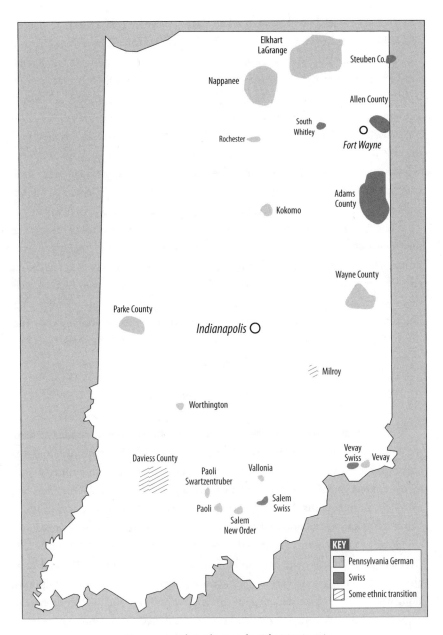

Map 4.1. Amish Settlements by Ethnicity (2006)

dialect of German they call *Swiss,* while those of Pennsylvania German descent speak the German-rooted, American-derived dialect known as *Pennsylvania German* (or Pennsylvania Dutch). The two dialects are decidedly different. As one Nappanee bishop explained, "It's like Spanish to us when they talk Swiss so fast to each other. We don't have a clue what they are saying." If Swiss speakers talk slowly, Pennsylvania German speakers can understand the general flow of a conversation, but they still find the vocabulary and elements of grammar unusual. For their part, the rare Swiss speaker who marries into a non-Swiss family or moves to a non-Swiss settlement typically picks up Pennsylvania German fairly quickly. Indeed, some anecdotal evidence suggests that Swiss speakers perceive their dialect to be inferior and believe that Pennsylvania German is a mark of status in the Amish world.[9]

While helpful in pointing to the presence of distinct dialects, the ethnic labels themselves are less precise terms than they are shorthand ways of tagging the two groups. Not all Pennsylvania German–speaking Amish have close Pennsylvania connections, nor are they necessarily any less Swiss in their European ancestry than those who today bear the Swiss name. And while migration streams did play a significant initial role in the formation of Amish ethnicity, contemporary constructions of peoplehood also stem from interaction with local contexts that have changed the ways ethnicity is understood and expressed.

Pennsylvania German–Speaking Amish

Pennsylvania German ethnicity emerged among the seventy thousand German-speaking people who immigrated to Pennsylvania during the 1700s. Although the bulk of these arrivals were Lutheran or Reformed in their religious commitments, their numbers included first-wave Amish immigrants as well as Mennonites and members of other faiths. Although these newcomers hailed from a variety of Rhine Valley states and would not, in that European context, have considered themselves a singular group, in North America they received the common label "Pennsylvania German" from British neighbors unfamiliar with the variety of Continental backgrounds the immigrants carried. Yet soon enough, those outsider perceptions, along with segregated settlement patterns, linguistic affinity, and the common treatment they received from colonial authorities, facilitated the invention of a Pennsylvania German ethnicity marked by distinct folkways, endogamy, and an American blended dialect.[10]

Amish sharing this East Coast ethnic experience founded settlements in the Midwest during the nineteenth century, and new arrivals to Indiana in the 1980s and 90s from Ohio, Pennsylvania, and New York have also come from this ethnic stream.

Their common speechways and interrelated migration histories tended to form broad patterns of similar folkways and symbolic separators, despite differences in local Ordnung and affiliation discipline. For example, by the early twentieth century Pennsylvania German–speaking Amish had uniformly adopted enclosed buggies as the means of family conveyance (even if some unmarried young people still occasionally use open buggies and adults sometimes go to town in spring wagons).[11] Although the precise style, size, and amenities allowed from place to place vary according to local Ordnung, the presence of *enclosed* buggies remains one of the easiest visual signs of an ethnically Pennsylvania German Amish community.

Swiss Amish

The Swiss Amish tradition in America traces its roots to the arrival of Amish directly from Europe in the Midwest during the 1830s-1850s.[12] Some sojourned briefly in Ohio, but by the 1850s two major groups had settled in Allen and Adams counties in Indiana, and from there launched related settlements in other states.[13] While some of these immigrants arrived in America directly from Switzerland, many more had lived for at least a generation in Swiss enclaves outside of the Swiss Confederation.

Perhaps the most commonly cited feature of Swiss Amish ethnicity is the Swiss dialect, which, despite its name, is not identical to the speechways of today's German-speaking sections of Switzerland.[14] Nevertheless, it is closer to that tradition than it is to Pennsylvania German.[15] (This fact may be at the root of the Swiss Amish reference to other Amish as "High Germans" and their dialect as "High German.") America's Swiss Amish forebears brought their speech patterns to relatively isolated language pockets in the Midwest, and while the dialect has changed over time, it did not grow out of an American melding and leveling of multiple dialects in the way Pennsylvania German did. Still, Swiss speech does vary somewhat regionally, and the Amish note that the Swiss spoken in Adams County sounds distinct—and is more intensely "Swiss"—than that spoken in neighboring Allen County.[16]

For the casual observer, the easiest visual way to identify Swiss Amish is by their use of unenclosed buggies in which riders sit in the open air. The particular style and shape of Swiss buggies is not uniform across all Swiss settlements or districts, but their lack of enclosure is a common feature.[17] One variation on this style is the presence in Allen County of "kid boxes." These small compartments on the back of the buggies provide a warmer, enclosed space in which small children may ride in winter.[18]

While the spoken dialects and differing buggy styles are important Pennsylvania

German and Swiss identifiers, they are but two of the many folkways that differentiate these ethnic groups. Swiss cemeteries, for example, mark graves only with narrow wooden stakes that include merely the initials of the deceased. While all Amish reject large decorative gravestones, Pennsylvania German-speaking Amish typically have erected modest stone markers that include the deceased's full name, death date, and age at death. Although some Swiss have now adopted similar stone markers, their traditional practice pointed to the fleeting nature of human life as the deterioration of the wooden stakes denied permanent memorialization.[19]

The Swiss have also maintained a European folk tradition of yodeling. Most common in Adams County, Amish yodeling is a musical style sung by all ages and by both men and women. The Amish have composed some yodels in North America, but many are of Old World origin. They yodel both German-language folksongs, such as "Mie Fater ish a Kahser Zieh" and "Tiggy, Tiggy," and English-language ballads, including "I left my Gal in the Mountain," "Blue Moon," and "Yodel Sweet Molly."[20] Many of these English lyrics are in the vein of traditional love songs or accounts of desperados—yodels that the church does not approve. The presence of such deviant English songs may be puzzling, but they point to the strength of the ethnic tradition among the Swiss group. Yodeling remains a form of recreation for some Swiss Amish families but is unknown among the non-Swiss.[21]

ETHNIC EVOLUTION

If Amish ethnic traditions are distinct, they are not fixed. For one thing, both ethnic groups have incorporated people of non-Amish background into their respective cultures. In the nineteenth century, non-Amish German-speaking immigrants (and some folks of British extraction) were able to join the church with less culture shock than might be the case for today's child of modernity who wishes to become Old Order. Surnames now common in Indiana's Pennsylvania German–speaking settlements, such as Lambright, Chupp, and Whetstone, descend from people absorbed into the Amish community in the nineteenth century.[22] Similarly, the Swiss settlements have incorporated families that did not share in the nineteenth-century European Amish migration saga, including Girod, Wickey, Schmidt, and Knepp, all of which have now become common Swiss Amish names after moving into ethnic circles from outside.[23]

Ethnicity also evolves as a result of interaction with outside contextual influences. For example, Pennsylvania German culture functioned differently in eastern Pennsylvania than it did in the Midwest. In Pennsylvania the Amish shared aspects of ethnic identity with the larger non-Amish Pennsylvania German population that surrounded them. In the nineteenth century many people spoke Pennsylvania German, and the dialect was hardly exclusive to the Amish. Similarly, Amish and non-Amish Pennsylvania German neighbors marked time with a series of ethnically recognized holidays rooted in Continental tradition, including Pentecost Monday and December 26 as a "Second Christmas"—holidays that set their rhythm of life apart from their English neighbors. Nor, for the most part, was their penchant for plain dress highly unusual among other Pennsylvania German religious folk who rejected ostentatious display and personal adornment. In many ways a Pennsylvania German ethnicity set the Amish apart in ways that often paralleled their religious separation from the world.[24]

In the course of the nineteenth century, as these Pennsylvania German Amish moved to the Midwest, their new context had an important bearing on the ethnicity they bore. For example, while they maintained Pennsylvania German as their primary language of family and church, they now spoke it outside its region of origin. In Pennsylvania they had shared the dialect with Lutheran and Reformed neighbors, but in the Midwest the Amish (and some of their Mennonite neighbors) were very often the dialect's sole speakers, so that Pennsylvania German now became a kind of religious signpost too. In Indiana, speaking Pennsylvania German almost always meant that one stood in the Anabaptist tradition—a new ethno-religious linkage that emerged in this new context. Moreover, the dialect continued to evolve in the Midwest and has developed into a distinct form of Midwestern Pennsylvania German that also marks its speakers in subtle ways as different from their East Coast religious relatives.[25]

The Midwestern context also modified the ritual calendar that separated the Amish from larger society. In the East, a larger Pennsylvania German cultural environment had encouraged the Amish to maintain European holidays such as Second Christmas as a way of standing apart from mainstream society. But in Indiana, the Amish found themselves in the midst of a culture that celebrated a commercialized form of December 25 and that pushed the Amish to think about other ways of showing temporal separatism. By the early twentieth century, they had exchanged a traditional Pennsylvania German Second Christmas for a new observance of "Old Christmas" on January 6. In so doing, they continued a sort of calendar distinction, but in a form that was a more relevant symbolic separator in their new environment.

This Midwestern evolution of Pennsylvania German ethnicity was especially evident to Amish who moved to Indiana in the 1990s from Lancaster, Pennsylvania, and settled in Parke and Wayne counties. Although communicating in Pennsylvania German with Indiana's native Pennsylvania German-speaking Amish is not a problem for recent arrivals from the east, they note differences in accent, pronunciation, and some vocabulary. The Lancaster newcomers also note with some puzzlement (though not criticism) the different ritual calendar in Indiana.

In some cases, the ethnic evolution of a settlement may be more dramatic. With very different results, the Daviess County settlement of twenty-two church districts in southwestern Indiana, and the Milroy settlements of four districts east of Indianapolis, have experienced some ethnic transition. Begun in 1869 by Allen County Swiss settlers, recent European Amish arrivals to Ontario, and Amish from Ohio (a few of whom had temporarily lived in Missouri), the Daviess County community initially bore the marks of the emerging Swiss tradition, belying the dominant place of the Allen County contingent.[26] Common surnames in the settlement still point to those roots, and patterns of marriage and visiting tie Daviess and Allen counties. But over the course of the twentieth century, the degree of Swiss ethnicity waned in the Daviess community, despite the general sense among many Amish there that their settlement is Swiss-related. For one thing, the settlement has undergone a remarkable language drift, and Pennsylvania German has displaced Swiss. This trend coincided with several other shifts in cultural folkway, such as the adoption of enclosed buggies in 1990. In some ways the community can now be described as both Swiss and not-Swiss.

The younger Milroy settlement has undergone a reverse set of changes. Begun in 1970 by Pennsylvania German households from Missouri, Ohio, and Wisconsin, the community was ethnically homogeneous until the 1990s, when it began attracting Adams County Swiss families. The reasons for the Swiss influx are complex, but the ethnic results have been clearer: The Swiss dialect has become more common and has not yielded place to the area's original Pennsylvania German. Travel to and from Swiss communities as well as business contacts with Amish in that ethnic circle are increasingly more common. Most aspects of formal Ordnung, however, such as the use of enclosed buggies, continue in Milroy's original tradition.

KIN AND CONNECTION

Ethnicity is bolstered and supported by many things, not the least of which are family networks. The presence and dominance of certain kin groups within each ethnic circle reinforces the notion of who "our people" are, with whom one is related, and to whom one looks for examples and advice on everything from starting a business to solving a church conflict.

While each settlement has its own peculiar constellation of surnames, there are

TABLE 4.2
Most common Amish surnames, by settlement and ethnicity

Pennsylvania German–speaking settlements

Elkhart-LaGrange	% of population	Nappanee	% of population	Kokomo	% of population
Miller	25	Miller	19	Herschberger	26
Yoder	14	Hochstetler[a]	12	Miller	22
Bontrager[a]	12	Borkholder[a]	10	Otto	18
Hochstetler[a]	5	Yoder	9	Bontrager	12
Lambright	4	Schwartz	5		78%
	60%		55%		

Swiss settlements

Adams County	% of population	Allan County	% of population	Daviess County	% of population
Schwartz	45	Graber	24	Wagler	25
Hilty	10	Lengacher	17	Graber	22
Wickey	8	Schmucker	16	Knepp	17
Eicher	7	Schwartz	10	Raber	9
Girod	6	Eicher	6	Stoll	9
	76%		73%		82%

SOURCE: Most recent settlement directories.
[a]Includes spelling variations, such as Bontreger, Borntrager, Hostetler, Burkholder, etc.

also broadly defined Swiss and Pennsylvania German names (see table 4.2). Amish people can easily identity the surnames common to each group. In the oldest settlements of each group, between 55 and 82 percent of people carry just five surnames.

Intermarriage commonly occurs not only within church affiliation but also within ethnic circles. However, there are a few notable exceptions that prove the rule, such as intermarriage between a handful of Adams County Swiss and Pennsylvania German-speaking Nappanee households. One of these unions produced an exceptionally large family, which, several generations later, had made the Swiss surname Schwartz more common in Nappanee than would otherwise be the case. Still the rates of ethnic intermarriage are low.[27] And since marriages also predict subsequent habits of family visiting and other kinship connections, endogamy reinforces the ethnic divide.

Naming patterns within families are another way that ethnic identity is reinforced, reminding children from an early age of their place in a larger community network. In that sense, child naming is also a primary means of propping up peoplehood within each group, although the particular means of doing so differs along ethnic lines.[28] Traditional naming patterns among Pennsylvania German Amish in Pennsylvania dictate that each child receive its mother's maiden surname as a middle name. This pattern leaves only the first name as an expression of individual choice on the part of parents, while the last two-thirds are ascribed.[29] The system also explicitly ties each child to both paternal and maternal family lines, making legal forms of address ethnic markers, as well. For example:

Parents: John K. Esh and Naomi B. Fisher
Children: Samuel F. [Fisher] Esh
            Amanda F. [Fisher] Esh

The Amish living in Parke and Wayne Counties, Indiana, who moved to the Midwest from Lancaster in the 1990s have, for the most part, continued this naming tradition.

In contrast, Pennsylvania German–speaking settlements with longstanding histories in the Midwest—for example, Elkhart-LaGrange, Nappanee, Kokomo, and related communities—evolved a different pattern, but one that also tied children to their families of origin with both middle initials and last names. These children typically received as their middle initial the first letter of their father's first name. Here the middle initial and last name connects only to paternal ancestry, but they still provide names determined by birth and not parental creativity:

Parents: Joe C. Miller and Emma L. Bontrager
Children: Anna J. [Joe] Miller
            Harvey J. [Joe] Miller

Among the Swiss, a more limited set of inherited surnames and accepted first names has actually produced more variety in naming patterns. Traditionally, middle initials are the same for all children in a Swiss family and are family-linked, but the middle initial may be the first letter of the father's first name, the first letter of the mother's first name, or the first letter of the mother's maiden surname. In some cases, children receive two initials, corresponding to both the father's and mother's first names:

Parents: Noah L. Girod and Barbara V. Eicher
Children: Emma N. B. [Noah and Barbara] Girod
            Ervin N. B. [Noah and Barbara] Girod

Given the smaller name pool among the Swiss—especially in the Adams County settlement—even the combination of parental initials and surnames does not provide enough practical distinction in a community filled with Schwartzes whose fathers' names begin with *J* or whose mothers' begin with *M*. As a result, some parents have given all their children the same arbitrarily chosen middle initial *X* or *Q*

TABLE 4.3
Elkhart-LaGrange settlement children with father's
first name as middle initial, by age cohort

Age cohort	
over 65	63.8% (N = 630)
50–65	59.0% (N = 881)
40–49	58.1% (N = 1025)
30–39	48.3% (N = 1487)
under 30	21.1% (N = 9087)

SOURCE: 1995 settlement directory

or *U*. This practice demonstrates a continued commitment to a tradition in which a middle initial—as much as a last name—is a marker of ascribed family identity, while giving a nod to the practical problem of identification in a community populated by relatively few extended family networks.

In some settlements, these patterns of naming are changing, suggesting that names are moving into the realm of creative choice and are less an ascribed marker of ethnic inclusion. In Indiana's older and larger non-Swiss settlements, parents increasingly lay aside ethnic naming patterns and bestow different middle names on each child, such as Brian Anthony or Alison Diane, thus leaving only the surname as a sign of the child's place in the community. This turn toward individuality in naming and a loss of the ethnic component is more pronounced in each generation, as illustrated in table 4.3.

INTERACTION AND IDENTITY

If ethnicity is strengthened and promoted through families and the ties created by marriage, visiting, and naming children, ethnic identity is reinforced through interaction with outsiders. But while it can, along with the patterns of geography and the practice of Ordnung, help define the Amish in relation to non-Amish neighbors, ethnicity plays a special role in providing a sense of Amish particularity vis-à-vis other Amish. The presence of two different ethnic groups within a broader church tradition—ethnic groups that do not break down exactly along Ordnung or other churchly lines—point to the distinction between church and family, between the bonds of blood and the bonds of baptismal water, and help fortify the fact that the Amish church is not synonymous with Amish parentage.

Ethnicity shapes one's view of the Amish world by directing ties to certain other groups and locations. When asked to name Amish settlements in other states, Indiana Swiss immediately mention other Swiss communities in Seymour, Missouri, or Quincy, Michigan, whereas the non-Swiss will mention Holmes County, Ohio;

Arthur, Illinois; or Lancaster, Pennsylvania. Testimony to the significance of these ties is the degree of ethnic isolation each group has had from the controversies that have troubled the other. For example, the mid-nineteenth-century *Dienerversammlungen* drew relatively few Swiss participants, and the controversial twentieth-century Amish mission movement bypassed the Swiss communities. Similarly, a bitter 1894 Adams County schism that produced the Amish Christian Church was little noticed outside Swiss circles.[30]

The combination of limited interaction and unfamiliarity with one another's problems has also produced a certain amount of stereotyping between both groups, especially with regard to the deviant behavior of unbaptized young people or the implied expectations surrounding business contracts. Those from Pennsylvania German–speaking settlements shake their heads at what they believe to be intemperate use of alcohol on the part of some Swiss, or what they perceive as a Swiss penchant for trying to make an extra dollar on every deal. Swiss Amish are apt to consider those they call "High Germans" too often allured by consumer goods and not sufficiently concerned with simple living. Regardless of the real differences among the Swiss and Pennsylvania German on such scores, the scope and scale of those differences is sometimes exaggerated in the casual remarks and even gossip that circulates within a given ethnic enclave.

The durability of dialects also points to popular Amish perception of the cultural refinement of each group. In cases of intermarriage, linguist Chad Thompson found, Swiss speakers more quickly adapt to Pennsylvania German than Pennsylvania German speakers do to Swiss. The differences seem to have little to do with the difficulty of learning each dialect and more to do with the Amish sense that Pennsylvania German—and its attendant culture—is somehow superior. At least some parents in ethnically mixed marriages believe that their children should speak Pennsylvania German because it is a more refined language than Swiss.[31]

Stereotypes function best at a distance, but even limited direct interaction, such as the few cases of ethnic intermarriage or migration from one ethnic stronghold to another, often provide opportunities for reinforcing popular notions of difference. In a recent and rather unprecedented migration, twenty Swiss households moved to the non-Swiss Elkhart-LaGrange settlement, where they clustered in seven church districts on the settlement's eastern and more conservative edge. All arrived between 1994 and 2002, and seventeen came from Adams County.[32] Elkhart-LaGrange natives credit the mini-exodus to mid-1990s church conflicts in the Adams settlement and the desire of people to "get away from all that controversy down there." Indeed, more than half the families came in 1997–99, as the Adams County

Swiss were suffering new rounds of schism. But from the standpoint of ethnic relations, it is significant that the Swiss arrivals have stuck close together, and their
coming served to confirm Pennsylvania German notions of contentious Swiss
church life and authoritarian bishops. Elkhart-LaGrange natives believe they can always tell who has "Swiss blood" simply by the way one acts and reacts, testimony
to the cultures expressed through ethnicity.

Yet the Amish do not always see their differences in a negative light. For example, some Pennsylvania German speakers who perceive the Swiss to be more blunt
and confrontational, credit this characteristic when asked to explain why the Swiss
have been disproportionately involved in Amish negotiation with the state on matters of private school recognition or the military draft. In such cases, the non-Swiss
appreciate what they term the Swiss willingness to "take matters head on."

This presumed difference in communication style illustrates some of the cultural variation behind the ethnic labels. Contrasting ideas of ecclesial authority are
another example of a commonly credited difference between the two ethnic
streams. Traditionally, the Swiss have vested more authority in their bishops as decision makers and agents of church discipline, sometimes even sanctioning excommunication by a bishop without the counsel of the rest of the district.[33] While this
characteristic certainly is not the sum of the Swiss approach to church life, it stands
in contrast to the habits of most other Amish, whose polity typically gives the congregation greater voice.

Given these and other differences in practice and perception, the two Amish ethnic streams show few signs of melting away, and even positive interaction can end
up highlighting a sense of the ethnic "otherness." For example, the Adams County–
born Swiss minister and bishop John L. Schwartz (1890–1993) served the church in
Nappanee nearly seventy-seven years. Despite his longevity in that community,
the highly respected Schwartz never lost his Swiss accent and was widely known
throughout the settlement for his distinctive-sounding sermons that set him apart
as "Swiss."

CULTURES IN CONTEXT

As the example of John Schwartz shows, ethnicity never stands alone as a marker
in Amish life. If Schwartz was prototypically Swiss, he was just as clearly something
more: a bishop responsible for overseeing faithfulness to the Ordnung in the Nappanee settlement that had a distinct history and was set in a local context populated
with particular neighbors, civic leaders, population pressures, and economic op-

portunities. All of these things and more were part of how John Schwartz was Amish.

Clearly, the three major internal identity factors considered thus far—migration history, Ordnung, and ethnicity—are not discrete. They are overlapping and cross-cutting, creating patterns of peoplehood that are varied and complex. But focusing only on these factors as a way of understanding Amish identity is inadequate, since the multidimensional character of any culture involves its interaction with wider contexts. And context supplies not simply a setting for Amish life, but also crucial components in the construction of Amish experience.

In the four chapters that follow, community case studies look at different settlements and groups of settlements, exploring how internal group factors and external contextual factors combine in complex ways to shape cultural identity.

Comparative Communities

Comparative Communities

CHAPTER FIVE

Elkhart-LaGrange and Nappanee Settlements

Each year millions of tourists crowd small towns in northern Indiana's LaGrange and Elkhart counties, seeking a few hours or a few days in what regional tourist bureaus bill as "Amish Country."[1] Whether in Nappanee's Amish Acres commercial and museum complex or at the sprawling Shipshewana Flea Market grounds twenty-five miles to the northeast, these visitors rarely encounter Old Orders directly, but they are sure to see some of the area's 23,000 Amish who share the rural roads and occasionally staff village retail shops and restaurants, and who populate the two large and all-but-adjacent settlements known as Elkhart-LaGrange and Nappanee.[2]

By almost any measure—numeric, cultural, or economic—the Amish presence in these north central Indiana communities is significant. The Elkhart-LaGrange settlement is the third largest anywhere. And unlike its more famous Lancaster, Pennsylvania, counterpart—a larger settlement but one that comprises a relatively small portion of the local population—northern Indiana Amish dominate area demography.[3] In LaGrange County, in fact, they account for about half of all residents.

Outsiders are not the only ones who associate the area with the Amish. Fellow church members in other parts of the United States associate Indiana with these two settlements—and with good reason, since the 123 church districts in Elkhart-LaGrange, along with Nappanee's 33 districts, represent 58 percent of Indiana's Amish population. The opinions of Amish living in this region carry weight across the state, symbolized by the fact that the chairman of the Indiana Amish School Committee has always been an Elkhart-LaGrange settlement resident, as has the state's representative to the National Amish Steering Committee.[4] While hardly unaware of other Old Order Hoosiers, the Nappanee and Elkhart-LaGrange churches bear a quiet self-confidence that suggests that they see themselves as standing in the center of the Amish tradition.[5]

In some important ways the Nappanee and Elkhart-LaGrange settlements are clearly different from one another. But in other respects they share similarities that reflect their common geographic and economic contexts as well as their shared ethnic heritage and understanding of Ordnung. Life in these two communities highlights the ways in which external economic and community forces interact with lively internal factors in forming dynamic Amish cultural identities.

SETTLEMENT ROOTS

Amish settlers began arriving in north central Indiana about the same time federal troops forced Native Americans from the region and encouraged settlement of white farmers from the East.[6] In 1840 a group of Amish land scouts from Somerset County, Pennsylvania, considered available acres as far west as Iowa City, before exploring options in Illinois and Indiana. "After inspecting this country [near Goshen, Indiana] which suited them very well, they agreed to make this region the future home for their church," remembered one of the earliest residents.[7]

Four southwestern Pennsylvania households moved to Indiana's Elkhart County in the summer of 1841, stopping briefly among coreligionists in Holmes County, Ohio. After building temporary homes south of Goshen, the Amish soon took up permanent claims in the eastern portion of Elkhart County and across the border in neighboring LaGrange County. Other Pennsylvania and Ohio families joined them, forming the nucleus of a settlement that would span the county boundary. In the fall of 1841 the group—which by then included a minister and a deacon—held its first church service, and regular Sunday worship gatherings began the next spring.[8]

Tensions among early arrivals marked the settlement's first two decades, and in local memory often seemed to pit more tradition-minded residents, who came from Pennsylvania, against those who haled from Ohio and had a penchant for change. Conflict as early as 1847 simmered for several years, and by 1857—almost a decade before the distinction between Old Order and progressive Amish surfaced in most other parts of the country—a schism divided the community.[9]

The Old Order wing of the church took root especially in LaGrange County; by 1866 it had formed two church districts there, and then two more by 1881. These four districts, along with one in eastern Elkhart County, constituted the Elkhart-LaGrange Old Order settlement in 1900. By 2003 the settlement had grown to in-

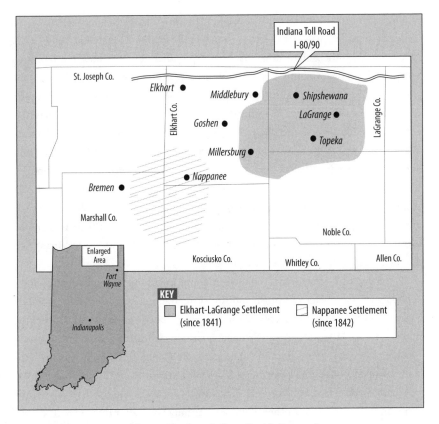

Map 5.1. Northern Indiana "Amish Country"

clude 115 districts, about one-third of which were located in Elkhart County and the balance in eastern LaGrange and the northern edge of Noble counties.[10]

The town of Nappanee, in Elkhart County's southwest corner, lends its name to the other sizable Old Order settlement in northern Indiana. To many visitors, and even to some non-Amish locals, the distinction between this settlement and the neighboring Elkhart-LaGrange settlement is fuzzy. Yet Old Orders themselves know that despite the proximity of the two, they bear key differences, including distinct origins. The first Amish arrived in what would become the Nappanee community in 1842, more than thirty years before the town of Nappanee itself was laid out and named.[11] But unlike their coreligionists a few miles to the east, who had followed a fairly simple westward migration from Pennsylvania and Ohio to Indiana, the Nappanee settlement had a more complicated genesis, including not only descendants of eighteenth-century Amish arrivals from the East, but also recent nineteenth-century European immigrants who had come directly to the Midwest.

Furthermore, the initial Amish attraction to the future Nappanee settlement had less to do with the presence of other Amish in the nearby Elkhart-LaGrange settlement than with the pull of non-Amish relatives. Shared blood lines, not baptismal vows, factored prominently in this early history. Take the case of Christian Stahly (1820–1909) and Veronica Housouer Stahly (1822–1897), the first Amish to make the Nappanee area their home.[12] An immigrant of 1835 from the German Palatinate, Christian Stahly settled initially in Stark County, Ohio, but soon moved to Ohio's Wayne County where he met Housouer, who was related to a network of Amish and formerly Amish Mishler and Keck families living in Ohio, western Pennsylvania, and Ontario. By the 1830s, members of the Canadian branch of this clan—who were no longer religiously Amish—had moved to northern Indiana. When the Stahlys and other Ohio Amish households—including several of Christian Stahly's brothers and his mother—joined them, beginning in 1842, they were following family ties, not specific churchly connections.[13]

The complex system of kin connection, sometimes interwoven with religion, resulted in an assemblage of Amish and Amish-related households that included European newcomers with surnames such as Ringenberg and Welty, along with the heirs of Yoder, Hochstetler, and Schlabach families whose ancestors had arrived in Philadelphia generations earlier.[14] The early Nappanee settlement was not especially compact and spanned northeast Marshall and southeast Elkhart counties. The originally swamp lands of northern Kosciusko County to the south of Elkhart became home to Amish and other white settlers only later, after they were drained.[15]

Like members of the nearby Elkhart-LaGrange Amish community, the Nappanee settlement suffered a division in the 1850s, with the conservatives aligning with the Old Order movement.[16] The Old Order group was overwhelmingly Pennsylvania German in ethnic composition (like the Elkhart-LaGrange settlement's population) and remained small throughout the nineteenth century, spawning a second Old Order district only in 1906. Over the course of the next century, the settlement expanded geographically—especially northeast and southeast—and grew in numbers so that by 2006 it included thirty-three church districts.[17]

Despite their different origins, the subsequent Elkhart-LaGrange and Nappanee stories in some ways paralleled one another. During the 1940s, for example, both settlements experienced the withdrawal of disgruntled members who formed so-called Beachy Amish congregations, identified by their adoption of automobile travel, less-traditional dress, and English-language worship in designated church buildings. Next, the "Amish mission movement" of the 1950s and 1960s roiled both the Elkhart-LaGrange and Nappanee Old Order communities, leading to the exodus of some younger leaders and leaving in its wake a more sectarian Old Order religious outlook.[18] Meanwhile, twentieth-century regional economic trends and school consolidation shaped occupational possibilities and educational options in both settlements.

Despite their proximity and complementary histories, members of each settlement maintain a distinct sense of themselves. Visiting between groups of young people and adults—and some intermarriage—does link the two communities, but the population of each remains overwhelmingly locally born and reared. Certain surnames predominate in each place, and local geographic orientations, professional services, commercial shopping opportunities, and school district boundaries also mark the two settlements, so that interaction with the wider world is different in each place. Not least, the relative size of the two settlements shapes their views of themselves and one another. The Elkhart-LaGrange settlement is almost four times larger than its neighbor and casts a bigger shadow in relationships with other Amish, the state, and the general population. Knowledgeable Nappanee Amish can still keep tabs on nearly all families in their settlement—something that is not possible for members of the Elkhart-LaGrange community.

One indication of the important difference that members make between the two settlements was a meeting in January 2001 in which leaders from the eastern-most Nappanee church district and the western-most Elkhart-LaGrange district agreed "that a church line between the [two settlements] should be established ¼ mile east of Elkhart County CR 25."[19] As both settlements continue to expand, residents foresaw their eventual geographic melding and took steps to ensure a friendly but clear distinction between the two. The two north central Indiana settlements may share a common ethnicity and a fairly compatible approach to Ordnung, but they remain rooted in different migration histories and kinship systems that perpetuate separate identities.

MODERATION IN ALL THINGS

A key feature of those identities is a shared history of churchly moderation that has discouraged conflict over Ordnung. Both settlements have experienced minor schisms through the years, but the number of disaffected members in each case has been relatively small. Perhaps more significantly, multiple affiliations within Old Order ranks have not developed here, and all church districts throughout northern Indiana maintain fellowship with one another. True, some dissenters have left the area in silent protest to changes they see coming too quickly or too slowly, but one of the marks of these northern Hoosiers has been consensus and forbearance. This temperament has in fact proven to be a point of distinction that is not lost on area

Old Orders. When they do recount stories of contention, the moral typically lies in the wisdom of staying with the church's mainstream majority.

A frequently cited negative example is that of Marshall County minister Samuel J. Christner (1888–1980), who in 1932 led sixteen conservative-minded families in breaking fellowship with the surrounding Nappanee churches, convinced that the majority was too technologically permissive. The onset of the Great Depression had forced some farm families to look for alternative sources of income, including taking jobs with non-Amish businesses in town or driving delivery trucks—changes to which Christner and his allies objected. Although the "Sam Christner Church" was not large, the division was bitter.[20]

In 1934 the Christner Church ordained Erlis Kemp (1897–1978) as minister, and two years later an Old Order Amish preacher from Mississippi moved to Marshall County to join the dissident group.[21] It soon became clear, however, that there was as much conflict within the Christner Church as between it and the larger Old Order body and that the new group lacked stable leadership. A year after his arrival, the Mississippi minister left for another conservative-minded settlement, and the Christner Church deacon soon followed him. Erlis Kemp, the recently ordained minister, rejoined the main Old Order group (only to defect again to the progressive Beachy Amish, signaling to Old Order observers the volatility of the Christner path). The Christner Church dwindled, and members left for other states. Christner, now the lone leader, moved away in 1947, bringing Nappanee's short-lived Old Order alternative to an end.

To the east, the Elkhart-LaGrange settlement witnessed a similar murmur of mid-century conservative dissent, but one that soon exited the area. Between 1953 and 1961 five ministers and a group of lay members from LaGrange County relocated to Kenton, Ohio, to establish a settlement that was decidedly more traditional in its use of technology and separatist in its interaction with larger society. Other LaGrange families moved to places such as Paoli, Indiana, with similar intentions. All of them objected to the shift toward factory employment in northern Indiana, which they saw as a sign of creeping "worldliness" that also expressed itself in less-traditional dress standards, an unrestrained youth culture, and greater openness to technological change. Similarly, some Amish sympathetic to New Order Amish values left the region in the 1980s and 1990s for New Order communities in places like Rosebush, Michigan, rather than establish a competing New Order church in northern Indiana.

The only break-away Old Order affiliation to remain within the Elkhart-LaGrange settlement emerged in the spring of 1987, when about a half-dozen households aligned with bishop Clemence J. Miller (1915–98) after a group of bishops called in to investigate controversy in Miller's church found his leadership to be the cause of the strife and silenced him. The roots and expression of the conflict were complex and involved Miller's opposition to liberalizing household technology, his support of strict shunning (*streng Meidung*) in contrast to the settlement's prevailing practice, and his seeking counsel from Swiss Amish leaders across the border in Michigan rather than yielding to the advice of ministers from within his own settlement. That Miller also appeared to support a highly innovative Amish entrepreneur who used attention-grabbing advertising only lowered Miller's status and made his support of traditional ways seem hypocritical to others. A decade later, the Miller group included a handful of older people and no children, and seemed headed for extinction.[22]

In each of these cases, a settlement mainstream rejected schism, and separatist groups quickly died out or left the area to embody their cause elsewhere. When today's Old Orders cite these cases, they hold them up as negative examples that in turn point to the dynamic center that holds current northern Indiana settlement life together. Some Amish in Elkhart-LaGrange and Nappanee even insist that their communities will not experience significant divisions, and many point out that they have no competing affiliations. Men and women here—though slow to criticize other Amish ways—mention with regret the multiple affiliations that exist among Old Orders in, say, northeast Ohio, or Indiana's Adams County, and are thankful that similar divisions have not formed here.

APPROACHES TO ORDNUNG

The resistance to division and sense of moderation that the Elkhart-LaGrange and Nappanee settlements value has not been imposed by a settlement-wide leadership scheme. If they have avoided the competing claims of multiple affiliations, they have not done so with an approach to Ordnung that assumes uniformity or unanimity.

The two northern Indiana settlements have retained a congregationalism that places the authority of Ordnung in district hands. Although church districts respect one another's views and differing convictions, they guard their congregational prerogatives. Modification of Ordnung surrounding technology, for example, has not occurred in a uniform way; there is no united front of resistance to change or embrace of innovation. For example, some church districts in the Elkhart-LaGrange settlement began using bottled gas as a heating and power source in the 1920s, while others did not accept it until the 1990s.[23] Kitchen refrigerators, bicycles, power lawnmowers, and bulk milk tanks are all things whose adoption and adaptation varied considerably from one place to another, yet have not led to a break in fellowship or to the birth of a new affiliations.[24] In 2002 near Shipshewana, a sixty-year-old man might eagerly describe his "new buggy with a gas heater, cup holder, arm rest with storage compartment, extra dropped storage under the seating for shopping, windshield wipers, battery-operated turn signals, foot brakes, and multiple rearview mirrors"; while a few miles away in another district, such amenities would not be found.

This polity pattern contrasts sharply with that of the Lancaster, Pennsylvania, settlement, where all the bishops, presided over by the senior bishop, meet twice a year to approve or reject changes percolating from below. Northern Indiana Amish are familiar with what they term the "Lancaster system of administration" and are quick to distinguish themselves from it, emphasizing their own inclinations toward district authority.[25]

In the 1960s, Elkhart-LaGrange leaders did begin holding an annual gathering of church leaders, but they have never expected that all ministers would attend every year. Furthermore, they take pains to point out that their gathering's chairmanship rotates and does not invest any one bishop with ongoing power or seniority. The meetings serve as a place for leaders to consult with one another, perhaps to get advice on settling local disputes, and sometimes to encourage more persuasive teaching on particular subjects through sermons. For example, a 2002 gathering held in the wake of the much-publicized broadcast of the documentary film *The Devil's Playground,* which featured the actions of deviant northern Indiana Amish teens, resulted in strong admonition against rowdy youth behavior.[26] But the settlement ministers' gatherings do not produce mandates on particular matters, nor do they dictate Ordnung decisions. The Nappanee ministers' meeting functions in a similar way. Begun about 1972, it features a rotating moderator, draws about 50 percent of eligible attendees in any given year, and provides a forum for fellowship and counsel, but not for issuing final administrative rulings.[27]

If the Amish here see virtue in maintaining community through cooperation and mutual forbearance, they also express some misgivings about the degree of Ordnung diversity. The growth of the northern Indiana settlements magnifies the multiple opinions found here. With 123 districts, the Elkhart-LaGrange settlement includes, by some reckonings, 123 different approaches to Ordnung and 123 different ways to be faithfully Old Order Amish. Yet the reality is less random than such a characterization implies. Because districts make decisions with an eye to neighboring opinion—either in deference or reaction to adjoining districts—recognized clusters of opinion emerge. Church members are aware of the contours of diversity and can locate patterns of practice. Referring to more restrictive understandings of Ordnung as "lower" and more progressive views as "higher," Amish com-

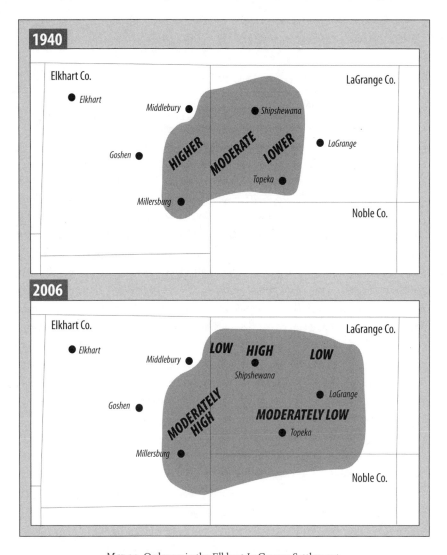

Map 5.2. Ordnung in the Elkhart-LaGrange Settlement

mentators add metaphors of elevation as they describe how the churchly landscape has changed (see table 5.1).

Local Elkhart-LaGrange memory reconstructs early and mid-twentieth-century Amish Ordnung in terms of a rough slope descending from west to east. At the time, those in Elkhart County—particularly its Clinton Township residents—had the "highest" churches and represented the settlement's progressive peak. Adjacent LaGrange County districts from Shipshewana to Topeka observed a moderate Ordnung, and those further east in Clearspring Township had the "lowest" Ordnung,

TABLE 5.1

Examples of "higher" and "lower" Ordnung in the Elkhart-LaGrange settlement

Low	High
Cautious about secular reading material	Use cell phones
Hire non-Amish drivers sparingly	Men omit suspenders
Avoid attending county fair	Take out-of-state sight-seeing vacations
Eat mostly home-preserved food	Buy more frozen food at store
Share community phone	More children enrolled in public school

meaning they were the most conservative. While maintaining common fellowship with one another, area Old Orders—especially young people looking for spouses with similar convictions—understood the lived differences. The more refined Clinton folks of the 1930s and 1940s, for example, referred to those from the "lower" eastern end of the settlement with the mildly derisive label "Clearspring Simmies."

The dynamic nature of Amish congregationalism, of course, means that none of these patterns were fixed. In the 1950s and 60s, as some key Clinton progressives left Old Order circles and committed conservatives moved out of LaGrange County entirely, the balance began to shift. Suburbanization and commercialization around the town of Shipshewana, coupled with a key church leadership change there in 1979, has led to the emergence of new center of "higher" (progressive) Ordnung in and around that village. At least partly in reaction, the two areas with the lowest Ordnung are now pockets on either side of Shipshewana—Howe to the east, and "the Barrens" area to the west. The Elkhart County portion of the settlement still bears some reputation for progressive inclinations, while the Topeka and surrounding area of southern and eastern LaGrange County feature moderately conservative expressions of Amish life.

Undoubtedly, the settlement profile will continue to evolve as districts make choices in informal conversation with their neighbors. Significantly, however, the most progressive and more traditionalist elements within the settlement show no signs of increasing their relative size and influence, apparently leaving the future of the community in the hands of those occupying the moderating middle ground. In those church districts generally regarded as being the most progressive, the percentage of children leaving the Amish fold is the highest, muting the liberals' future influence. Those widely seen as adhering to the most conservative Ordnung have the least number of children leaving the faith, but their potential impact on the settlement is limited by the fact that they have the highest rates of migration out of the settlement. Disappointed with the progressive drift of the community but uninterested in betraying their heritage of avoiding schism, they handle conflict by moving away (see table 5.2).

TABLE 5.2
Defection and migration of adult children, Elkhart-LaGrange settlement (%)

	Defection	Migration out of settlement
Districts with lowest Ordnung ("conservatives") N = 219 adult children	7	22
Districts with highest Ordnung ("progressives") N = 781 adult children	31	8

SOURCES: Amish informants' consensus on the most conservative districts (two clusterings of 10 districts) and the most progressive districts (cluster of 12). Percentages are of adult children of all members in these districts as listed in the 2002 settlement directory. Data from the 1995 and 1988 directories yield very similar results; these are long-term Elkhart-LaGrange patterns.

A similar pattern of congregationalism, coupled with another set of historical dynamics, produced a different Ordnung topography in Nappanee. There, mid-twentieth-century observers noted that the northwest portion of the settlement—often called Burkholder Corner—had the settlement's lowest Ordnung, while the opposite, southeastern area, was less tradition-minded.[28] During the past three decades, however, the degree of diversity within the Nappanee settlement has declined. The annual minister's meeting has promoted a certain level of common conversation, though the body mandates no settlement-wide changes. Instead, leaders attribute the growing convergence to a general trend toward adopting a higher Ordnung everywhere in the settlement. "Most [other Amish] people would probably say we're liberal here," conceded one bishop.

In part, this convergence may be linked to a common loss of agricultural ways of life most closely tied to traditional Ordnung observances. In that respect, the Nappanee community, like its Elkhart-LaGrange partner, reflects the shift away from farming that characterizes almost all Amish settlements in North America. The nature and degree of that shift in northern Indiana, however, are distinctive.

REGIONAL CONTEXTS

The regional contexts in which Old Order communities exist are as significant for shaping their identities as their Amish convictions. Although Amish informants can easily differentiate themselves from their Ohio and Pennsylvania counterparts in terms of church administration and affiliation, economic markets have also played major roles in contemporary Indiana Amish life. Occupational opportunities reflect these realities and in turn create their own patterns and possibilities of interaction with the wider world.

The Amish have never been economically isolated or self-sufficient communities. Nineteenth-century families, overwhelmingly engaged in agricultural pursuits, appear to have diverged little in practice from their non-Amish farm neighbors. In 1860, among LaGrange County's Newbury Township farm families, Amish households stood near the norm of area agriculture. They owned average numbers of horses and sheep, raised typical crops of corn and hay, and produced normal amounts of butter.[29] In the late nineteenth and early twentieth centuries, Amish farmers also participated in the region's cash crop, commercial peppermint.[30]

As population growth put pressure on land prices and then availability, northern Indiana Amish responded by forming new settlements in other Midwest and plains states. Between 1892 and 1905, for example, families from Nappanee moved to Hubbard, Oregon; Mylo, North Dakota; Carrington, North Dakota; White Cloud, Michigan; Gibson, Mississippi; and Newton County, Indiana.[31] Some households may have picked up stakes to escape family disagreements or church conflicts, but migration was primarily a way to maintain or improve economic status.

That strategy changed during the Dust Bowl and the Great Depression as many of these newer settlements, often established on marginal land or some distance from access to rail lines, folded.[32] As families began to move back to Hoosier communities they had left a few years or a few decades before, they carried the message that launching new farming enterprises was risky and that remaining by traditional hearths—even if that meant taking up nonfarming jobs—might be the surer path to stability. During the late 1930s some younger Amish men in the Elkhart-LaGrange and Nappanee settlements began working in local factories, at area grain elevators, and—in a few cases—driving delivery trucks. Hard-pressed churches conceded driver's licenses to men who otherwise had no work, provided they drove only when they were on the job and working for a non-Amish employer who owned the vehicle.[33] In exceptional cases, Nappanee household heads hard-hit by Depression economics took government-sponsored jobs through the Works Progress Administration.[34]

A number of factors conspired to make farming less viable as the twentieth century wore on. Population growth—both Amish and non-Amish—continued to squeeze available acres and spike land prices. With the loss of the commercial mint market, an important cash source evaporated, leaving farmers with dairying or crop farming on the modest scale afforded by the region's eighty-acre farms. In the Nappanee settlement, after 1960 some districts permitted farmers to rent their land to tractor-farming non-Amish neighbors while the Amish owners took day jobs in town. That option was never approved by churches in Elkhart-LaGrange, which may have slowed the transition away from agriculture there, accounting for its somewhat higher—though continually declining—share of farm families.[35]

After 1972, when new state dairy regulations mandated milk cooling in bulk milk tanks that required home-generated or utility-provided electricity, some churches balked, opting instead to continue using water-cooled cans even if it meant shipping lower-priced Grade B milk. But this choice also weakened farm profits. Unlike the Lancaster, Pennsylvania, Amish, whose settlement-wide decision-making structure had allowed for the adoption of bulk tanks when similar regulations came into play there, the patchwork nature of Amish polity in northern Indiana meant that no such settlement bargain would be struck with milk marketers. Instead, the Amish exodus from farming in northern Indiana only picked up steam. In the late 1970s several Amish entrepreneurs joined Mennonite businessmen in sponsoring a local cheese-making establishment—Das Deutsche Käse Haus—to provide an outlet for Grade B milk. Although the project was quite successful in itself, it did not boost the number of Amish farmers.[36]

By the late 1980s, farming had become a minority pursuit among Amish men in both the Elkhart-LaGrange and Nappanee settlements, and factory work was the norm.[37] One bishop, noting the irony of the situation, laughed that now "we have to take our children to the steam shows [museum reenactments] to show them what thrashing is!" Although some families have retained acreage and continue to plant and harvest crops during evening hours or on Saturdays while the household head earns a living on the factory floor, the percentage and absolute number of full-time farmers continues to slide.

But the difficulties in farming were coupled by the ease with which men could land industrial jobs, the comfortable wages they provided, and the lack of labor union restrictions. "Once they get used to that weekly pay check it's hard to give it up," one Nappanee church leader conceded.

When area Amish men looked for jobs outside the agriculture sector, it was no surprise that they turned to factory work. Industrial manufacturing, especially of recreational vehicles and prefabricated homes, is a remarkably large part of the region's economy. Amish men turned to factory work because it was the type of wage labor the local economy offered, and they have remained in such jobs roughly in proportion to their non-Amish working neighbors (table 5.3).

If the Amish occupational profile in northern Indiana reflects its economic context, it diverges sharply from the Amish experience in almost every other part of North America. With the exception of Geauga County, Ohio, where a sizable number of Old Order men work in non-Amish owned industry, factory work is all but unknown in the Amish world.[38] In most other places, Amish-owned microenterprises lodged at or near home and employing immediate family members or neighbors have been the Amish alternative to farming. While the number of small busi-

Illustration 5.1. A young, unmarried man rides his bicycle to work at a factory. In the Nappanee and Elkhart-LaGrange settlements, boys and men of all ages regularly wear knit caps. Source: Courtesy of the Mennonite Historical Library/Joel Fath.

TABLE 5.3
Manufacturing as a percentage of all jobs, 2000

All workers		Amish workers (household heads under 65)	
United States	14.2		
Indiana	23.4		
LaGrange County	49.7	Elkhart-LaGrange settlement (2002)	52.9
Elkhart County	52.0	Nappanee settlement[a] (2001)	59.4
Kosciusko County	47.6		
Marshall County	42.0		

[a]The Nappanee settlement spans Elkhart, Kosciusko, and Marshall counties.

nesses in Elkhart-LaGrange and Nappanee has increased during the 1990s, that occupational option has done little to dislodge the attraction of factory work in northern Indiana—and certainly has not achieved the status that it has in Pennsylvania or Ohio, where small shops are clearly the most popular alternative to agriculture. In those areas it is commonplace to say that factory work is antithetical to Old Order life and that such work spells the end of Amish society. The experience in northern Indiana, however, suggests a more complex relationship (table 5.4).

TABLE 5.4

Occupations of Amish household heads under age 65 (%)

Elkhart-LaGrange settlement

	1995	2002
Farmer	25.4	17.4
Factory	54.0	52.9
Carpentry/construction trades	4.1	7.5
Shop owner/worker	9.7	16.5
Other	6.7	5.6
	N = 2139	N = 2735

Nappanee settlement

	1993	2001
Farmers	11.7	8.3
Factory	58.8	59.4
Carpentry/construction trades	8.8	6.3
Shop owner/worker	9.7	15.8
Other	11.0	10.3
	N = 556	N = 679

SOURCE: Settlement directories.

THE EFFECTS OF INDUSTRY

Despite their heavy involvement in industry, Elkhart-LaGrange and Nappanee Amish men and women are far from fond of such work. They can quickly list its negative aspects, including the intense pressure of assembly line performance. "The line keeps moving," one employee explained. "It just keeps moving whether your piece fits or not!" In addition to the general stress of the factory floor, Amish hands cite the crude language and occasional drug use on the part of non-Amish coworkers as a bad influence—especially on Amish-reared young men who have not yet joined the church.

And yet these criticisms are part of a larger picture that belies simplistic caricature. A clear sense of separation persists, even in the midst of such close elbow-rubbing with the dominant economy. Amish men choose to hire on with firms that employ large numbers of fellow church members, in effect creating ethnic subcultures at work. Some factories have 50 to 70 percent Amish staff, and even those that employ relatively few Amish draw a fifth of their workers from Old Order ranks.

Amish workers spend their break time and lunch hours with fellow church members, talking about Amish life in Pennsylvania German and interacting in only a limited way with non-Amish coworkers. Indeed, it is likely that Amish factory employees work in more of an ethnic cocoon than do those whose home-based businesses—while seemingly more separate—frequently require ongoing English-language interaction with non-Amish customers, suppliers, and shippers.

This does not mean that the impact of industrial work is negligible. The contours of Amish life in northern Indiana have been shaped by their unusual reliance on factory labor. For example, the Amish ritual calendar has bent to the demands of standard work weeks and seasonal production schedules. Weddings, traditionally held on Tuesdays or Thursdays in November, no longer reflect that rural rhythm, and are likely to occur almost anytime of year and often on Saturdays, when most male guests have the day off. Even the annual settlement ministers' meetings convene on Saturdays, since so many bishops, preachers, and deacons are factory workers.[39]

Work in large factories with layers of management and specialized employee tasks also open the possibility of new forms of status being introduced into Amish society. If in the past a person's status was related to success in farming and raising children who join the church, it may now come from being a foreman or crew leader or from operating computer-aided quality control equipment Monday to Friday.[40]

The prevalence of industrial work also has implications for the practice of mutual aid. Since only Amish who are self-employed or work for an Amish employer are exempt from Social Security, a sizable portion of the community is now linked to the federal system of old-age pensions. While the church discourages those who pay into the system from collecting benefits when they reach age eligibility, anecdotal evidence suggests many do cash in—at least enough to concern Amish leaders in other states who fear that the Elkhart-LaGrange and Nappanee practice may jeopardize Old Order exemption that was based on the contention that Amish wanted no part of the system.[41]

In addition, steady wage labor in the Elkhart-LaGrange and Nappanee settlements has also introduced significant cash flow into family pockets. Factory jobs provide a steady paycheck and require no investment other than a lunch box on the part of their employees. (In contrast, Amish entrepreneurs may make handsome profits but must plow those earnings back into their businesses.) Discretionary disposable income pays for decorative landscaping that would be uncommon around homes in most other settlements and allows for restaurant meals and sight-seeing trips taken during paid vacation time—another employment perk not found on the farm. Nor does one have to be a factory hand to feel the impact. Area Amish business owners find it difficult to offer competitive wages and benefits to lure employees. "The high paying factory jobs force us to pay higher wages," complained one Topeka entrepreneur.

The impact of industrial life on Amish society has come to be reflected even in

Illustration 5.2. Landscaping and paved driveways typify the "Amish suburbs" that reflect the affluence of an industrial lifestyle. Source: Courtesy of the Mennonite Historical Library/ Joel Fath.

the spatial structure of the settlement. Suburban-style tract housing for Amish factory worker families—two-story, attached-garage homes on half-acre lots, each with a small horse barn and pasture—are now commonplace in Nappanee and Elkhart-LaGrange. A paved driveway and basketball hoop for the children are more likely than the sizable vegetable gardens that once marked Amish properties. Such homes have sprouted not only along country roads in lots carved from farm fields, but also in what amount to "Amish suburbs"—subdivisions developed from former farms and including new streets lined with rows of Amish-owned houses. These Amish suburbs keep ethnic life close, as interaction with fellow church members is more immediate than ever, but it also symbolizes the social and familial changes that factory work has brought to northern Indiana Amish life, and sets their settlements apart.

Indeed, Amish observers comment on the pressures that industrial work places on families, since fathers are away from home and children may grow up without regular or meaningful chores. To date, the size of families headed by factory workers has not declined in a statistically significant degree. So the task of occupying the six to seven children who compose the typical factory worker's family falls exclusively to the wife and mother. "It's not good," one parent confessed. "Older boys who are home from school and would be doing chores are out on the road on their bikes." She added, "We contend more with material things. Things that used to be a luxury for the older folks who had saved money are now a necessity for the young folks just starting out."

Observers note other changes in the nature of women's work. As wives shift more of their energies to child care, rearing, and discipline, they may not have to spend as much time on traditional tasks of food production and preservation. As one Shipshewana Old Order woman put it, "We have adapted to city life. . . . Around here there is a lot less gardening and canning being done today than there was years ago. People simply go to the store and purchase food that they used to take the time to can."

For their part, some single women have also taken jobs in area factories—sometimes in the offices, but also doing things like driving forklifts in inventory warehouses. Upon marriage, women leave this sort of wage labor, but its presence provides a way for young women to build up independent, pre-marriage earnings that are less likely in other settlements without this occupational option.

But if industrial employment has brought change to Amish Country, it has hardly meant the end of Amish society. Retention rates for children of factory workers are no lower than the settlement average.[42] In some ways, factory work may even buffer the influence of the wider world more than some other alternatives. The fact that industrial work seems so alien to its Amish participants paradoxically makes it easier for employees to separate themselves from their work. Factory wage-earners owe their company nothing beyond their stipulated hours and are not emotionally invested in their jobs. Industry is a means to an end: a way to make a living in forty hours so that one can return to the Amish world for the rest of the week.

Moreover, the fact that factory work takes place on alien turf, using equipment provided by non-Amish employers, means that it tends not to exert the same pressure for technological change in the home as do Amish home-based businesses. Unlike Amish entrepreneurs, whose competitive edge may hinge on the need to introduce production innovation or cell phone technology into the home environment, the very separation of factory work from home holds that sort of change at bay. So although fathers' work away from home may be problematic for family life, removing work from the home also shields the home from certain pressures and does not expose children to the sort of regular interaction with non-Amish customers and salespeople that may accompany life with a family-run small business.[43]

EDUCATIONAL ENCOUNTERS

Amish children are central to another notable feature of life in the Elkhart-LaGrange and Nappanee settlement, an attachment to area public schools. In this case, as with involvement in the industrial economy, the implications of Amish interaction with the world are more complex than first impressions suggest.

Despite a 1920s conflict over compulsory attendance that saw some fathers spend time in jail rather than send their fifteen-year-olds to high school, positive relations between local school administrators and Amish parents marked most of the twentieth century.[44] In contrast to their fellow church members in Lancaster, Pennsylvania, who rapidly abandoned public school participation in the 1940s and 1950s, the majority of Amish parents seemed satisfied with the rurally oriented, relatively small public grade schools of Elkhart, LaGrange, Marshall, and Kosciusko counties and only gradually warmed to the idea of private schools.

The first Amish school in Indiana opened in 1948 near Middlebury in the northwest corner of the Elkhart-LaGrange settlement and was initially staffed by a non-Amish teacher and later by an Amishman recently arrived from Plain City, Ohio. One more school followed in the 1950s, and several in the early 1960s. The 1967 consolidation of the Westview School District in LaGrange County prompted the opening of a dozen new Amish schools in three years as parents sought to keep their children from bus rides to distant facilities, but the majority of Amish youngsters continued to enroll in public systems.[45] Many Amish families lived near small towns with modest-sized elementary schools, and their "scholars"—as the Amish refer to school students—were able to walk or bicycle to school. Within the Westview District, one K-8 elementary in rural Honeyville gradually took on an almost entirely Amish student body because of local Amish population growth, while continuing to be staffed by non-Amish public school teachers who followed district curriculum.

The first Amish school in the Nappanee settlement opened in 1951 when parents retained an abandoned Marshall County school as an alternative to having their children bussed west to the city of Bremen.[46] Parents launched a half-dozen schools in the late 1960s in the wake of public school consolidation, but then the movement all but halted, and only one more school opened during the next twenty years. In the late 1970s about half of all Nappanee Amish pupils were in public schools.

The number of private schools in both settlements expanded notably in the 1990s and early 2000s, and Amish observers explain that a growing concern about public classroom access to the Internet and the increasingly divergent lifestyles of English classmates have prompted more parents to opt for Amish schools, despite the sub-

TABLE 5.5
Amish children enrolled in public and Amish schools, Elkhart-LaGrange and Nappanee settlements

	Total number of school-age children	Amish school enrollment	Percentage enrolled in Amish schools
Elkhart-LaGrange			
1979–1980 school year	1,931	999	52
2001–2002 school year	3,316	2,039	61
Nappanee			
1977–1978 school year	577	304	53
2001–2002 school year	856	680	79

SOURCE: 2001–2002 population data were taken from directories; estimated number of school-age children was derived by counting the number of children born between July 1, 1987, and June 30, 1995; July 1, 1965, and June 30, 1973; and July 1, 1963, and June 30, 1971. Amish school enrollments taken from Indiana State School Committee informant and *Blackboard Bulletin* (Nov. 1979, 12–13) and *Blackboard Bulletin* (Dec. 1977, 12–13).

stantial extra costs involved. Both northern Indiana settlements have shown a slow but steady rise in support of private schools, though the growth has been stronger in Nappanee, where in the early twenty-first century about 80 percent of scholars attended Amish schools, while in the Elkhart-LaGrange settlement about 40 percent (more than 1,200 children) were still public school students (table 5.5).

School supporters credit the broader support within the Nappanee settlement to stronger endorsement from church leaders there. The smaller size of the Nappanee settlement has made a spirit of common cause easier to achieve, despite the congregational autonomy that continues to animate church life there. The size of the Elkhart-LaGrange community may make unity of opinion more elusive.

Indeed, while the recent rise of private schools in the region is significant, when compared to other Amish settlements such as Lancaster, Pennsylvania, the more striking fact is the continued loyalty of northern Indiana Amish to public schools. Some Amish public school patrons even quietly dismiss parochial schools as inferior and cite their children's need to "learn to get along in the world" by rubbing shoulders with non-Amish classmates. The fact that the Amish make up such a large percentage of the total population—and a disproportionately larger share of the school-age population, thanks to their sizable families—bolsters their sense of security in a mixed environment and means that Amish students in public schools are never without Old Order peers, even when they are outnumbered by non-Amish classmates.[47]

One result of the continued participation in public schools is that a good share of Amish children grow up with non-Amish school friends who, in many cases, continue to be at least neighborly acquaintances well after Amish students withdraw from formal education at the end of eighth grade. School contacts help cement local ties, further coupling area Old Orders to their non-Amish community. Indeed, public school participation is probably a more significant link to outsiders than the industrial employment of adult Amish men.

At the same time, an increasing percentage of Amish children *are* attending private schools, suggesting that the crucial childhood years in Amish Country are now more often spent in a church-and-family-defined context that assumes Old Order values and reinforces Ordnung assumptions. This development suggests that increasingly, northern Indiana Amish society will have fewer significant relationships with surrounding society, despite continued participation in non-Amish employment settings. Indeed, given the significant role that private schooling plays in shaping children and inculcating Old Order faith, the shift to Amish schools suggests that contemporary Amish society is more enclosed—in meaningful ways—than ever before, despite the continued prominence of factory employment or the growing popularity of supermarket shopping trips and restaurant meals. Such forays into the wider world, in fact, are perhaps less threatening to Amish social stability now precisely because of the privately controlled schooling context for Amish youth. The economic "opening" and educational "closing" of Amish society are in this case simultaneous developments.

TOURIST TRADE AND TRENDS

A different sort of encounter, but one with a similarly distinctive northern Indiana edge, is that accompanying the region's tourist trade. Midwestern Amish-theme tourism is a more recent phenomenon than its East Coast cousin, emerging in institutionalized ways only in the late 1960s. The 1970 opening of Amish Acres near Nappanee marked a major new stage in this development, and the advertising and notoriety it has generated have done much to popularize the area with visitors from Chicago and Detroit to Indianapolis and Cincinnati. During these same years, the local animal auction in the LaGrange County village of Shipshewana transformed itself into one of the Midwest's largest weekly flea markets, drawing thousands of attendees each Tuesday and Wednesday.[48]

While the connection in visitors' minds between area Amish and consumer pursuits is by no means straightforward, it is clear that the presence of a resident Amish population lends a certain wholesome legitimacy to recreational commerce.[49] The local tourist bureau and wider business community have picked up on these themes, marketing north central Indiana as "Amish Country" and, in fact, using the term

Illustration 5.3. A small number of Amish are directly involved in the tourist trade. Source: Courtesy of the Mennonite Historical Library/Joel Fath.

Amish in their advertising more regularly and consistently than do their counterparts in Lancaster, Pennsylvania, where the tourist trade is more likely to offer up the ethnic term *Pennsylvania Dutch.*[50]

For most Elkhart-LaGrange and Nappanee Amish, however, direct connections to tourism are limited. Tourism is heavily concentrated in very specific parts of both settlements, and most Amish do not live at those centers of attention. Some Amish were involved in the establishment of Menno-Hof, a nonprofit, Mennonite-run visitors' center in Shipshewana, which aims to give a historically accurate presentation of Amish life. But even in this case, most Amish kept their distance. Otherwise, relatively few Old Orders participate directly in tourist trade. A handful immediately adjacent to Shipshewana and Nappanee own stores that cater to visitors, and some young women work in area restaurants or as motel housekeeping staff. Generally, however, Amish in the vicinity steer clear of traffic congestion and avoid the clusterings of tourist establishments.

But even if few Amish have immediate ties to tourism, that hardly means Amish throughout the settlements are unaffected by the trade. The presence of Amish-theme tourism shapes Old Order identity in both places. The added attention Amish residents receive from regular visitors bolsters their sense of separation and of being different. The fact that hundreds of thousands of spectators see something intriguing in Amish life is not lost on Old Orders, who comment on the fact that "we didn't realize what we've got here, until we see all the tourists coming."

Moreover, tourism presents and reinforces images of a more traditional way of life than actually exists among the area's Amish, since tourists expect Old Orders to be barefoot farmers, not industrial workers. Visitor literature promotes pictures of a bygone agricultural life that now characterizes only a small minority of the area's Amish population.[51] The tourist industry does not highlight the fact that the typical Amish father works in a plant producing motor homes or that Amish mothers may buy more food at Wal-Mart than they grow in gardens. Paradoxes abound here, since steady Amish population growth has outstripped available farmland and helped push Old Order families into occupations and ways of life that—if widely known—likely would not impress prospective tourists as the focus of a worthwhile vacation destination.

Regardless of the accuracy of the bucolic agrarian images, the Amish are well aware that their presence bolsters the local economy and generates significant tourism-driven tax revenue—as much as $74 million a year in the late 1990s.[52] The growth of tourism has, in that sense, tied the Amish here more tightly to their local community and their non-Amish neighbors, rather than alienating them. If some critics in the past complained that the Amish were "free-loading" on the back of modern society by refusing to participate in the military or were otherwise not pulling their civic weight, the symbiotic relationship now runs both ways. The northern Indiana economy needs the Amish presence to function at its expected level. And by defining the region as Amish Country, tourism underscores for Amish residents that this is *their* home, suggesting that non-Amish residents just might be the interlopers. It also suggests a commitment on the part of area civic leaders to ensure the survival of the Amish in this place.

MANAGING CHANGE

Occupational changes, population pressures, and their related social implications place stress on the Elkhart-LaGrange and Nappanee Amish, especially since new developments often occur in areas of life without stable or well-defined Ordnung traditions. Managing change in this context is not easy, and in recent years it has prompted creative responses and reinvigorated a few older strategies, all of which help explain the continuing health of these settlements and the way they understand themselves.

One important means of directing change has come through the establishment of modest church-related institutions. Hardly examples of bureaucracy, most of these organizations feature extremely low overhead, typically functioning on volunteer labor out of a home office or kitchen desk. They also remain lay-driven, even when they have the informal blessing of some church districts. Keeping ministers and bishops off the boards not only respects the heavy church commitments these leaders already have but also keeps the organizations formally separated from the church itself—a move that underscores the Old Order avoidance of denominational hierarchy. And while church-centered financial help for families hit by fire or facing major medical bills has been common for decades and is a feature of many Amish communities, new northern Indiana mutual aid programs suggest some of the distinctive features of these settlements.

One of these modest organizations is the Amish Mutual Mortgage Fund (AMMF), which formed in the Nappanee settlement in 1990.[53] Using an initial pool of money from settlement investors, AMMF offers loans to young married couples from the Nappanee settlement for the purchase of a first home. The program works as a revolving fund, with the payments coming back into the account, as well as some modest return for the original investors and charitable disbursements to local Amish schools. Because of the low overhead, the fund can offer interest rates below those available commercially. As well, borrowers need not take out life insurance policies—a requirement many banks insist upon but that violates Amish religious sensibilities—before obtaining an AMMF mortgage. Though AMMF was rooted in a desire to help young people get a financial start, it was not driven by the demands of skyrocketing farm process, since by 1990 very few Nappanee young people were interested in farming. The fact that Nappanee Amish established AMMF to assist nonfarm families signaled their understanding that these households represented the future of the community.[54]

A somewhat different program emerged in 1995 in the Elkhart-LaGrange settlement. Known as Bruder-Hand, this revolving loan fund offers start-up loans to Amish families who wish to launch home-based businesses that involve the entire family and provide a viable alternative to work in industry. While taking a job on the factory floor requires no investment and little financial risk, entrepreneurship can command significant up-front cash. One organizer described the program as a way of "getting fathers established at home so they wouldn't have to work away." While the seed-money scheme clearly echoes traditional Amish mutual aid efforts, the birth of Bruder-Hand in this region points to the settlement's distinctive occupational profile that makes structured support of small business necessary—in sharp contrast to other Amish communities where such agricultural alternatives need little encouragement.[55]

Two years after Bruder-Hand's founding, Amish business leaders launched another sort of community project—a medically staffed birthing center to provide an alternative to expensive hospital obstetrics wards. Dubbed the New Eden Care Center and located in LaGrange County's Eden Township, the project was a joint endeavor of Amish and non-Amish players. Area medical doctors and certified nurse midwives now deliver babies there. An Amish contractor put up the building, and Amish donations provided project seed money. Since the building is fully electrified and has other modern amenities necessary for medical care, the structure is not legally owned by Amish individuals. However, in key symbolic ways New Eden clearly remains Amish; for example, the rooms do not have televisions, and extended family provide the new mothers' meals. A small board of Amish men donate their time toward managing the property and keeping finances in order. Though employing non-Amish staff, including registered nurses, New Eden maintains remarkably low overhead, and a three-day maternity stay costs only about $500. Some four hundred children are born there each year.[56]

A project that required even more cooperation with outsiders and exhibited a good deal more innovative spirit was Rest Haven on the campus of Oaklawn, a major mental health center in Goshen. While psychiatric medicine has long had an awkward relationship with Old Orders—many seeing the potential benefits, but many others fearing the secular and individualistic underpinning of this modern science—most Amish have been relatively slow to access mental health services. Rest Haven provides a hospital setting for Amish patients where their concerns about mass media, dress, gender distinction, and other matters are taken seriously. Nightly hymn singing and devotions are part of the scheduled routine. Non–Old Order therapists who speak Pennsylvania German are on staff, and family members enjoy expanded visiting privileges.[57] Certainly, Rest Haven has not won the endorsement of all Amish in the area, but its presence is testimony to the generally progressive bent of these settlements and their fairly well-connected network of relationships with the local community. In 2005 a group of area Amish who endorsed the Rest Haven model began Pleasant Haven, a long-term residence facility for recovering mental health patients. Pleasant Haven has fewer clinical overhead costs and is more affordable for Amish clients without insurance. Amish house parents help staff the home, and church districts in the Elkhart-LaGrange and Nappanee settlements take turns holding Sunday church services at the site.

While the structure and function of these new institutions continue Amish traditions of low-key bureaucracy, they also have been the product of a new class of lay leaders who function in an entrepreneurial mode unavailable to bishops and ministers bound by more restrictive Ordnung guidelines. They also forge settlement-wide contacts as they work with mortgages, business loans, and birth records among younger families and keep in touch with the rising generation.

But while these new institutions provide a different way of managing change than that offered by the ministry, the profile of church leaders in northern Indiana is also changing, suggesting another way in which these Old Orders are thinking about how best to chart their collective future. Bishops, ministers, and deacons in the Elkhart-LaGrange settlement are being chosen at younger ages.[58] Of those ages fifty and older, the average age at ordination was 40. Those under fifty were ordained at an average age of 32. This tendency to nominate younger men for leadership posts suggests that members are entrusting their church to the care of those most familiar with contemporary economic or technological realities.[59] Indeed, the rising ministerial class also reflects the new occupational realities in northern Indiana, with leaders under age forty being factory employees in more than 60 percent of the cases.

Significantly, however, new leaders share another characteristic that was less common among ministers of a generation or two ago: an increasing percentage are sons or grandsons of ordained men. Whereas less than half of the bishops, ministers, and deacons ages sixty-five and older had this sort of pedigree, growing numbers of each younger cohort do, with about 70 percent of the youngest age group sharing this trait. As the community entrusts leadership into younger hands who toil in less traditional work places, they also nominate those who come from families with proven loyalty to the Ordnung. In doing so, they may be banking on these ministers having the sort of experience that will better enable them to negotiate change and adapt to the evolving environment, while being grounded in tradition. Interestingly, that grounding is signaled more often in terms of genealogy than in an individual's decades of personally demonstrated submission to the dictates of Ordnung-regulated farm life.

DYNAMIC IDENTITY

Life in the Elkhart-LaGrange and Nappanee settlements remains dynamic, given their sizable population; Ordnung diversity; economic profile; and evolving schooling, leadership, and mutual aid patterns. By many measures, the region's Amish are thriving; clearly, this is the case economically. Indeed, when asked how he would characterize the Nappanee settlement to someone unfamiliar with it, one bishop's immediate response was "It's a place where you can get a job."

The prosperity here has made it, in many ways, easier to be Amish. With a broader range of employment options, one no longer needs to be a successful farmer or face the prospect of moving away or leaving the church, as may have been the case in the early twentieth century. Expanded occupational options likely explain, in part, the rising retention rate for Amish children in these settlements. Only about 80 percent of those born in the 1920s and 1930s joined the church, while 95 percent of those of the most recent generations have done so. Retention success has not been even though, and the Amish are quick to note that commercial wealth may be a culprit here too. The churches around Shipshewana, which are most closely associated with up-scale town life, have by far the highest rates of defection.[60] More pointedly, the Amish teens and young adults shown using illicit drugs in the 2002 documentary film *Devil's Playground* were introduced to their behavior in non-Amish work settings where they also earned cash to sustain their habits.

The two northern Indiana settlements are also remarkably diverse by Old Order standards. The range of technology use—from self-generated electricity on some properties to ice boxes and woodstoves in others—matches a similar range of practice in other areas of life. Some families regularly spend evenings at Wal-Mart filling shopping carts with consumer goods, while other households make a principled choice to keep their children out of such establishments. A few Old Order church districts hold bi-weekly Sunday school sessions to promote Bible study, but the vast majority have not adopted this innovation in church life. Some Amish here spend summer Saturday afternoons waterskiing on nearby lakes; others limit socializing to work frolics, volleyball games, and quiet Sunday afternoon visiting.

All of this diversity makes life in these settlements unusually hard to generalize but uncommonly rich to observe. This is especially so because the diversity has not produced schisms of competing affiliations. Indeed, this sense of forbearance on the part of those who differ has become a mark of the understanding and practice of Ordnung in these settlements, tested over time and expressed through a commitment to congregational polity. Mutual submitting and a balancing of local autonomy and wider settlement opinion give Amish life in this region its distinct character.

Nappanee and Elkhart-LaGrange Old Orders are also relatively well-connected to the surrounding non-Amish community, and to a notable degree, they do not construe separation to mean withdrawal. Their long attachment to the public schools—with attendance rates that are still high in comparison to most other Old Order communities—is one indicator of this, as are their high rates of employment in non-Amish workplaces. Certainly, Amish school attendance rates are on the rise, and Amish men who work in factories report that they spend their days in an ethnic subculture of Amish co-workers. Nevertheless, these forms of social engagement with wider society point to a sort of quiet, corporate self-confidence. The focus of state tourism and an indirect source of local tax revenue, the Amish know that they are as critical to the success of their non-Amish neighbors' way of life as that larger society is to their own.

These characteristics that serve to locate this version of Amish life may not be readily apparent to the tourists who visit northern Indiana or to all of the region's non-Amish residents, but they are clear to Old Orders themselves. Certainly, they know that their experience is different from Amish life not many miles to the southeast. Those historic Swiss settlements offer another equally valid, but decidedly different, Amish identity.

CHAPTER SIX

Swiss Settlements
of Eastern Indiana

Indiana's Swiss Amish possess a clear sense of identity that is simultaneously self-assured and yet always in the shadow of their better-known Pennsylvania German–speaking religious cousins. Ask an Amish person in the Swiss settlement near the southern Indiana town of Vevay to name the largest Amish settlements in the state, and they are apt to cite those in Adams and Allen counties, and perhaps in Daviess County. Mention the Nappanee community, which rivals Adams County's in size, or the Elkhart-LaGrange settlement that dwarfs all of them, and the Swiss conversation partner may react slowly, as if being reminded of places they had not called to mind in many years. Their few comments on these communities suggest that these other settlements exist in a parallel Amish world.

At the same time, one need not push very hard to find Swiss Amish people freely and easily describing themselves in contrast to their non-Swiss coreligionists. On this score they get considerable help from outsiders. Picture books, commercial tourism, academic studies, and popular images typically overlook the Swiss Amish, focusing instead on enclosed buggies, the Pennsylvania German dialect, and other markers of Amish ethnicity drawn from non-Swiss communities.[1]

Some Swiss welcome this sense of Anabaptist anonymity, while others express a mild resentment toward this assumed second-class status. "When we visit [Amish] settlements in other states and say we are from Indiana," one Swiss school teacher chuckled, "everyone thinks we are from [Elkhart or LaGrange Counties]. Allen County is just not what other Amish think of when they say Indiana."[2]

As noted in chapter 4, the Swiss are not an Old Order affiliation, though they share some roughly similar approaches to Ordnung. Rather, Swiss ethnicity has

emerged out of shared history and common traditions among a people who populate eighteen settlements in several states. For outsiders, perhaps the most easily
identifiable symbol of Swiss Amish life is the use of unenclosed, or "open" buggies.
Many Amish themselves are quick to suggest that the Swiss are "less fancy" or that
their clothing is more traditional—men using hook-and-eye fasteners on shirts as
well as coats or always wearing hats, often even when working indoors. Others cite
the dialect difference between the two ethnic streams. For their part, the Swiss usually refer to Pennsylvania German speakers as "High Germans"—presumably because they perceive that dialect as closer to standard German than their own, but
perhaps also because it reflects their sense of ethnic minority status. "High German" signals a sort of normative standard from which the Swiss diverge.[3]

The Swiss Amish in eastern Indiana's Allen and Adams Counties, along with
their diaspora of related communities, lend their own hues to the Amish mosaic,
even as they themselves are divided by differing affiliations and various interpretations of Ordnung. Their understanding of unity and uniformity has produced a particular Amish identity with implications for church life, relations with the state, and
occupational pursuits. Interacting, in turn, with local contexts such as urban Fort
Wayne and sparsely settled Adams County, these factors shape Swiss patterns of
practice and change.

FAMILY RESEMBLANCES

In the twenty-first century, eighteen Swiss Amish settlements include ninety-two
church districts scattered across seven Midwest and Mid-Atlantic states, but more
than half are in Indiana, and all are in some way tied to the communities in Allen
and Adams Counties.[4] These two settlements stand as parents to the Swiss Amish
diaspora. The Allen and Adams settlements are no more twins than the Elkhart-
LaGrange and Nappanee communities profiled in the previous chapter. But viewed
from a distance, or in the light of academic scholarship that often neglects Swiss
Amish culture, it is clear that the Swiss share a host of family resemblances, beginning with common immigrant origins.

Identifiably Amish settler surnames began showing up in Adams County in 1840
and in Allen County in about 1844—about the same time that Amish households
were arriving in Elkhart, LaGrange, Marshall, and Howard counties. But the composition of the Allen and Adams counties' Amish population was distinct, since the
vast majority were first-generation immigrants. This was especially true after arrival in Adams County of some thirty-eight European households beginning in 1852
and the coming of twelve families—many tied to an extended Graber clan—to

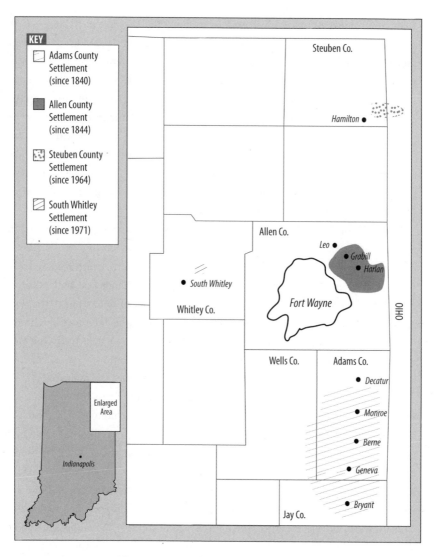

Map 6.1. Swiss Settlements in Eastern Indiana

Allen County in the next years.[5] Kin ties in these settlements did not run back to colonial Pennsylvania, nor did many Allen and Adams Amish have connections to the emerging Indiana settlements dominated by those from the Pennsylvania German–speaking ethnic stream.[6] These patterns and the new arrivals' linguistic distinction laid the groundwork for ethnic differentiation.

Mid-nineteenth-century church developments reinforced the ethnic divide. Few

Allen and Adams counties Swiss leaders attended the *Dienerversammlungen* of the 1860s that were watershed events for Pennsylvania German–speaking churches and precipitated the "Old Order" separation from the change-minded majority. Most nineteenth-century, second-wave European Amish outside Allen and Adams counties embraced change and assimilation, so when the Swiss Amish in those counties chose the Old Order path, they left behind most of their immigrant cohort in other parts of the country.[7] Religiously, that left the Swiss of the Allen and Adams settlement aligned with an Old Order camp otherwise dominated by Pennsylvania German speakers who descended from colonial-era immigrants—Amish with whom the Swiss held little in common culturally. As a result, the Swiss expression of the Old Order way remained rather isolated.

During World War II, for example, alternative service assignments in lieu of the military threw Amishmen and progressive Mennonites from around the country together into government-established work camps. For many Amish draftees from the Pennsylvania German ethnic stream, it was an experience that blurred settlement identities and even prompted a significant number of defections to the Mennonites. For the Swiss, however, the dialect and other cultural difference heightened their sense of separation from other Amish, and virtually none defected to the Mennonites, whose life apparently held even less attraction.[8] Moreover, the mid-century mission movement that rocked most Old Order communities and realigned Old Order parameters in many places made hardly a ripple in the Swiss settlements.

Instead, the defining events in Swiss Amish history have often been without parallel in other Amish places. In 1894 in Adams County, for example, the Old Order church lost about two-thirds of its members when the son of the settlement's lone bishop formed a group known as the Amish Christian Church. Founder David Schwartz (1862–1953) combined some traditional Anabaptist teaching with his own revelations from God to create an unusual mix of perfectionism and separatism. Convinced that it was the only true church, the group rejected all outside fellowship and harshly condemned those who remained in the Old Order faith. It also drew sharply negative reactions from non-Amish neighbors, who considered it a cult. Before breaking apart in 1936, the Amish Christian Church had put local Old Orders on the defensive in a way that those in few other settlements anywhere have experienced.[9]

In reaction to this 1894 schism, the Adams County Old Order bishop sought to retain close control of those who remained in his flock and resisted allowing his church to separate into two districts, even when its membership grew beyond the capacity of members' homes to accommodate everyone. Only in 1929 and 1938 did the settlement birth a second and third district. Until then, worshipers packed hosting homes on Sunday mornings, with many having to sit in upstairs rooms and unable to hear the preaching downstairs. Complicating matters in Adams County was a set of unusual family and leadership dynamics. From the mid-nineteenth to the mid-twentieth centuries, bishop leadership in the settlement passed from father to son for three generations.[10]

Swiss settlements also exist in regional contexts that mark them in distinctive ways. The Old Order community in Allen County is on the edge of metropolitan Fort Wayne, a city of 206,000 residents with several thousand more in peripheral suburban communities. The Allen County Amish live closer to a major urban center than any other Old Orders in America and have had to contend with things like sharply rising land values and complicated zoning ordnances. They also have easy access to a wide range of consumer retail establishments. Despite living next to a large city, however, the Allen County Amish have not become a major focus of tourism, perhaps because of the relatively limited size of their settlement—only seventeen districts in 2006.[11]

Adams County, by contrast, remains sparsely populated. However, many non-Amish neighbors there share with the Amish a sense of Swiss ethnicity. The towns of Berne and Geneva boast ethnic Swiss heritage festivals and business districts with stylized Swiss chateau storefronts and signs. In the early twenty-first century, Berne civic leaders had even announced plans to construct a full-scale replica of its European namesake's imposing Glockenspiel. For the Swiss Amish in these places, being Swiss has a religious, Anabaptist component, to be sure, but it is hardly limited to the Amish themselves. Swiss Reformed (now United Church of Christ) congregations, for example, represent their ethnic heritage in ways that are different from the Old Orders, but a similar ethnic attachment crosses denominational lines in a way that Amish elsewhere in Indiana recognize.[12] A modest Amish-themed tourist attraction (not Amish-owned) named Amishville exists outside Berne, but Amish-specific tourism remains largely undeveloped and is rivaled by the area's more general Swiss heritage attractions.[13]

A mix of motivators, from the search for more land to a desire to avoid church conflicts, has sparked out-migration from the historic Swiss communities. Already in 1869 Allen County church leaders John and Jacob Graber led a group to southern Indiana's Daviess County, perhaps in the wake of a disagreement with their brother Peter, who was the Allen settlement's bishop.[14] However, most out-migration has occurred since the mid-twentieth century. Allen County Amish started the Norfolk, New York, settlement in 1974, which in turn gave rise to others in Clyde, New York (1979); Linesville, Pennsylvania (1985); and Quincy, Michigan (1977).[15] Distressed by rising land prices in Allen County, several families left the Fort

Wayne area in the early 1970s for South Whitley, Indiana, about forty miles west.[16] In 1947 Adams County households moved to a new community in Bowling Green, Missouri, which has since grown into a sizable settlement; others formed a Seymour, Missouri, settlement in 1968. Staying closer to home, several Adams County families in 1981 organized a settlement near Salem, Indiana. Five years later some of these Salem Amish relocated again, this time to near the town of Vevay in Switzerland County.[17] The list of Swiss Amish settlements extends beyond these, but what is significant is that Swiss Amish sensibility has been a key component of the migrants' cultural baggage.

TRADITIONAL TEMPERAMENTS

While a history of migration has produced a particular network of Swiss settlements connected by kin ties and common memory, what makes these Amish distinct is the sense—among themselves and others—that they share cultural characteristics that express their traditional temperaments in recognizable ways.

For outsiders, this sentiment sometimes comes across as aloofness. "You will discover if you're around the Swiss," said one Elkhart County Amishman who has an unusual number of Swiss contacts, "that they are suspicious people." Other Amish outside Swiss ethnic circles speak of Swiss clannishness or of a reticence to engage in business contacts with other Amish. Those looking on at Swiss life credit them with being especially tradition-minded, given to disputes over Ordnung, and uneasy with compromise.[18]

From the Swiss perspective, such traits color a different picture, rooted in theological commitments and serving as a logical expression of separation from the world. When asked to describe the differences between his people and those living in the nearby and much larger Elkhart-LaGrange settlement, one Swiss leader from the northeastern Indiana Steuben County settlement replied, "Well, I could go into a lot of detail on that, but I'm not sure I should. I guess it comes down to the fact that the Swiss require repentance before acceptance." He meant that the Swiss Amish have traditionally practiced *streng Meidung* (strict shunning) in which excommunicated members remain "in the ban" until they return to the church in humble submission. If those disciplined refuse, or if they join another denomination or even another Amish affiliation, they are shunned for life. This level of discipline is not observed by most non-Swiss Midwestern Amish, who typically "lift the ban" in cases where the excommunicated subsequently show themselves to be a members in good standing of related "plain churches."

While the number of such banning and shunning cases is quite small in any settlement, the principle remains an important symbolic mark of distinction for most Swiss. Among other things, it serves as a churchly line of demarcation to limit the exchange of ministers to the circle of churches who share this value and thus also channels much of the friendly visiting and social networking that follow such religious links. Those limitations, in turn, put the brakes on inter-settlement interaction among young people, reducing the chances of forging new marriages and family ties that might otherwise draw these communities together.

To others, *streng Meidung* also symbolizes a deeper commitment to tradition and to a conservative Ordnung. The Swiss believe that other Old Orders rejected *streng Meidung* in the late 1800s out of ecumenical concerns, not wanting to offend nineteenth-century Mennonites (with whom some former Amish affiliated) by suggesting that these progressive cousins were somehow beyond the Anabaptist pale. Such sentiment may have been appropriate in the days when Mennonites and Amish shared more in common, some Swiss aver, but today it merely reflects an unhealthy spirit of tolerance and an inability to uphold church discipline. One Swiss deacon says he has talked to other Amish who admit that *streng Meidung* is in the Bible, but they want to honor their ancestors [who gave up the practice] and continue to work with the Mennonites. "But if the ancestors would come back today" and see the worldly Mennonites, the deacon speculates, "they would say 'Whoa! That's not what we intended.'" By holding to strict shunning, the Swiss signal their disciplinary independence. They are not drawn into implicit approval of the choices of other groups.[19]

This desire to hew close to tradition, even in unpopular or uncomfortable situations, has also characterized Swiss determination in confrontations with government. The most articulate World War II–era Amish statement of conscientious objection and refusal to participate in the military, for example, came from the pen of a blacksmith near Berne, Indiana, named David L. Schwartz (1909–89). Schwartz authored the pamphlet "Articles of Faith of the Old Order Amish Mennonite Church" and distributed it to Amish men facing local draft boards.[20]

During the postwar years the Swiss played key advocacy roles in various Amish conflicts with the state, especially on conscription and parochial school issues. By 1966 when the National Amish Steering Committee was formed to serve as a liaison to the federal government on behalf of all Amish settlements, men from Allen and Adams Counties filled two of the National Steering Committee's three slots— a dramatic overrepresentation of Swiss influence on this national board. Although the Steering Committee began its work with military matters, it quickly broadened into a wide range of church-state issues, taking up federal, state, and local concerns and conflicts.[21]

One of the reasons other Amish looked to Swiss leadership on such issues was that the Swiss had pioneered, in many ways, the struggle for public recognition of Amish schools.[22] Although there had been resistance to high school attendance in the 1920s among some LaGrange County parents and an Amish school had quietly opened in northeastern Elkhart County in 1948 and near Nappanee two years later, the major Indiana conflict over schooling surfaced after 1959 in Allen County.[23] Old Order parents there opposed parts of the public school curriculum, including certain subject matter in science classes and physical education dress codes. Arrests of parents and students followed as officials objected to both the uncertified Amish school opened there that year and to the fact that Amish teens were not attending high school.

For the next eight years Allen County parents held out against local and state government coercion, and made repeated trips to Fort Wayne and then Indianapolis to press their case.[24] One leader later explained his determination: "For some reason I just pressed on. I wasn't going to let it rest." In Adams County to the south, Swiss families resisted the county's 1953–54 school consolidation and fought with truant officers trying to enforce high school attendance. In one case, a boy named Samuel Schwartz holed up in a corn crib and threw corn cobs at a truant office trying to catch him; the boy's father went to jail.

Back in Allen County, a father named David Schwartz was among those whose persistence and willingness to go to the state capital ultimately resulted in Indiana's 1967 education agreement with the church. The agreement, which has remained in force since then, was brokered by sympathetic Superintendent of Public Instruction Richard Wells and an Amish group headed by Schwartz.[25] Certainly, the confrontation had its amiable moments—for example, Allen County Amish parents hosted Wells for an evening meal in one of their schoolhouses—but the Swiss penchant for "taking matters head on," as one Amish observer from outside their circles put it, was also a factor.

Support for Amish schools is strong in the old Swiss communities, and complete in the newer, outlying settlements (see table 6.1). By 2001–2002 almost all children in Allen County attended parochial schools, and about 80 percent of those in Adams County did. But even the lower Adams County number masks the way the Amish there have driven a hard bargain with public school administrators. To retain even modest Amish enrollment, the South Adams public school district has established some special classrooms without computers, televisions, and certain reading material that Amish parents found objectionable. Amish parents in the Elkhart-LaGrange and Nappanee settlements who send their children to public schools do so largely on the school's terms; the Swiss are less keen to make such concessions.[26]

TABLE 6.1

Amish children enrolled in public and Amish schools, Adams and Allen counties settlements

	Total number of school-age children	Amish school enrollment	Percentage enrolled in Amish schools
Adams County settlement			
2001–2002 school year	1,352	1,049	78
Allen County settlement			
2001–2002 school year	630	607	96

SOURCE: Population data from directories, with estimated number of school-age children derived by counting the number of children born between July 1, 1987, and June 30, 1995. Amish school enrollments taken from Indiana State School Committee informant.

If Swiss Amish determination set the stage for the emergence of private schools in their communities (and throughout the state), local context also shaped those schools in important ways. Even during their fight to gain legitimacy, the Allen County public districts typically provided bussing for Amish children to Amish schools, extending to Old Orders the same benefits that the influential Catholic and Lutheran parochial schools of the greater Fort Wayne area had earlier secured. While the Amish initially had to pay a small fee for this service, the transportation soon became a public expense.[27]

Bussing, in turn, allowed for another unusual feature of these schools: Amish school consolidation, of sorts. Rather than a score of small buildings scattered across the settlement, the Allen County community has only seven schools, and most are remarkably large by Amish standards. Several have four rooms (with two grades per room), and in one case, two two-room buildings share the same property. These multi-room schools each have a senior male teacher who serves as the school principal—a role and title unique in Amish education.[28]

Concern that bussing may not always be available in an age of shrinking public school funding and a desire for schools to be closer to students' homes have led to some recent Amish reassessment of this school pattern. Explained one former teacher and school leader, "We're trying to work away from big schools. We're downsizing."[29]

SETTLEMENT SCHISMS

While some observers praise what they see as the Swiss tenacity in standing up to the state and crafting parochial school systems that reflect their values and draw on regional resources, other outsiders criticize another aspect of Swiss culture: an understanding of unity as uniformity that—at least in the opinion of some Old Order onlookers—has produced a plethora of schisms. Unable to abide divergent

Illustration 6.1. One of the unusually large Amish school buildings that exist in the Allen County settlement. Public school bussing of Amish private school students in this community has resulted in several Amish schools with more than a hundred students. Source: Courtesy of Thomas J. Meyers.

practices, Swiss Amish churches cluster in relatively narrow affiliations of like-minded folks. As a Swiss deacon explained, contrasting his people's traditional notions with the greater diversity of practice that he sees in the Elkhart-LaGrange settlement, "If you think differently than them, they say 'OK. God will judge.' But the Swiss think, 'If you're not like us then you're out in left field.'"[30] Other Swiss Amish, bitter about their churches' approach to discipline even as they remain loyal members, are less charitable. "In this community excommunication is used as a club," one Berne Old Order lamented. "I feel that excommunication is for a brother or sister who has left the Christian way of life. It is to remind him that he was a brother and we want him back." But in Swiss churches, this man lamented, it is a tool for separation as much as for reconciliation.

Scholars might entertain a different appraisal of such divisions. Observers of other social groups have used the metaphor of a musical repertoire to describe how ethnic communities deal with dissent.[31] Like a body of work that musicians learn well and fall back on when asked with little notice to play something, communities also have repertoires of behavior on which they draw when they find themselves under stress. For the Swiss Amish, schism has become an accepted—if still publicly regretted—piece of their cultural repertoire. Seen in this way, schism is not a failure of group dynamics, as it might be among some other Amish, but is the expected result of recognizing differences in applied faith. In other words, it is not enough to credit a tendency to schism among the Swiss to the presence of authoritarian leaders or a culture that does not shy away from confrontation—significant as these factors may be. Rather, these factors themselves also draw on a repertoire of behaviors that make schism an understood response to difference. In this scheme, maintaining churchly ties in the face of differences in lived practice holds no virtue over schism—indeed, such amity may be seen as a sign of hypocrisy. In other words, here schism is grounded in important values of obedience, faithfulness, and conviction, and expresses strength rather than failure.

Differing circumstances and contexts, though, result in cultural repertoires that play themselves out in various ways. In Allen County, for example, Amish schisms—while sharp—produced groups that moved out of the Old Order orbit—an Apostolic Christian Church in 1862, an Egly Amish group after 1865 that became a Defenseless Mennonite Church, and the so-called Lengacher church that organized in 1943 and eventually affiliated with the car-driving Beachy Amish.[32] The remaining Old Order party was never large and was surrounded by formerly Amish entities, perhaps allowing Swiss separatism in this case to focus on common Old Order boundaries.

In Adams County, on the other hand, division has been common *within* the Old Order camp, resulting in geographically overlapping affiliations within the settlement. In the early twenty-first century, the forty districts of the Adams settlement were aligned in five distinct affiliations, the two largest of which date to the mid-1900s.

The general outlines of today's Adams County affiliations go back to 1944, when Jacob L. Shetler (1899–1976) and his wife Amanda Hershberger (1898–1987) moved from Mount Hope, Ohio, to a farm near the Adams County town of Monroe. Because the Shetlers had left their former church affiliation in Ohio on difficult terms, they placed the Adams County Old Orders in a particularly Amish ecumenical bind. On one side were those who said that to welcome the Shetlers would be disrespectful and insulting to the Ohio Amish, whose discipline should be honored. Reciprocal respect was key to maintaining informal Amish equilibrium, they argued. Those who disagreed—and they included the aged bishop, Joseph A. Schwartz (1867–1949)—felt that since the Adams County churches were not in fellowship with the Ohio church in question, it made no sense for them suddenly to adopt the Ohio group's discipline in this case and shun the Shetlers. Matters were made more complicated, however, by the fact that the Adams County settlement was pursuing fellowship ties with a small (and eventually defunct) Amish church in Jay County,

Indiana, that *did* wish to observe the Ohio discipline and insisted that the Adams church shun the Shetlers.

As long as he lived, bishop Joseph Schwartz was influential in keeping the church open to the Shetlers and resisting the pressure from Jay County, but after his death, his son (and, coincidentally, successor as bishop), Joe L. Schwartz (1893–1982), steered the church toward a stricter discipline, including a move in 1953 to remove the Shetlers from fellowship.[33] Thereafter, two distinct subgroups known as the "Shetler" and the "Joe L." groups came into being. In subsequent years the Shetler churches were relatively more open to technological innovation (though still fairly conservative in comparison to Elkhart-LaGrange or Nappanee standards), while the Joe L. group—which by 1992 represented about 60 percent of the settlement's districts—remained relatively more traditional, for example, rejecting natural gas refrigerators. Indeed, in some ways the Joe L. Ordnung is now less flexible than it was at mid-century.[34]

Other disagreements have produced more recent divisions. In the mid-1990s two splinter groups emerged, one each from the Shetler and Joe L. affiliations, and a small fifth group formed under the leadership of the grandchildren of Sam Christner (the controversial one-time Nappanee leader discussed in chapter 5).[35] Today the Joe L. affiliation counts about half the settlement as members, the Shetler group claims a third, and the other three affiliations together comprise about 15 percent.

One practical result of these schisms is that church districts have not always divided because they have grown too large, but because of internal disagreements over which affiliations to pursue. Districts that in other settlements would divide only if they grew too large for area homes sometimes split well before reaching that density in Adams County. Indeed, the average number of households per church district is one of Indiana's lowest, apparently as a result of affiliation-driven, rather than growth-driven, division (see table 6.2).

Settlement and affiliation identities rest in an uneasy relationship. For example, the Joe L. and Shetler groups continue to share the same cemeteries (which predate

TABLE 6.2
Households per church district, by settlement

Settlement	Number[a]
Adams County	25
Allen County	47
Daviess County	47
Elkhart-LaGrange	31
Nappanee	27

SOURCE: Settlement directories.
[a]Average number of households per church district

Illustration 6.2. Swiss Amish traditionally marked graves with wooden stakes, ensuring that no one would receive permanent memorialization since the stakes inevitably rot away. Source: Courtesy of Thomas J. Meyers.

their division), but they send their children to separate parochial schools (whose establishment came after 1953) and thus limit contemporary interaction between their two camps. The settlement does produce a common settlement directory, but its contents reveal the reality of competing affiliations.[36]

The implications of Swiss schism, exported through migration or communicated through traditional channels of fellowship and religious reciprocity, affect Amish relations more broadly. Adams County settlers to Indiana's Salem community in 1981 found themselves in conflict with one another and their parent settlement. In that case, the minority forestalled outright division by leaving the area for the Switzerland County town of Vevay in 1986. But soon that new Vevay settlement split into two small, non-fellowshipping church districts, each with its own school.

The Steuben County settlement in northeastern Indiana also shares a history of schism, migration, and contention. Adams County Swiss who had moved to Bowling Green, Missouri, beginning in 1947 and later aligned themselves with the "Joe L." affiliation (after it emerged in Indiana), left Missouri for Camden, Michigan, and then relocated back to Indiana in 1964. There, near the Steuben County village of Hamilton, Swiss households from Allen County who shared the "Joe L." affiliation's disciplinary convictions joined them. Despite the formal churchly ties, discord prompted those who had come from Allen County to leave the Steuben settlement for DeGraff, Ohio, in the early 1990s.

The partial dissolution of the Steuben settlement highlights the related but different roles that affiliation and Ordnung play in Amish life. On the one hand, the Allen County churches had long before sided with the Adams County "Joe L." group in affirming *streng Meidung*. Yet over time, the two bodies diverged in their application of technology-related Ordnung. Allen County is much more progressive on technology adaptation and is generally more open to innovation than is the Joe L. group. (Indeed, Allen County practice parallels much more the Adams County Shetler faction, although, given the hierarchy of Amish Ordnung values, the churches' stands on excommunication trumps other concerns.) In the end, while a shared theology of church discipline initially made the Steuben settlement possible—bringing together those Amish who stood in formal fellowship with one another—their disagreements on other aspects of Ordnung eventually rendered the project unworkable. Simply put, if a common Ordnung surrounding church membership and ritual is necessary for establishing fellowship, it is not sufficient to maintain a stable and successful blended settlement.

OCCUPATIONS AND ORDNUNG

Questions of church fellowship are not the only elements in the evolving lives of Amish communities. Contexts—geographic, economic, and social—all play significant roles. For example, the Old Orders who moved to Steuben County did so because, according to one resident, in the early 1970s the county offered, at $400–$700 an acre, the cheapest land "for what you get" anywhere in the state. Indeed, the interplay of Ordnung and the Swiss settlements' surroundings shape what it means to be Amish in these communities, and shifting patterns of employment are one window onto these dynamics.

Other Amish tag the Swiss as notably slow to modify traditional Ordnung understandings.[37] The Allen County settlement, for example, continued hand-milking dairy operation until 1992, and such dairying is still the only method permitted in certain Swiss communities. Despite some variation from place to place, other broad patterns emerge from generalized practices. Telephones are typically more distant from the home than in most non-Swiss settlements, with shop and business phones often relegated to separate buildings away from the work space. Telephone utilities still receive requests to install community "phone shanties" shared by six to ten families in lieu of individual business phones.[38] Cell phones are more vigorously discouraged. And the Swiss unenclosed buggies typically lack the interior amenities found in their enclosed-carriage cousins. In one notable way, though, the Allen County Amish have expressed some creative adaptation within traditional constraints. As early as 1965 one entrepreneurial farmer installed a belt-driven alternator on his buggy to recharge the battery used to power the rig's safety lights, and he later added alternators to other Allen County carriages. The innovation drew no protest since it expressed the virtue of frugality by making the battery last longer.

As is the case in settlements almost everywhere, farming as a means of making a living is on the decline among the Swiss Amish. Knowledgeable estimates put the number of families supported by farm income at less than 10 percent. There are fewer than a dozen full-time farmers in Allen County, and perhaps only one apiece in the outlying Salem, Vevay, and Steuben settlements. Regional economic factors, along with the limits and historical development of church Ordnung, have shaped the available alternatives.

A few non-unionized factories near Decatur provide employment for a small number of Amish men in the northern part of the Adams County settlement.[39] Otherwise, industrial employment is all but unavailable on Amish terms or forbidden by the church—in stark contrast to the Elkhart-LaGrange and Nappanee settlements, where such work has become a majority pursuit. But neither have the Swiss eagerly turned to establishing home-centered shops and businesses, largely because the more restrictive Swiss Ordnung surrounding technology at or near home has limited the efficiency and profitability of such enterprises. Instead, mobile carpentry crews that work for non-Amish clients and can use the tools of the trade on alien turf without overstepping church boundaries have been the chief occupational alternative. Even in places where home-centered technological taboos have softened in recent years, such as Allen County or among the "Shetler" Old Orders in Adams County, the pattern of trading plows for power saws was already well-established. Even in the South Whitley settlement, launched by Allen County families desiring more farmland, carpentry work began taking younger men in the 1980s, and by 2000 it was the most common trade among household heads.

As many as 80 percent of working-age men in the Adams County settlement are employed in carpentry, traveling to jobs well beyond their immediate area. It is not uncommon for crews to work in Indianapolis or to travel to other sites a hundred miles away. Since many contractors pay travel time, workers do not necessarily mind long-distance jobs. In some cases, construction workers stay at a workplace for several days in a row, lodging in motels, even though the church officially frowns on this sort of separation of fathers from their families.

Most Swiss carpenters work for Amish-owned outfits in which a non-Amish employee owns the trucks and power tools. Often Amish entrepreneurs purchase such items and then sell them—sometimes even at a loss—to the non-Amish employee. While some observers see this arrangement as hypocritical, from the Old Order perspective the arrangement publicly demonstrates the business owner's respect for Ordnung provisions and also places the owner in a vulnerable and therefore humbled position, since the non-Amish party can legally leave with the tools and truck at any time.

In Allen County, Amish men also have focused on carpentry work. Local memory places the first man to take up such work in about 1935, but the large-scale shift to construction followed only in 1970, as land prices rose dramatically and the Ordnung surrounding agriculture remained static, severely limiting dairy herd sizes. (It was during the 1970s that Allen County families began the South Whitley daughter settlement, which more eagerly embraced bulk milk tanks and other innovations in an effort to forestall the shift away from farming—a shift the new community delayed, but did not halt.)

Like their Adams County compatriots, Allen County carpentry crews also work on jobs many miles from home in Indiana, Ohio, and Michigan. Close proximity to metropolitan Fort Wayne provides more work closer to home. Upscale urban neighborhoods also provide a market for other kinds of mobile work groups in Allen County. Unmarried young women and teens have formed cleaning crews of three or four people, including a non-Amish driver. Efficient housekeeping operations can clean six to eight houses a day.

The urban environment also provides more opportunities for spending the cash that carpenters, contractors, and cleaning crews bring home. Observers note that Allen County Old Orders near Fort Wayne frequent restaurants much more than their Swiss cousins in other settlements where restaurants are less common. An Allen County custom kitchen contractor, with the aid of a non-Amish driver, might visit potential customers to place bids in the evening but take his entire family along and stop for supper on the way home. Occasionally, day laborers who spend every day on the road—sometimes many miles from home—complain that their wives want to go out to eat in the evening, while they just want to stay home. In households with at-home businesses, such gendered differences are reportedly less common.

Home-based small businesses—while still the minority pursuit among the Swiss—are more common in Allen County and among the Adams County "Shetler" group because of their relatively more liberal Ordnung surrounding technology at or near the home. Allen County bishop Eli Wagler (1893–1963) is still remembered for counseling men, for the sake of their families, not to work away from home; but only a modest percentage of Swiss men have followed such advice. Church leaders have seen a greater danger in opening the door to technological innovation in the home itself than in keeping it more at arm's length—even if that working distance necessitates household heads leaving home to work in the non-Amish world.

The contrasting combinations of context and Ordnung in Allen County and the small Steuben County settlement just to its north illustrate different Swiss approaches. The Allen County community has, by Swiss standards, a relatively progressive Ordnung governing home shops, although even here shops of some size use only line-shaft power to operate sophisticated equipment that in larger Pennsylvania German–speaking settlements would run on hydraulic or pneumatic power. Such relative Swiss caution, however, is balanced by the Allen County Amish's adaptation of 12-volt battery power and willingness to employ as many as 6–8 people. One firm that produces precision hydraulic nuts and elbow valves for non-Amish firms uses a large diesel engine (mounted on a spring bed to keep the shop from vibrating) to run a line shaft under the shop floor, which in turn powers belts to various overhead shafts that run a host of machinery. Natural lighting from windows and skylights provides most of the illumination, but so does a number of what the Amish here call "third-world lights"—fluorescent lights that run on twelve-volt battery power. Though his formal education ended with eighth grade, this entrepreneur has repeatedly adapted and improved equipment designed by university-trained engineers, in one case designing a new system to salvage and recycle the oil and shavings produced by the metal tooling and milling process.

Despite the cutting-edge technology in the shop, there is still much handwork that would be mechanized in non-Amish businesses, such as finishing parts and measuring finished parts for quality control by hand, and shipping products without the aid of automatic packaging—all of which ensures work for family members, which is more important to such enterprises than larger profits. More importantly, however, the business owner had retained a cloak of humility, directing compliments away from himself and his business. Marks of Swiss conservatism appear in the glossy catalogue that reveals the firm's acceptance of credit card sales but not phone orders, informing customers: "Traditionally, normal telephone service is not available, please respond by mail."

But although technological flexibility opens the Allen County settlement to the possibility of small businesses, local civic restrictions also hamper such pursuits. The necessarily more rationalized and bureaucratic approach to local government that exists around a metropolis of a quarter-million people has produced zoning and land use regulations that effect this settlement on the city's edge. Frequent frustrations with zoning restrictions on small shops and at-home businesses has ebbed and flowed through the years.[40] At one point in 1995, officials from Fort Wayne called in Lancaster, Pennsylvania, civic leaders to explain the so-called Heritage Preservation zoning models the Pennsylvanians had developed.[41] Even so, zoning pressures have continued to be problematic in Allen County and are another part of the local context that conspires to make mobile carpentry crews an attractive alternative to agriculture, despite relative churchly openness to shop innovation.

The situation in Steuben County, a sparsely populated area just to the north, is markedly different. Here local zoning restrictions are not an important factor, and Ordnung plays a different role.[42] Like most other Swiss churches, the group here takes a more tradition-minded approach to allowing technology in and around the home, but the result has not been to push men into the world of mobile work crews because the Steuben Ordnung also prohibits men from working away from home. The result has been a proliferation of very modest home-based businesses—rough sawmills building shipping pallets, and the like.[43] After one sawmill began employing three families, the church stepped in and forced each household to open its own mill. While one effect of this ruling was to spread business energy more evenly across the settlement, its basic motive was to ensure that parents and children worked together at home, a variation on the themes that animate Swiss life.

ETHNIC AMISH IDENTITY

In important ways, the Swiss live Old Order lives akin to those of Amish people elsewhere. But the ethnic component that colors that life in its various regional contexts marks the Amish mosaic in recognizable ways. Among other things, it serves as a reminder that ethnicity, while not an independent variable in the Amish experience, is not exactly the same thing as the religious convictions that animate Old Order life. Durable identities rooted in immigration stories, migration patterns, and kinship networks have been important factors in charting Amish history, even as they interact with Ordnung and local economies in complex ways.

Ethnicity regulates basic interaction with other Amish—whether marked by dialect differences or limited churchly relations. Likewise, cultural patterns of confronting conflicts "head on" have given the Swiss a reputation that earns both respect and criticism from other Amish. The Swiss are far from isolated; and in fact, a few Adams County church districts torn by conflict have even invited Nappanee bishops to offer counsel and an outside perspective on their strife. Nevertheless, for a people whose patterns of visiting and informal interaction have been key to community, the Swiss Amish world has remained distinct from the larger Amish scene. For some Adams County Swiss, in fact, ethnicity may orient them toward non-Amish Swiss neighbors as much as to Pennsylvania German–speaking Amish in other places.

Yet ethnicity is not the same as church Ordnung, and even Swiss settlements that share ethnic affinity are not always agreed on church discipline or the appropriate use of technology and interaction with the world. From highly segregated Steuben County families to Adams County household heads who enter non-Amish working environments every day, choices reflect both contextual factors and longstanding Swiss sentiments.

Swiss traditionalism persists even in channels carved by change. For example, while recent decades have witnessed a modest shrinking of family size in the Elkhart-LaGrange, Nappanee, Kokomo, and other Pennsylvania German–speaking settlements, that development has not followed among the Swiss. While only a few Swiss engage in full-time farming, their family sizes have remained large—even in urbanized Allen County (see table 6.3).

All of these patterns are part of the Swiss sense of being something of an alternative Amish expression. While other Old Orders may quietly criticize aspects of Swiss culture as divisive or worldly, such critiques themselves illustrate the different standards and assumptions at play in Amish circles, since many Swiss would see

TABLE 6.3
Family size, by settlement

Settlement	Average number of children for women over age 45	Ethnicity
Adams County	9	Swiss
Allen County	8	Swiss
Daviess County	8	Swiss in origin
Elkhart-LaGrange	7	Pennsylvania German
Nappanee	7	Pennsylvania German
Kokomo	6	Pennsylvania German

SOURCE: Settlement directories.

themselves as the bearers of a conservatism and separatism that have resisted the influence of worldly ways quite well. Certainly, different Amish groups do not view each other as competitors in a game of faithfulness, but they do understand themselves in relation to one another's expressions of faith—expressions that include attention to Ordnung and that are shaped by ethnic culture and environmental contexts that are not always understood by those living elsewhere.

The role of local contexts—understood well or not—is especially apparent in the process of transplanting a settlement hundreds of miles from its original home. The experience of Lancaster, Pennsylvania, Amish who moved five hundred or more miles to Indiana in the 1990s with their own interpretations of Ordnung and ethnic attachments, highlight these themes.

CHAPTER SEVEN

Transplants from Lancaster, Pennsylvania

Late in the evening the moving trucks rolled into the Wayne County, Indiana, farm lane. The new owners—an Amish family from Lancaster County, Pennsylvania—were one of more than a dozen households in 1995 to relocate to this fledgling Lancaster outpost in the Midwest, begun just a year before. The entourage unloading that night had brought the household goods, farm animals, and equipment that the family needed to begin a successful farming enterprise; but the new arrivals also carried critical cultural baggage, including commitments to a Lancaster Ordnung and a set of assumptions that kept them closely linked to those they had left behind. The Wayne County Amish, like a similar settlement of Lancaster Amish begun in Parke County, Indiana, in 1991, were recreating Lancaster life from southeastern Pennsylvania, five hundred miles away. From the use of gray buggies that contrast strikingly with the styles and black color found among Amish in the Midwest, to the less visible but more significant network of kin connections and business transactions that weave the lines of travel and trade into particular patterns, these two young and demographically thriving settlements were obviously Lancaster transplants.

Yet these "daughter settlements" (or, in Lancaster Amish parlance, "sister settlements") were not simply clones of their churchly parent, nor were they isolated from their new regional contexts. For example, from the start they received some help in constructing barns and homes from Hoosier Amish in the Adams County, Milroy, and Daviess County settlements, and they instinctively turned to those same places for their initial blacksmithing, harness supply, and buggy repair needs. Then, too, the migrants differed in some significant ways from those they had left behind in Pennsylvania—not the least of which was their willingness to move away from the stable Lancaster settlement. Indeed, the establishment of these new communities highlights the roles of context and culture in shaping Amish life. In this case, a new Midwestern environment absorbed, bolstered, and transformed deeply etched memories of a distinctive Lancaster heritage.

PENNSYLVANIA HERITAGE

Without doubt, Lancaster is home to the world's best-known Amish population. The subject of popular travelogues already in the nineteenth century and for most of the twentieth century a focus of East Coast tourism, the area known as "Pennsylvania Dutch Country" annually receives some four million visitors.[1] Moreover, the Lancaster Amish have captured a disproportionate share of academic attention as well, and almost all popular interpretations of Amish life come through a Lancaster lens.

For the Amish in Lancaster—and elsewhere—the southeastern Pennsylvania settlement carries a distinctive reputation. Accurate or not, Lancaster Amish are thought to be religiously traditional, technologically progressive, and financially well-off. Due to its public notoriety and its proximity to Washington, D.C., the Lancaster settlement also has traditionally taken the lead in diplomatic dialogue with the federal government, and a Lancaster Amishman has always chaired the National Amish Steering Committee, the group's liaison on church-state matters.

Though they share a Pennsylvania German dialect and an eighteenth-century immigrant past with a majority of Midwestern Amish, the Lancaster church has in some ways become an ethnic group in its own right. While Midwestern Amish history was marked by inter-regional migration and marriage that link settlements across space, the Lancaster church remained remarkably settled, self-contained, and self-sustaining, so that today many customs (such as gray-topped buggies) and surnames (such as Stoltzfus or Fisher) have become Lancaster exclusives.

The Lancaster sense of self reflects and is also reflected in the southeastern Pennsylvania settlement's structure. Strikingly less congregational in organization than most of their Midwestern counterparts, the Lancaster Amish typically grant each bishop oversight of *two* church districts, halving the number of top leaders in the settlement and creating a leadership pool that has—thus far—been small enough to maintain something of a consensus around a settlement-wide Ordnung. Controversy in 1909 and 1966 resulted in minor schisms, but the seceding party in each case was very small and never seriously threatened the health of the mainline Old

Order church.[2] Indeed, when Lancaster Amish speak about "the church," they just as often mean the whole settlement as their local district. The published church directory of the Lancaster Amish illustrates this sensibility. In contrast to Midwestern settlement directories that are organized by district and then list families within those district divisions, the Lancaster directory alphabetizes all households in the entire settlement in a single 372-page listing, making the settlement itself—and not the church district—the primary unit.[3]

Leaving this Lancaster "family" to move elsewhere has never been common. Public school conflicts provoked a minor migration into neighboring Maryland in 1940, but otherwise, heading out of the heartland was rare until the later 1960s. Even then, when a handful of new settlements branched out, they involved few families and were located within Pennsylvania itself. Then, during the late 1970s to the late 1980s, out-migration all but ceased. So interest in leaving Lancaster—and even more, in establishing settlements in states some distance away—has been a remarkable recent development.[4]

One way to begin understanding Indiana's "Lancaster Amish" is to consider their motives for moving.[5] Although each family who migrated had its own reasons and motives were admittedly mixed, a cluster of factors emerge. Chief among these was a desire for available, affordable farmland. Rising prices in southeastern Pennsylvania left some young people without the opportunity to farm, and parents of youngsters worried that some day their children would be unable to plow the soil. As a result, migrants tended to be younger families, though there were also a smattering of established households. Some families had rented land in Lancaster and were looking for the opportunity to buy; others already owned farms in Pennsylvania but sold them to acquire additional Midwestern acres for the next generation. In addition, several Lancaster Amish entrepreneurs of considerable means sold highly successful businesses and moved to Indiana with the hope of allowing their children to experience agriculturally centered lives. Although not everyone who settled in Indiana's Parke and Wayne counties ended up farming, the desire for farmland drove Lancaster migration plans. And since the initial core group of families had these interests, the process of selecting a new home was guided by concerns for soil suitability as much as price per acre.

Farmers and non-farmers alike also cited related land-use and population concerns, such as Lancaster's traffic congestion, suburbanization, and resulting zoning strictures that increased property taxes, hindered some agricultural work and home-based businesses, and reduced the quality of life. The attraction of a more rural and isolated environment in central Indiana proved appealing, whether one's occupational future was specifically agricultural or not. "Here [in Indiana] you can drive for miles without meeting a car," one Parke County woman reported. "It's so relaxing."

In fact, demographic and economic pressures often were only one piece of a larger sense of unsettledness that migrants had felt in Lancaster and that went deeper than the fact that there were more cars on the road or fewer farms in the center of the settlement. "One Sunday morning [when we lived in Lancaster] we were going to church, and we went by the Turkey Hill [convenience store] and it was packed," one man began, when asked why his family had settled in Parke County. "And then in his opening [sermon] that morning the minister talked about the 'running to and fro' in the world, and how we need to keep a simple life. And I thought, yes, that's true. We used to have a simple lifestyle here in Lancaster, but now it's go, go, go. Stores are open seven days a week and [non-Amish] people are shopping and working all the time. It just doesn't quit." In Parke County, in contrast, he and others found an environment they characterize as "laid back" and "less rushed." While observers would probably see that his family continues to uphold a strenuous work ethic and engages in activity that keeps their children busy six days a week, their schedules are more easily governed by Amish values than by the demands of modern efficiency.

Then, too, the misgivings migrants had about the general direction of Lancaster County culture often paralleled a general unease with aspects of the Lancaster church itself. The size of the old settlement, some felt, militated against church unity and fellowship, and ran the risk of reducing Amish affiliation to a set of identifiable behaviors instead of a set of mutual relationships. "We have more oneness here," a single woman living in Parke County said, characterizing what was different about the Indiana daughter settlements. The new communities are small enough that everyone knows everyone else and appreciates a sense of fellowship.

Among other things, the limited size has meant that young people's activities are more closely monitored. Unlike the Lancaster settlement, where hundreds of teens and young adults socialize in more than a dozen distinct youth groups, some with a reputation for deviant behavior and each with a fair degree of autonomy, in the Parke and Wayne communities the small number of young folks in each place form a single "crowd" and activities are known and watched by adults. "There were too many things to contend with in Lancaster County for the young folks," one Parke County mother explained.[6]

In the late 1980s these desires for relief from demographic, economic, and cultural pressures, coupled with an interest in seeing a closer sense of church community and discipline emerged in conversations among a handful of Lancaster families. Interestingly, many of the first to express interest in migrating lived in southern Lancaster County, a portion of the settlement relatively less encumbered by the pressures they observed in other parts of the community and that they feared were moving their way. The group also included a young deacon from the west-center edge of the settlement, who contacted Ivan Glick, a farm equipment salesman and agriculture historian well known in the area, to ask if Glick would help them locate land elsewhere. Glick, in turn, contacted Mennonite real estate agent Hiram Hershey; and the two men became cultural and, in the case of Hershey, legal brokers for the Amish, making contacts on their behalf and working to facilitate and smooth migration. The two outsiders began surveying agricultural real estate possibilities in dozens of locations.

SETTLING IN INDIANA

In 1989 Glick contacted Parke County's Agriculture Extension agent of twenty-six years, George Waltz, and asked about the land market. As it became clear that Parke County fit much of what the Amish were looking for in climate, agronomy, and price, the brokers asked Waltz to visit Lancaster and discuss farming possibilities in more detail. There he met with about fifteen interested households in the basement of an Amish farmhouse and informally fielded questions about soil, weather, and markets. Glick and Hershey then visited Parke County alone, and in early 1991 went back with a van full of Amish "land shoppers" on an exploratory trip.

Parke County offered an appealing rural landscape, though it was not simply a less-populated version of Lancaster. Large, cash crop farms characterized Parke County's agriculture; the sort of small-scale dairying with which the Amish were familiar had faded several decades earlier. Any Amish newcomers would have to install or refurbish dairy barns and divide larger tracts into more manageable parcels (see table 7.1).

Nevertheless, the exploratory group was favorably impressed and quickly turned serious about establishing a new settlement there. Indeed, one night members of the party sat up in their motel room until 2:00 a.m., hammering out common understandings of a church Ordnung that any future Parke County community would adopt. In general, they expected to adhere to the same church rules that guided life in Lancaster. But they did agree to ban tobacco growing and any use of tobacco products—both customs that were tolerated in Lancaster. In addition, to keep farming on a family-labor scale that assures enough work for all hands and to stem the pressure for labor-saving mechanization, they decided that farms would be limited to thirty-two milking stanchions. A family could have more than thirty-

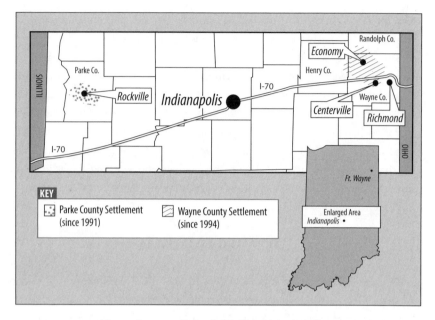

Map 7.1. Lancaster Pennsylvania Transplants in Indiana

TABLE 7.1

Comparison of Lancaster County, Pennsylvania, and Parke and Wayne counties, Indiana

	Lancaster Co., Pa.	Parke Co., Ind.	Wayne Co., Ind.
Size (sq. miles)	946	445	404
Population (2000)	470,658	17,241	71,097
Population density/sq. mile	498	39	176
Number of farms (1997)	4,556	471	814
Average farm size, acres (1997)	86	401	212
Average farm value/acre, including buildings (1997)	$5,578	$1,600	$1,939

SOURCE: U.S. Census 2000; U.S. Department of Agriculture 1997 Census of Agriculture.

two cows if they wished, but the inconvenience of taking the animals in and out of a limited number of stanchions would discourage larger enterprises.[7] The new settlement clearly would be a Lancaster "sister settlement," but one whose members were especially sensitive to "clean living" and the pressures associated with accumulated wealth.

Soon the Amish began negotiating the purchase of several of the more than forty farms on the market that summer, acquiring a half-dozen before the summer crop season was over. The first two families moved to their new Parke County acres in December 1991, and thirteen followed the next year. Households buying existing homes set to work remaking them into Amish dwellings, removing electrical light fixtures, replacing electrical appliances with natural-gas powered ones, and tearing out wall-to-wall carpeting.

Meanwhile Parke County locals were learning more about their new neighbors. Initially, some residents had misgivings, wondering whether the Amish pay taxes or if they buy from local stores. For his part, realtor Hershey donated an educational documentary film and several scholarly books about the Amish to the Rockville, Indiana, public library, and shortly before the first Amish families arrived, Hershey, Waltz, and three Amish men who were about to move to Parke County formed a question-and-answer panel to address local queries at a public meeting. This sort of interaction seemed to assuage concerns. The Amish took the opportunity to explain their beliefs and reasons for moving. In the panel session they were "quite frank," one observer recalled, "in saying that they hoped Parke County people would not promote tourism around their presence."

For some residents the matter of most concern was land values. Coming out of the agricultural depression of the 1980s and with few children interested in farming, a number of older landowners were happy to sell their farms at better-than-expected—though not extraordinarily high—prices. But some younger locals working rented land were disappointed, knowing that the arrival of the Amish would boost values and encourage retiring farmers to expect better prices. While the first two-dozen-or-so transactions ran through Hershey's office in Pennsylvania, the Amish soon were making purchases through Parke County realtors.

"This is a pretty conservative community," observed one non-Amish resident with decades of experience in the town. "It's hard to accept change, and you would hear some grumbling around the edges about the Amish." A few longtime residents were sure dairy farming was a thing of the past and scoffed at Amish hopes of reviving milking in Parke County. At the other extreme were the aggressive efforts of several local banks to obtain Amish clients whose wealth they unrealistically imagined. A decade later, retired agent Waltz saw the Amish arrival as a positive part of the area's agricultural development. "I feel like it's been good for Parke County," he concluded. If they bucked the regional trends with smaller farms and more of a dairy focus, he noted, they boosted business for veterinarians, created a market for used farm equipment, and engaged in new construction that has obviously increased property tax receipts.[8]

The Amish themselves had a general sense that most longtime residents welcomed them as an economic asset. Indeed, a story circulated among Amish households back in Lancaster that when a new Parke County arrival went to the courthouse asking for a building permit, the clerk admitted he had not issued one for years. Though of doubtful authenticity, the story communicated something of the difference the Amish perceived between life in Parke and Lancaster counties. And indeed, the new community was taking root in a place with a decidedly different economic profile from southeastern Pennsylvania. One of the first Amish families to move to Parke County discovered that between the time they had purchased their land and when they relocated, the paved road in front of the house had been ground up and converted to a gravel road, since a shrinking county tax-base was preventing the county from upkeep of paved roads. Taxes were also lower and zoning regulations much less restrictive than in Lancaster.

Within a few years, the success of the Parke County community led rather directly to the establishment of a new Lancaster-rooted settlement in Wayne County, across the state from Parke. Not only had Parke residents proven the viability of establishing a Lancaster sister settlement in the Midwest, but Lancaster visitors to and from the Parke community passed through Wayne County as they traveled Interstate 70. Again, the Amish worked with Glick and Hershey, who had checked out opportunities in several other states but recommended exploring Wayne. In conjunction with a Centerville, Indiana, realtor, the pair brought groups of land shoppers to east-central Indiana, where the prospective purchasers asked more detailed questions about rainfall, agronomy, and land availability.

The purchase process proceeded much as it had in Parke, only a bit more quickly. Like Parke County, Wayne County's agricultural economy had been in slow but steady decline, and a significant number of older farmers or absentee owners had been unable to find buyers. In August 1994 the first Amish family arrived, settling near the village of Economy, west of Richmond. Eighteen households followed in 1995. As in Parke County, the newcomers purchased existing farms and modified them to fit their needs, refitting or refurbishing barns for dairy operations. In some cases, purchasers built entirely new dairy barns, and some new arrivals had to build new homes, too, since large farms were divided into smaller parcels that lacked any structures.

Both settlements grew quickly. In 1996 the Parke community counted thirty-seven families and divided into two church districts. By 2002 some eighty-two households comprised four districts there. For its part, the Wayne settlement's growth prompted its church to divide in 1997 and again in 2002, at which point the community was home to some sixty families. And while travel back and forth between the new settlements and eastern Pennsylvania has been regular, there has not been any significant permanent return migration back to Lancaster.

ADJUSTMENTS AND ASSUMPTIONS

If settlement proceeded fairly smoothly, adjusting to new surroundings took more time—both for the Amish arrivals and for longtime locals. The Amish appreciated their new rural setting, but they had to get used to the more geographically dispersed nature of their settlement. Some goods that were readily available in Lancaster, such as the naphtha gas they used for indoor lighting, could not easily be had, and families turned to propane.

For many area residents the Amish were a bit of a novelty, but most were pleased that anyone was moving to regions that had seen little economic or population growth in some time. A vocal minority of longtime residents in both counties complained that Amish buggies damaged the roads and called on county government to impose a county buggy license fee. While the Amish admitted they would pay if required, they objected to the fee and pointed to other southern Indiana communities without such an imposition. Such licenses were unknown in Pennsylvania and took the newcomers off guard, symbolizing to some a sign of resentment on the part of locals.[9]

Despite the debate over license fees, most actions pointed to amiable acceptance. Area banks and businesses put up hitching rails for buggies. Locals agreed to provide "taxi" service for Amish travelers needing to make longer trips. When officials took the initiative to have horse-drawn vehicle warning signs posted for motorists on county roads, the Amish saw it as a gesture of good will. Similarly, they noted with appreciation the fact that the business communities generally did not promote Amish-theme tourist attractions.[10] For example, in the early years of the Parke County settlement, an Amish woman offered to sell baked goods at a store in Bellmore. Sales rose when the storeowner advertised the items as Amish-made. Despite stronger sales, the woman requested that he remove the sign—which he did—even though sales then declined. While Web sites and printed material from tourist trade groups in both places make occasional references to the Amish, neither has tried to capitalize on its new population.

If locals gave the Amish a bit more breathing space than the church had experienced under the bright lights of mass media marketing back in Lancaster, the Amish in Parke and Wayne counties also observed a somewhat greater distance between themselves and their new hosts. Many of the habits and boundaries that regulate Amish interaction with the world are the product of relationships that have evolved over generations, and in the absence of that sort of shared history, the migrants tended to be less engaged in formal community relationships. Lancaster Amish men, for example, have long been active in Pennsylvania's system of volunteer fire companies, while those in Wayne and Parke County are not. Then, too, the Amish feared engendering resentment among those unfamiliar with their life and tried to avoid calling too often on non-Amish neighbors. Indeed, one of the few aspects of Parke County Ordnung that differs from Lancaster's pattern is Parke's permission of electricity-powered chest freezers. In Lancaster County, Amish households rent space in community frozen food lockers or rent freezer space from non-Amish neighbors—situations that are unavailable in Parke County or lack tradition there.

Amish economic pursuits capture the combination of continuity and adaptation that marked the emergence of these new settlements. Since one of the chief motivations was the desire to secure farmland (and not just a rural locale), it is not surprising that about sixty percent of households in Parke and Wayne counties are engaged in agriculture (see table 7.2).[11] Indeed, they are perhaps the only Indiana settlements in which majorities are farming.

The sort of farming they pursued—small-scale dairying—was unlike the cash cropping that had come to dominate these areas prior to the Amish arrival. As a result, local farm supply dealers initially did not stock inventory that the newcomers were looking for, leading the Amish to order goods from Lancaster merchants with whom they had longstanding connections and only gradually to transfer business to Indiana retailers. Yet if the Amish farming practices differed from those of their new Parke and Wayne neighbors, they also diverged from fellow farmers back in Lancaster, since the Indiana settlers could not rely on tobacco as a cash crop to prop up milk profits.[12] A notable number have turned to commercial produce growing, establishing contracts with regional and national supermarket chains to supply pumpkins, tomatoes, or peppers.

The preponderance of farmers gives these sister settlements a different feel from that of their more small-shop-and-business-oriented kin in eastern Pennsylvania. With less pressure from an entrepreneurial class to adapt new technologies and less

TABLE 7.2
Occupations of household heads, age 64 and younger (2002),
Parke and Wayne settlements

	Parke County	Wayne County
Farming	57%	59%
Carpentry/building trades	18	31
Small businesses/shops	16	7
Other	9	3
	N = 79	N = 58

SOURCE: *Church Directory of the Lancaster County Amish,* 2 vols. (Gordonville, Pa.: The Diary, 2002).

disposable income from wage-earning jobs, Indiana's Lancaster settlements may rest more comfortably with traditional Ordnung expectations. Seasonal cycles and weather patterns more directly orient people's lives, and large families have plenty of work for children. Most families expect the next generation to follow them in farming. The Amish know what local land is expected to be for sale and talk openly about where the settlements will expand geographically to accommodate new acreage.

Not every farming effort has been successful. In both new settlements a handful of would-be farmers have had to turn to other lines of work. Then, too, from the start a few households engaged in other occupations, and some later settlers arrived with no intention of tilling the soil. Amish firms, such as a Parke County harness and tack shop or a Wayne County construction crew that specializes in dairy barns and other farm structures, soon sprang up to meet settlement needs, though they also serve non-Amish customers. And the range of nonfarm business has expanded. Parke County's Amish operate a fabric and shoe store, along with blacksmithing, woodworking, carriage making, and harness shops; and Wayne County is home to several woodworkers and furniture builders. Several Parke County families have launched a small outdoor farmers' market just east of Rockville. Perhaps the most unusual Amish enterprise was one Wayne County family's operation for two years of a small restaurant in Centerville.

Despite this diversity, the number of home-based businesses is actually rather modest, especially compared with the Amish economic scene back in Lancaster, where small businesses located at or very near the home have become the clear alternative to farming and in some districts outnumber functioning farms.[13] Many of those Lancaster shops produce wood or metal products for wholesale dealers, or supply the local tourist trade with fabric crafts or furniture. Enterprises in infant settlements, however, face the challenge of breaking into established markets. The Amish in Wayne County, for example, found that Midwestern retailers already had contracts for Amish-built gazeboes and lawn furniture from suppliers in the larger Pennsylvania and Ohio settlements that could provide the product volume that retailers needed. Creating new accounts with start-up Indiana firms was less appealing even if they were geographically closer.

As a result, although some small shops do flourish among the Lancaster transplants, a more common agriculture alternative is work on carpentry crews. Such mobile work crews are hardly a rarity back in Pennsylvania, but they play a proportionately larger role in Parke and Wayne counties. The Wayne County settlement, for example, has three such crews, two of which do work mostly for Amish clients—a demand that remains high as new settlers move in and need to construct,

Illustration 7.1. Although dairy farming was the occupational aim of most of the Lancaster transplants, a number have established home-based shops and retail businesses. Source: Courtesy of Thomas J. Meyers.

expand, or remodel property—and a third that takes mostly non-Amish jobs, working as far away as Indianapolis. Some men also work for non-Amish contractors. In any case, construction work has provided ready opportunities in central Indiana since the new settlements themselves produce steady demand and because local contractors—unlike, say, furniture craftsmen—are not in competition with Amish entrepreneurs in larger, established settlements to the east.

The relative lack of Amish-owned businesses has also precipitated more contact with non-Amish retailers and forced more frequent trips to town. "In Lancaster we had more things among our own people," noted one Parke County man. "You could hook up a team [and go get things] without losing a whole day." For some services, such as buggy repair, harness, and horseshoeing, settlers initially traveled to other Indiana Amish settlements: to Daviess County from Parke, and to Adams County or Milroy from Wayne. Gradually, such firms emerged among the Lancaster people themselves. And the transplants continue to buy some items, such as buggies, hats, and bonnets, from Amish businesses in Lancaster itself, since these symbolic separators reflect the Lancaster Ordnung and are not available from Midwestern Amish producers, who adhere to different styles, colors, and standards.

Amish concern for their children's education also accents the dynamic of continuity and change in the creation of new communities. One of the first things the new arrivals did was to make plans for private schooling. Within a year of each settlement's start, residents had constructed schoolhouses. Parke County's first teacher in 1992 haled from Lancaster, and in 1995 Wayne County secured its first schoolteacher from Parke. Households never considered sending their children to area public schools, with which they had no historic relationship. Moreover, unlike some of the large Indiana Amish settlements in which a significant minority of children enrolls in public schools, the Amish in southeastern Pennsylvania have long universally supported their own private schools. Briefly, a developmentally disabled Wayne County Amish child did attended a public school special education classroom, but in 2001 the Amish there set up a special education room in one of their schoolhouses, and the student transferred out of the public school setting. By 2005 the Wayne County settlement had six schools, and Parke County had seven. In each settlement, one of the schools included a special education classroom.[14]

Illustration 7.2. A Lancaster-style schoolhouse in Indiana. Source: Courtesy of Thomas J. Meyers.

In virtually every way, these schools follow the Lancaster pattern—from the curriculum to the physical shape and layout of the building. Replicating even the building design and floor plan was important enough for the Lancaster transplants that they expended notable energy gaining approval in Indianapolis. The process took more time than they expected, since the state was accustomed to approving only Midwestern-style Amish school buildings. Nevertheless, the effort was part of establishing Amish identity in a new context—maintaining old ways necessitated learning new procedures—and of alerting the state to the fact that the Amish are not all cut from the same cloth.[15]

If the new arrivals continued to think of their school buildings in Lancaster terms, their orientation to the east was notable in other ways too, and they sometimes proved problematic. For example, when a new settler in Wayne County began a residential construction renovation project, he instinctively followed Pennsylvania building code guidelines with which he was familiar. Unfortunately for him, they differed in small but significant ways from those in force in Indiana. Complicating the picture and underscoring the fundamental problem that precipitated the conflict, the Wayne County Amishman contacted the *Pennsylvania* representative to the Amish Steering Committee—the church-state liaison group—for help in mediating an issue with Indianapolis. The advice from five hundred miles away only hampered resolution. Eventually, the Indiana Steering Committee representative became involved and helped ease the tension, but the episode illustrated the depth of Lancaster-oriented identity among those who, at some level, seemed to act as sojourners even in the process of putting down permanent roots.

CHURCHLY CONNECTIONS

The confusion surrounding how best to interact with state building codes was soon settled, but the incident pointed to a deeper reality: The connections between Amish communities are not primarily geographic, important as proximity may be. The meaning of memory and migration are critical factors in Amish sensibilities, and sometimes those ties are mediated through the church and its Ordnung.

The Amish in Parke and Wayne counties have intentionally maintained an Ordnung virtually identical to that recognized by their sister churches in Lancaster. Buggies are gray, and dress patterns mirror those in the east. Worship services follow Lancaster protocol.[16] As a practical guide to faithfulness, the Ordnung connects these Indiana churches to the Pennsylvania heartland in visible ways, continually reminding members and onlookers alike of their sister settlement relationship. Equally important, a common Ordnung functions as a symbol of spiritual unity across space. The churches in Lancaster and their diaspora are in fellowship precisely because they pursue the same way of life no matter where they reside.

In fact, the very structure of the church in the Lancaster sister settlements facilitates connection and commonality. For example, the Lancaster pattern of leadership selection encourages the ordination of bishops who are older, which has the effect of limiting churchly autonomy of newer settlements. Taking seriously biblical injunctions requiring leadership candidates to have nurtured their own children in the faith, Lancaster churches typically reserve the office of bishop for men who have at least one child who has become a church member.[17] Given the fact that children's baptism usually falls in the late teen years, even the youngest potential bishop candidates are in their mid-to upper-40s. Since new settlements most often attract younger families, the likelihood of quickly achieving ecclesial independence is diminished, since there often are no eligible bishop candidates in a new settlement.

As a result, for almost seven years the Parke and Wayne counties relied on the services of Pennsylvania bishops, who traveled to Indiana to provide semiannual communion services and to perform all baptisms and weddings. And since communion and baptism are rites that require commitment, or recommitment, to the Ordnung, these services took on specific meaning when undertaken in the presence of authoritative Lancaster eyes.

In contrast, many new settlements planted by migrants from historic Midwestern communities, such as Elkhart-LaGrange, could achieve churchly autonomy more quickly, since they were free to ordain resident bishops without the limitations that restrained their Lancaster brethren.[18] The Parke and Wayne communities, on the other hand, were tethered longer to their one-time church home. Only in 1998 did Parke County have a resident bishop; the Wayne settlement followed two years later.[19]

Other structural factors also keep transplanted Lancaster church order relatively unified, such as the tradition of granting a bishop oversight of two church districts. A bishop's practical need to balance opinions in two places often militates against change and puts the brakes on an individual district that might be unusually change-minded. The smaller number of bishops per settlement also allows for easier communication and coordinated agreement among bishops.[20]

Such agreement emerges in twice-yearly *Dienerversammlungen* (ministers meetings), which all the bishops from Lancaster sister settlements attend.[21] Held in Lancaster County itself, the meetings aim to articulate and uphold a common Ordnung among all the churches. Unlike similar ministers meetings' in larger Indiana settlements, where attendance is not mandatory and decisions are only advisory, the Lancaster gathering draws all leaders and outlines commonly agreed-upon commitments. Although the Amish maintain a congregational form of church government, some Lancaster-related Amish do refer to the *Dienerversammlung*, in English, as "the bishops' conference"—pointing to the semi-synodical polity they employ. Amish in other parts of Indiana recognize the difference too, with many commenting on the Lancaster circles of churches as "more hierarchical than we are."

The bishops from Parke and Wayne counties dutifully attend the Lancaster bishops' conferences and reaffirm each spring and fall their commitment to carrying out the Lancaster Ordnung.[22] Travel to Lancaster itself—a symbolic return of the diaspora in the convocation of bishops—along with the substance of discussions, means that the leadership meetings anchor the Indiana transplants in a tight network of churchly relationships and ground their day-to-day life in the authority of the Lancaster Ordnung, allowing little room for settlement innovation. Even the small changes that the Indiana communities have made—such as Parke County's permissiveness on chest freezers—had to meet with bishop approval in Lancaster first.[23]

THE TIES THAT BIND

Critical as such churchly cues remain, they are not the only ties that bind. The role of family in linking settlements, and the resulting travel and visiting that those links engender are crucial in orienting new settlements. The fact that these transplanted Amish communities stem from common geographic roots compounds the connections produced by kinship.[24] Leaving family behind in Pennsylvania was one of the difficult aspects of migration that residents cite. Feelings of loneliness and isolation certainly vary in intensity and typically diminish over time, but even those who have lived in Indiana for a decade remark on the continued draw of family ties and their wish to visit Lancaster more often than they are able. Especially wistful are the handful of older adults with grown children and grandchildren who remain back in Pennsylvania. One mother suggested that the strain of separated family members made the resettlement process more difficult for women. When her husband said that "it didn't take long 'til this [Wayne County] felt like home. We made it home," his wife interjected, "For the men it's different, I think. Women feel more for their family back in P.A."

Family rituals—especially weddings—are the most common occasion for travel between Indiana and Pennsylvania. Parke and Wayne counties' Amish residents report that most families make two such interstate trips a year, one during the fall wedding season and another at some other time. Such trips often last five to seven days and may involve several households together contracting with a non-Amish van driver. Less often a driver will transport a group made up only of women or young people from several households. Public bus transport between Indiana and Pennsylvania is also common.

Unlike many other Midwestern Amish communities, where weddings take place throughout the year, the Lancaster tradition concentrates all marriages into a period stretching from the last week of October through the first few days of December. The large number of marriages in such a compressed period of time helps facilitate the kind of kinship interaction that the interstate travelers prize, since a week's visit during November likely allows one to attend several weddings and see literally hundreds of friends and relatives. And weddings, unlike funerals, lend themselves to planned travel that is less rushed. Nevertheless, it is clear that churchly commitments still trump family ties. Households will forego attending a relative's wedding early in the Pennsylvania wedding season if it would mean missing their Indiana church district's October communion service.

For their part, the Indiana settlements have modified their own wedding season, holding most marriages in mid-October or in mid-December—in effect, bookending the Lancaster season—so as to allow Pennsylvania kin more easily to attend these Midwestern events. And relatives from the east travel to Indiana for other occasions too, such as to help a new mother after childbirth.

In any case, attendance at weddings in Pennsylvania or Indiana remains a key way relationships between the sister settlements remain fresh, even for children born and raised outside Lancaster. Indeed, weddings themselves can be events at which formal courting takes place, the first step in the formation of another generation of genealogical links among the Lancaster network of communities. Such long-distance dating relationships, in turn, produce their own set of occasions for interstate travel.

As the Indiana sister settlements grow, however, some members predict a decline in the amount of inter-settlement interaction. In 2002, for example, one keen observer counted as many courting couples within the Wayne County settlement as couples in which only one member lived in Wayne. A growing population, diversification of extended families, and the rising generation's acclimation to Indiana all point to the possibility of more intra-settlement marriages and at least a slight decline in "running back and forth" to Pennsylvania on the part of young people. "We know how hard it is to live here and have family back there," one Hoosier transplant couple confided. "I hope more young people stick with marriage partners from our own churches here."

Even so, few expect an end to regular inter-settlement visiting, given the fact that new households continue to arrive from Pennsylvania and that the Lancaster diaspora traditionally has maintained close fraternal bonds. However, those bonds typically run through Lancaster itself, so that often there is more travel between each of the Lancaster Indiana settlements and Pennsylvania than there is directly between Parke and Wayne counties. The intra-state ties that have developed, generally revolve around the cooperation needed to maintain Amish schools or relate to the state, while family bonds pull toward Pennsylvania.

TRANSPLANTED IDENTITY

The identity of Indiana's Lancaster transplants is located in a web of relationships that are themselves rooted in migration memory, church Ordnung, and a Lancaster-esque ethnicity. Interaction with non-Amish neighbors, links to Lancaster, ties to other Indiana Old Orders, and the relationship between the Parke and Wayne counties settlements themselves, all define what it means to be Amish in these places.

Given their recent vintage, relations with the non-Amish local community are fresh and dynamic, currently cordial but open to misunderstanding. Unlike the context in eastern Pennsylvania, with its nearly three-century tradition of Amish and non-Amish interaction and negotiated cultural understandings, these Hoosier locales are still places where Old Orders are a novelty. The transplants must be more self-consciously Amish as they explain their desire for private schools, work with local banks, bargain for exemption from buggy licensing, and make arrangements with neighbors to secure drivers for longer trips. Things that had grown routine in Lancaster now commanded more time and thought. The Amish find themselves more often in the position of humble petitioner—a position not foreign to the Amish spirit but now accentuated in new ways.

For their part, the local non-Amish communities were familiar with popular Amish commercial and media stereotypes before they ever had real Amish neighbors, and when the new arrivals came with a special interest in agriculture, they confirmed some of those traditional images. Still, the possibility of misunderstanding and miscommunication is notable where such direct encounters are still new. All of this has helped produce an Amish identity at once more articulately engaged with the world, and more diffident and retiring.

A second set of relationships that sheds light on this transplanted identity is the link to Lancaster. The ties here are strong, including kin connections and frequent travel to the place that symbolically anchors their church and plays a leading role in determining the Ordnung that manages everyday life in Indiana. Undoubtedly, the Amish in both Parke and Wayne counties all know more people in the Lancaster settlement a third of a continent away than they do in any of the geographically closer Ohio, Indiana, or Illinois Amish communities. The fact that most Hoosier transplants make semiannual—and in some cases, more frequent—trips to eastern Pennsylvania means that Lancaster functions not just as a symbolic center of identity but as a living demonstration of Amish life. And that life is shared, via the Ordnung, back in Parke and Wayne counties, as families drive gray buggies, adhere to Lancaster dress codes, and otherwise visibly demonstrate their solidarity with the churches on the Atlantic seaboard in ways that other Midwestern Old Orders immediately recognize as different. The churches within the Lancaster diaspora all share in the Lancaster-administered Amish Aid Plan and Church Aid Plans for mutual assistance in the event of fire and storm loss or health care costs. While such mutualism begins with the local district's alms fund, larger costs are born by the Lancaster network.[25]

Indeed, a Lancaster identity emerges even in the context of describing differences. Members can immediately list the handful of differences that distinguish them from their eastern Pennsylvania brethren, but they do so in a way that underscores their sense that these variations are minor exceptions to the rule. In general, the transplants are very hesitant to criticize their Lancaster kin, even though most can just as quickly enumerate what they see as the positive characteristics of their slower pace of life and small settlement size in Indiana. Even when commenting on the evils of tobacco or the deviant young people back in Lancaster in ways that implicitly critique the home community, the criticism is almost never direct and is very often coupled with a confession of imperfection on their own part.

A third set of relationships—those with members of other historic Indiana Amish settlements—provide another means of placing the Parke and Wayne groups in the wider Old Order world. By most measures, the number of such deep and defining relationships is few. Certainly there is a good deal of curious interest on all sides. Amish in other parts of the state know about the Pennsylvania settlements and have a general sense of the outlines of their Ordnung, but they know relatively few individuals within these communities well. For their part, Parke and Wayne Amish are aware of other Hoosier settlements, though they often are less sure about the specifics of size, exact location, or Ordnung details.

Not surprisingly, only a few have traveled to the Elkhart-LaGrange or Nappanee settlements, and just a handful from those areas have been to church in Parke or Wayne County. True, the first Parke and Wayne arrivals instinctively turned to neighboring Amish settlements in Daviess or Adams counties for blacksmithing or harness repair work—even bypassing nearer non-Amish neighbors who provide such services—but the number of ongoing, significant business contacts with other

Indiana Old Orders have never become critically important to the economy of the Lancaster-spawned settlements. And although the Lancaster Amish are in full fellowship with a sizable portion of the state's Swiss churches (owing to their common practice of *streng Meidung*), the Lancaster folks remain openly curious about the Swiss in ways that betray the actual distance between the two ethnic groups, despite a certain theological kinship.

Most of the few strong friendships that have emerged between Lancaster transplants and other Indiana Amish revolve around common interest in private schools. Annual school directors' meetings draw participants from around the state and provide a forum for discussing matters ranging from legal compliance to classroom discipline. These meetings rotate from settlement to settlement, and Parke County hosted the 1997 gathering, while Wayne County hosted the 2001 meeting.[26] The intense and focused nature of these meetings has forged some key cross-community friendships, but in relative terms, only a handful of Amish participate regularly in such events.

Meetings of Amish schoolteachers themselves occur more often—typically every six weeks—and might have become a venue for more frequent inter-settlement interaction, but that has not occurred. At one point the Wayne County Amish teachers met with schoolteachers from the Allen County settlement to the north. Both groups highly value their private schools, and the Wayne teachers were impressed with the quality and seriousness of the Allen County schools. Nonetheless, differences in daily practice trumped geographic proximity and mutual academic respect. The Allen County schools use hand-held calculators with some mathematics lessons and had adopted a number of newer, updated textbooks, which seemed to signal a slightly more progressive curriculum. Instead, teachers from the Wayne and Parke settlements meet together to discuss classroom issues and share teaching ideas. When it comes to regular interaction among teachers around practical matters of school concern, the Lancaster settlements have ended up talking to themselves.

And yet these gatherings of schoolteachers are something of an anomaly in the pattern of interaction *between* Wayne and Parke counties. Although the Amish in both places feel a greater bond with one another than with other Indiana Old Orders, they do not visit back and forth with any frequency. It is much more common for residents to visit Lancaster County, Pennsylvania—five or six hundred miles away—than to visit each other. The young people rarely go back and forth, and few marriages have linked the two communities. For now, Lancaster remains the hub that connects these outlying settlement spokes.

The nature of these overlapping and intersecting relationships reveals the state

of an evolving Amish identity. Connections between the local non-Amish community and the Lancaster, Pennsylvania, parent settlement are high, while ties to other
Hoosier Amish and between Parke and Wayne counties themselves remain under-
developed. The story of migration and the ties of Ordnung remain firm and give
this culture specific shape. Local contexts are also crucial in situating Amish identity and have facilitated and even justified the ways in which these settlements have
deviated from the Lancaster norm, permitting a silent but recognizable critique of
life in the Lancaster heartland.

A clear sense of being part of a diaspora—a larger imagined community—coupled with a commitment to putting down new roots in particular places combines
to define these transplants in important ways. If this identity nurtures a sense of
separation, neither fully Lancaster nor firmly Midwestern, it has allowed for selective interaction with new neighbors and, to a lesser extent, with other Amish in the
state.

Inter-settlement interaction and the significance of that interaction in shaping
Amish identity figures prominently in the experience of four settlements that exist
almost on top of one another in south central Indiana—communities considered
in the next chapter.

CHAPTER EIGHT

The Paoli-Salem Communities

The southern Indiana barn raising attracted Amish participants from four different settlements in Orange and neighboring Washington counties. Some of the men arrived in enclosed buggies; others came in open ones. Half of the carriages bore bright orange triangles indicating a Slow Moving Vehicle (SMV), and half did not. A few of the workers had hired English drivers to bring them to the site, while others would not have countenanced such a move. Many had long beards, though a few sported tightly trimmed beards. Some of the men wore wide suspenders, others wore narrow ones, and still others wore no suspenders at all. A majority of the group spoke Pennsylvania German, while the rest conversed in Swiss. About half the men saw nothing wrong with sharing tobacco as a common pleasure of the work day; others refused smoking and chewing on principle and would not work in the presence of those who did.

These Amishmen had come together around a common building project as people committed to helping one another and extending mutual aid. Yet the differences in appearance, custom, taboos, and communication were striking reminders of the diversity of practice and the complex web of relationships negotiated among the various people who claim the Amish name.

South central Indiana is home to an intriguing Amish arena. Around the towns of Paoli and Salem, four different settlements exist side by side in an area with a radius of perhaps fifteen miles. Each settlement has a distinct history and represents a particular approach to Ordnung. Nor are the four groups all of the same ethnic background. Making sense of these differences challenges many of the popular and academic assumptions about Amish life and raises provocative questions about the nature of Amish identity.

A central tenet of Amish faith is separation from the world. Yet the ways in which the Amish variously mark that separation distinguish Amish groups from one another as much as from the rest of society. Identity can be shaped as much by perceived differences and similarities among settlements as by conscious comparison with mainstream culture.

The Amish often describe their practices with the vocabulary of "high" and "low." A "lower" church is more conservative and more traditional than a "higher" one. The term "lower" also calls to mind the Amish value of humility, or lowering oneself in relation to others, thus suggesting that those in higher churches—rather than being more fully developed or mature—are actually flirting with dangerous values.

Academic observers have picked up on this linear imagery and used it more rigorously than the Amish have. Constructing a spectrum of conservative-to-progressive or traditional-to-liberal Amish groups, observers have postulated ladders of acculturation and Anabaptist escalators of adaptation.[1] Such a one-dimensional model, however, imposes too narrow a view of the elements that are important to Amish life and limits one's ability to see the many different ways in which convictions cluster and cohere. Linear models also reveal the ways in which modern minds—intentionally or not—measure the Amish with fundamentally progressive assumptions that may not be best suited to Old Order realities.[2]

The weakness of lining up Amish groups on a conservative-to-progressive continuum becomes especially evident when considering the four settlements around Paoli and Salem, Indiana, which illustrate the complex relationships that shape Amish identities. Critical factors in the construction of identity often fail to combine in ways that can be expressed in linear fashion. Moreover, consistency is in the eye of the beholder. Those who take traditionalist positions on technology may not do so when it comes to more innovative social custom or theological discussion. Similarly, one's stance on appropriate occupations may not signal one's openness to tampering with worship patterns or engaging with potential religious converts. And differences in ethnic culture complicate any comparisons.

NEIGHBORING SETTLEMENTS

The south central Indiana counties of Orange and Washington are home to five distinct Amish settlements, four of which exist almost on top of one another and are

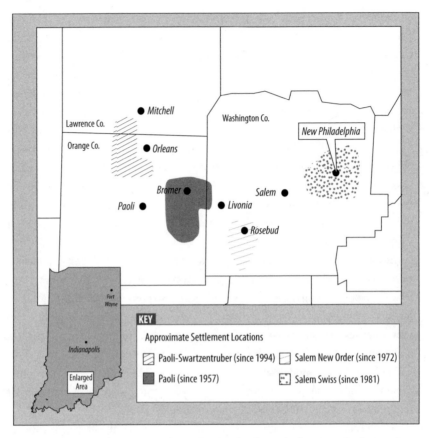

Map 8.1. The Paoli, Paoli-Swartzentruber, Salem New Order, and Salem Swiss Settlements in Indiana.

considered here.[3] To the east of the Orange County seat of Paoli lies the oldest of the communities, which for convenience will be called the Paoli settlement. Just to the north of the Paoli group, near the town of Orleans, is a Swartzentruber settlement related to the Swartzentruber Old Order affiliation in Ohio and elsewhere.[4] The area west of the Washington County town of Salem is home to a so-called New Order Amish settlement, while a settlement of Swiss Amish exists just to the east of Salem.

Paoli Settlement

The first of what would become a cluster of Amish settlements in south-central Indiana began in 1957, when three families moved to farms east of Paoli in Orange County and were joined the next year by three more. The founding families came from different places—Elkhart-LaGrange and Nappanee settlements in Indiana; Mercer County, Pennsylvania; and a Jay County, Indiana, settlement that was then in the process of dissolving. If the geographical background of the group was diverse, the pull to Orange County was a common commitment to reconfigure Old Order life in particular ways. At mid-century the Amish who formed the Paoli settlement were concerned both to stem technological and occupational changes moving through the larger, older communities and to bring about moral reform, especially among Amish youth. The remote location in Orange County promised to be the place where they could build their new Amish ideal.[5]

The Paoli Amish were committed to a "low" Ordnung (very traditional) for regulating most aspects of family and community life. Technological innovation and nonfarm employment remain strictly limited, as is casual interaction with surrounding society. Homes are remarkably modest. At the same time, the Paoli church was somewhat innovative in the strictures it placed on equally traditional Amish customs surrounding youth activities and the place of unbaptized teens. Paoli parents would not tolerate the antics that had traditionally accompanied young people's gatherings in the older settlements. Nor was tobacco use—another old custom among many Old Orders—permitted in Paoli. The forthrightness with which the Paoli church held their particular combination of traditional and novel commitments left them in fellowship with only a modest circle of other equally small settlements formed about the same time. Since 1991, the Paoli settlement has consisted of two church districts.

Salem New Order

Very near the Paoli settlement is a New Order Amish community whose members live west of Salem in Washington County. The New Order Amish of Salem date their origins to 1972, although their church has a rather complicated set of beginnings. The first residents included families of Amish and conservative Mennonite background, and initially the formal affiliation and direction of the group was not clear-cut. Through a series of developments—including the arrival and departure of more households from various places—the church increasingly took on a New Order Amish identity and eventually moved into New Order circles of fellowship and accountability.[6] Stemming in part from its unusual origins, the New Order church in Salem meets for worship in a church meetinghouse rather than in members' homes. They are the only Amish in Indiana to do so.[7]

Nationally, the New Order Amish movement emerged from a 1960s Amish emphasis on Christian conversion that used language many Old Orders criticized as individualistic. New Order proponents—who at first resisted that label—saw the teaching as both biblical and a necessary means of bringing young people to faith. Condemnation of smoking and of courting traditions in which dating teens were left unchaperoned in private bedrooms became rallying issues for New Order sympathizers. In 1966 resistance to the New Order agenda sparked churchly division in Ohio. Thereafter, a distinct and identifiable circle of New Order churches emerged, centered in Ohio but with districts in a dozen states.[8] Today there are more than sixty church districts in the United States, including two in Indiana.

The New Order emphasis on "spiritual values" has in some ways undercut the ability of Ordnung to regulate "externals," and New Order Amish sometimes express concern that a distinctive way of life may actually be an avenue of "works righteousness" and a temptation to earn salvation by following custom. While the New Order Amish still strive to live a simple life and use horse-drawn transportation on the road, they typically are much less restricted in their use of technology and less traditional in dress than other Amish. Also distinctive is the New Order tendency to offer more rational explanations of faith and practice in place of unarticulated deference to tradition.[9]

Salem Swiss

East of the town of Salem lies the Swiss Amish settlement that includes two church districts. The first families moved there in the fall of 1981. The next year more households arrived, including a resident bishop. These newcomers were from Indiana's Adams County community—one of the state's Swiss Amish ethnic centers. The quest for affordable acreage in a rural setting was one migration motive, and Washington County offered it. In addition, some of the early arrivals shared a desire to liberalize certain aspects of Ordnung—such as larger-scale turkey-raising operations not permitted in their Adams County affiliation.[10]

New Swiss arrivals have boosted the population through the years, but churchly debates have prompted others to leave, including the original three Salem settlement households. In 1986 Salem Swiss Amish families started the Vevay settlement in southeastern Indiana's Switzerland County. Certain kin ties still connect Salem to Adams County, to the Vevay community, and to other Swiss settlements in the Midwest, but for the most part the Salem Swiss church has few links of formal fellowship with other Swiss communities. Dialect and Swiss-specific customs, such as open buggies and particular dress styles, visually mark the Salem Swiss population.

Swartzentrubers

The fourth settlement in the area began in 1994 when four households associ-ated with the Swartzentruber affiliation moved to Orange County, settling north of the older Paoli settlement. The Swartzentrubers represent an ultra-traditional Old Order affiliation with roots in a 1913 eastern Ohio *streng Meidung* controversy. While most of the churches in the Wayne-Holmes County settlement were not inclined to practice strict shunning, bishop Samuel E. Yoder (1872–1932) had insisted on it. Perhaps personality conflicts added to the impasse, and a group of Amish media-tors from Indiana and Illinois were not able to resolve the conflict, which resulted in a final break of fellowship by 1917. Yoder's more traditional approach to church discipline, it turned out, was coupled with an equally conservative appraisal of up-dating Ordnung in any way. His supporters soon became known for their resistance to innovation in household technology, farming practice, dress, and worship liturgy. The group received the nickname "Swartzentruber Amish" in 1936—four years after bishop Yoder's death—when its two key leaders coincidentally bore the Swartzentruber surname.[11]

In the 1940s and 50s the Swartzentruber subgroup began daughter settlements in Ohio, Tennessee, and Ontario. New communities in other places followed, and during the 1990s a notable surge in new Swartzentruber communities took place. The Orange County settlement drew on this Swartzentruber diaspora. The first two families in Indiana came from the Wayne County, Ohio, Swartzentruber heart-land. The next two moved from the Gladwin, Michigan, community; and subse-quent arrivals hailed from Ohio and from Heuvelton, New York. Indiana Swartzen-truber Amish families continue to have contact with relatives in these and other settlements of their affiliation. In 2004 the Swartzentruber settlement in Indiana had grown to include two church districts.[12]

COMMON GROUND AND DIVERGENT CHOICES

All four Amish settlements in Orange and Washington counties recognize one another as Amish. They use horse and buggy transportation on the road, and those who farm do so with horses.[13] They extend mutual aid to one another through joint work in occasional barn raising "frolics" across settlement lines.

Local context also impresses certain similarities on all four groups. For example, none of the children in these settlements attend public schools. While the highly conservative-minded Paoli and Swartzentruber families might be disinclined to

TABLE 8.1
Amish settlements in Orange and Washington counties

	Swartzentruber	Paoli	Swiss	New Order
Local arrival	1994	1957	1981	1972
Early settler origins	Ohio, Michigan, New York	Various Indiana and Pennsylvania	Adams County, Indiana	Various Midwest and Pennsylvania
Districts today	Two	Two	Two	One
Transportation on the road	Horse and buggy	Horse and buggy	Horse and buggy	Horse and buggy
Farming	Horses	Horses	Horses	Horses; tractor use around the barn
School enrollment	All in Amish schools	All in Amish schools	All in Amish schools	All in Amish schools

trust public schools in any case, the fact that these settlements exist in communities without a deep history of Amish involvement in public education is the key factor that keeps all four committed to Amish schools. But while the Amish are united in their support of private schools, each of the four settlements maintains its own set of buildings and teachers—illustrating the clear lines of distinction that exist among them, even in areas of common conviction. Those differences, though, form complex patterns of interaction and separation (see table 8.1).

It would be tempting to align the differences on a continuum formed by the ultra-conservative Swartzentrubers on one end and the progressive New Orders on the other, with the Paoli church very close to the conservative end of the spectrum and the Swiss somewhere in the middle. By some measures, this scheme makes sense. The Ordnung surrounding technology use, for example, seems to follow such a pattern. Swartzentruber and Paoli church members have no easy access to telephone service; in emergency situations they will use a pay phone or a non-Amish neighbor's phone. The Swiss also reject individual telephone ownership, but have established community phone booths that several families can share to make outgoing calls. Since the booths are located at some distance from any private dwelling, they cannot easily be used for receiving incoming calls that disrupt the rhythms of family life. In contrast, the New Order Amish have telephones in their homes, and some even list their phone numbers on business signs and in their church directory.

Other uses of technology also form a ladder stretching from "low" to "high" Ordnung practice. The "low" Swartzentrubers milk cows by hand and use oil lanterns rather than pressured gas lamps. Chain saws, bicycles, and power lawn mowers are off-limits. Small gasoline or diesel engines can be used to pump water or operate washing machines. The Paoli church follows a similar Ordnung with regard to technology. Swiss practice is more flexible, with shops employing line-shaft power to operate several machines at once. New Order homes and businesses observe a "higher" Ordnung, for example, using bottled gas appliances and lighting as well as hydraulic and pneumatic power sources to operate shop equipment.

At first glance, carriage styles seem to fit this conservative-to-progressive continuum as well. The Swartzentruber and Paoli churches, for example, drive buggies without rubber tires, protective storm fronts in winter, or the bright orange SMV signs. Neither group uses electric lights on their buggies, though their buggies are equipped with a small driver's side hook on which a lantern can be hung at night. In contrast, New Orders drive closed buggies much like those used by mainstream Old Order groups in Ohio and northern Indiana: carriages with sliding doors, rubber tires, protective storm fronts for winter weather, SMV markers, and battery-operated electric lights and turn signals. But attempting to place the Swiss in such a scheme poses a problem. Unlike any of the other three Pennsylvania German groups in the area, the Salem Swiss church members follow the traditional Swiss pattern of using open buggies. This represents a different tradition and is neither more conservative nor more innovative than an enclosed buggy.[14] The introduction of ethnic differences complicates an Ordnung continuum that assumes variations on the same customs.

Migration histories and contexts also have bearing on the visual expressions of identity. Although the Paoli and Swartzentruber churches both adhere to a remarkably low technology Ordnung, their homes are quite different. Both groups ban carpeting, window curtains, indoor toilets, and other amenities, but the physical appearance of their homes diverges considerably. In part because the Paoli church founders were leaving settlements they feared were becoming too worldly and affluent, the Paoli group has intentionally minimized the attractiveness of their homes, in many cases adopting an almost dowdy look. The Paoli settlement exists, in some ways, in conscious discontinuity with those Amish communities where neat vinyl siding, landscaping, and cement driveways prevail.

The Swartzentrubers, in contrast, moved to Paoli intending to create a community that was in continuity with their Swartzentruber traditions from Ohio. Rather than reacting against another settlement, the Swartzentrubers set out to closely imitate their parental patterns. New Swartzentruber homes are large, two-story frame farmhouses similar to those traditionally found in eastern Ohio. They sport extended wrap-around porches and sometimes daylight full basements. Indeed, Swartzentruber homes typically are larger and more imposing than the nearby Swiss and New Order homes, though the New Orders have a variety of interior

Illustration 8.1. The very modest homes in the notably conservative Paoli settlement reflect the low Ordnung of these churches. Source: Courtesy of Thomas J. Meyers.

TABLE 8.2
Technology use and public appearance, Orange and Washington counties

	Swartzentruber	Paoli	Swiss	New Order
Telephones	No easy access	No easy access	Community phone booths	In homes; public numbers
Power sources for machinery, tools, and equipment	Very limited	Very limited	Permissive away from home, limited at home	Permissive
Buggy style	Enclosed	Enclosed	Open	Enclosed
Household amenities	Few	Few	Few	Many
Houses— appearance	Large in size, imposing	Modest size, dowdy in appearance	Modest size, some neat, some dowdy	Modest size; some landscaping

amenities and some modest landscaping that none of the other groups would allow. The Swiss houses are modest in size. Those of newer construction, especially, are neat in appearance but quite plain. The style and appearance of Amish homes in each settlement does say something about the identity of each group, but not in a way that can be easily or meaningfully compared on a continuum that parallels other Ordnung choices (see table 8.2).

SOCIAL LIFE, CUSTOM, AND TRADITION

If the Paoli and Swartzentruber groups share some things in common when it comes to traditional approaches to technology, they part ways in the area of social life and custom, mixing the meanings of traditional and innovative, "low" and "high" Ordnung. In fact, on issues about which they feel strongly, members of the Paoli settlement and the Salem New Orders share significant common ground—a situation surprising to onlookers gauging Amish fellowship only in terms of buggy style and dress standards. If the New Orders have not left tradition unquestioned, neither has the Paoli settlement in certain cases. Both groups, for example, are committed to moral reform of traditional folkways, including the exclusion of tobacco and the promotion of tightly controlled youth activity, free from rowdy behavior or the hint of promiscuity.

As one New Order leader characterized the Paoli group, "They think like us, but they wouldn't explain it the way we do." Such an appraisal may suggest a closer affinity than actually exists, but the comment is telling. Indeed, people from both the ultra-conservative Paoli and progressive New Order churches engage in informal religious fellowship. New Order young people will attend Sunday evening "singings" held in Paoli homes. New Order parents approve such social interaction because they know the evening will be well supervised and maintain a spiritual atmosphere. Paoli leaders apparently welcome the New Orders for similar reasons, believing that the New Order youth will be well-disciplined. New Order adults who sometimes accompany the youth characterized the Paoli singings in positive terms. "We were received very well. We had fine fellowship with them," noted one. Yet the interaction does not flow both ways, and Paoli youth do not attend singings in New Order homes. Home environments there, with telephones and other marks of modernity, would make Paoli visitors uncomfortable. The Paoli group is secure enough in its own turf to admit New Order visitors, but it does not venture beyond the bounds of its own separatism.

For their part, the Swartzentruber and Swiss youth activities follow traditional channels, with minimal interference from parents and few public qualms about the generations-old customs surrounding unchaperoned dating, including so-called "bed courtship."[15] Tobacco use, too, is regarded in these circles as part of rural life and protests against it merely the troublesome complaints of those dissatisfied with the wisdom of past generations. Similarities of opinion on these points among Swiss and Swartzentruber folks are the result of parallel thinking about tradition and not the product of creative interaction. Indeed, there is no evidence that mem-

TABLE 8.3
Social custom and tradition, Orange and Washington counties

	Swartzentruber	Paoli	Swiss	New Order
Tobacco use	Yes	No	Yes	No
Alcohol use	Permitted	Forbidden	Permitted	Forbidden
Tightly controlled youth activities	No	Yes	No	Yes
Courting rituals	Traditional, unchaperoned group and individual meetings	Regulated group gatherings; parents choose partners	Traditional, unchaperoned group and individual meetings	Regulated group gatherings; chaperoned dates
Dialect	Pennsylvania German	Pennsylvania German	Swiss	Pennsylvania German

bers of these two groups regularly communicate at all. The ethnic and dialect differences compound the Ordnung differences to keep churchly fellowship and communication to a minimum (see table 8.3).

In some settings, though, Swartzentrubers and Swiss customs defer to the demands of other groups. At cooperative projects such as barn raisings, members of the Paoli church will not participate unless Swiss and Swartzentruber men "put away" their tobacco. Abstinence on the part of all is a condition of their cooperation. While New Order workers are equally public about their refusal to smoke, they are less confrontational. In at least one case, nonsmoking New Orders worked along side tobacco-using Swiss and Swartzentrubers until members of the Paoli church arrived—at which point all tobacco disappeared for the duration of the project.

INTERACTING WITH THE WIDER WORLD

Though separate from the world, Amish communities are never isolated. Economic ties, neighborly contacts, and conversation with inquiring religious seekers are among the ways Amish consciously interact with larger society. The rural Orange and Washington counties context leaves members in environments remote from major population centers. Occupational possibilities are curtailed, given limited retail customer bases, very modest tourist traffic, and a dearth of major industry. These absences may have been part of the region's attraction for the Amish who moved here, and they continue to shape the sorts of economic opportunities that are available.

Both Swartzentruber and Paoli churches emphasize farming as a way of life, and the majority of both groups live on farms, though a range of sideline businesses supply income for most families, either in lieu of farming or as a supplement to it. The "low" Ordnung of both groups bridles technology and offers only a modest array of such businesses: saw mills, furniture crafting, wooden basket making, and small retail stores. Some Swartzentruber men work as carpenters but only take jobs within buggy-driving distance; a few work for a non-Amish-owned slaughterhouse doing manual labor.

The Paoli group is the most limited in its occupational interaction since that church forbids married men to work away from home. While unmarried teens can find employment in construction trades, household heads may not. The Paoli Amish seek to keep family life central, to curtail involvement with outsiders, and to avoid the lure of higher paying jobs elsewhere.[16] In contrast, married Swartzentruber men do not have to be self-employed at home as do their Paoli neighbors. Remarkably, in spite of the severely limited ability of these groups to advertise or take telephone orders, retail requests for things like furniture keep these intentionally small-sized shops busy. In neither group do women or girls work outside the home, though a married Swartzentruber woman without children might operate a modest retail store without compromising her place in the community.

Only one New Order household near Salem is engaged in farming, though a church leader there wistfully wished more would engage in agriculture, citing the farm as a good place to raise children. Instead, most New Order men work in small businesses, a greater range of which are possible, given the more flexible approach to technology and telephone ordering and marketing. The regional environment directs most New Order businesses toward lumber, wood craft, and carpentry lines. Despite their more advanced equipment—from forklifts to pneumatic jigsaws— the New Order Amish share something in common with their Paoli and Swartzentruber neighbors to the west. The New Order Amish self-consciously try to minimize what they see as the negative influences of secular society by encouraging household heads to find employment among fellow church members. They do not work "away" for non-Amish firms, though some carpenters do jobs for non-Amish customers.

The Salem Swiss Amish are in some ways the most different in their more ready acceptance of working "away." Like Swiss Amish elsewhere, they are less reticent to engage in mobile carpentry crews that take household heads out of the community for most of the day to work on construction jobs at some distance. Almost all the Salem Swiss Amishmen are carpenters, and they routinely hire drivers to shuttle them to job sites. A few families have modest home-based manufacturing shops in which they build hickory rocking chairs or other wood products. Without the hydraulic- or pneumatic-powered equipment that their New Order counterparts might use, these Swiss firms run machinery from a simple, single-engine line-shaft source. The absence of readily available telephone service within the business would suggest that these firms would focus on marketing through established wholesale outlets, but anecdotal evidence points to surprising numbers of word-of-mouth retail orders too.

As decidedly rural people, none of the Amish in Orange and Washington counties spend much time in towns, but they offer a modest range of appraisals of such ventures. New Orders see the opportunity to interact with non-Amish town residents as part of their Christian witness. A friendly word and cheery face are ways of spreading the peace of Christ in everyday conversation. Members of the Paoli Amish settlement, however, view town life as potentially threatening. "Town is not for our people," notes one leader, citing vices of wasting time in stores, gossiping on the street corner, and drinking coffee in area lunch counters. Members of the Paoli districts go to town rarely, consolidating errands as much as possible. Observers note that often only male household heads make the trek, shielding children from its influences by having them stay at home. Swiss and Swartzentruber families are more apt to go to town as an entire family, viewing the outing as a bit of a break from the weekly work routine, but they rarely spend much time in town or have lengthy interactions with others. In both cases the intense orientation to kin group and church dampens interest in social conversation with outsiders. Indeed, Swartzentruber and Swiss individuals rarely offer more than a curt acknowledgement to a greeting initiated by a passing New Order Amish person when they meet in town.

In some communities a source of interaction with non-Amish neighbors comes in the form of hired drivers who transport Amish passengers on trips that are longer than possible in a horse and buggy. Neither Swartzentruber nor Paoli Amish hire private drivers for local trips other than the most extreme of medical emergencies (in which case, non-Amish neighbors would undoubtedly not charge for the service). For planned trips of some distance, both groups use public bus lines. Until 2005, a route from Louisville, Kentucky, to Bloomington, Indiana, ran through Paoli. Since that time, these Amish need to hire drivers to take them to the bus terminal in Louisville, Kentucky.[17] Since pleasure trips are off-limits, such travel typically takes place only in the case of funerals or visiting close relatives who live in other settlements. Swiss and New Order Amish members more readily hire drivers to take them on longer trips, preferring such transport to public buses. Non-Amish neighbors with vans often work as "taxis" in such Amish communities, perhaps shuttling people to town or even driving for interstate trips between settlements.

Swiss mobile carpentry crews employ non-Amish drivers on a daily basis to take them to work sites outside the settlement.

A highly self-conscious form of interaction with the world comes in the form of conversations with religious "seekers" who express interest in joining an Amish church. The Amish may counsel seekers to live among them, observing firsthand if their way of life is really as attractive up close as it is from a distance. In addition, church leaders will discuss doctrine and biblical understandings with them. Few seekers end up joining the church, though such incorporation into the church through baptism does occur on occasion. While serious inquiries are few and no Amish settlement is overrun with seekers, some communities receive more than others. For their size, the Paoli and Salem New Order settlements probably receive more inquiries from seekers than any other communities in Indiana.

In the case of the New Orders, the attraction for outsiders is likely the New Orders' verbal articulation of belief, coupled with their willingness to use English and otherwise accommodate themselves to the needs of outsiders until they have become comfortable with Pennsylvania German. The relatively progressive New Order approach to technology also means relatively fewer changes in lifestyle for converts. The Paoli group, in contrast, demands much more in terms of shedding modern conveniences, yet in that way it also proves attractive to others by offering a life that in many ways runs closest to the sectarian ideal outsiders expect from the Amish. Very restrictive in technology use and sharply separated from the world, the Paoli group also upholds strict moral standards with a sort of rigorous logic that makes more sense to the modern mind than the tradition-guided customs of the

TABLE 8.4
Interaction with the world, Orange and Washington counties

	Swartzentruber	Paoli	Swiss	New Order
Work location	At home or away	Married men must be self-employed at home	At home or away	At home or for another church member
Type of work	Farming, small businesses, slaughterhouse	Farming, sideline/supplemental businesses	Shops, farming, carpentry	Small businesses
Regularly go to town	Yes	No	Yes	Yes
Paid transportation	Public bus; hired driver only to bus terminal	Public bus; hired driver only to bus terminal	Hire private drivers	Hire private drivers
Inquiries from seekers	No	Yes	No	Yes

Swartzentrubers. In fact, despite their equally separatist way of life, the Swartzentrubers receive almost no seekers, and in fact, would be less inclined to interact with them. For its part, the insularity and in-group orientation of the Swiss settlement east of Salem has not attracted seekers either (see table 8.4).

FRATERNAL LINKS

Not only interaction with larger society but also contact with other Amish churches reveals differences among the four settlements. None of the four groups are "in fellowship" with another; they do not exchange ministers or attend one another's worship services (although as mentioned above, the Paoli group accepts New Order attendees at their evening youth "singings"). Each settlement is part of a circle of other Amish church districts that provide accountability and reciprocal recognition of leadership. The Indiana Swartzentruber community is in fellowship with a portion of the Swartzentruber affiliation scattered over several states, while the New Order church at Salem is part of a circle that includes Indiana's other New Order district near Worthington and all other New Order districts nationwide that reject tractor farming and public utility electricity. The Salem Swiss settlement has a somewhat smaller group of fellow districts, given the history of division that has marked the Swiss diaspora. The Paoli settlement also has a limited range of fellowship; its Ordnung commitment to "low" technology and a reformist approach to social customs are absolute and find few equal partners. Fewer than a dozen districts in Ohio and Michigan fit these criteria.[18]

One of the factors in determining church fellowship is the Amish view of the ban and its permanence. While the New Order group will, in certain cases, lift the ban and end its social dimension of shunning, none of the other three groups do. All practice *streng Meidung* (strict shunning), which calls for the lifelong status of excommunication for the unrepentant. To date, no one in the four settlements has left his or her church to join one of the neighboring groups. Were that to happen, it would likely produce a serious breach of trust and ill will among the groups involved and sour cooperative community work. In some cases, individuals moving in from other communities have to negotiate local interpretations of the ban, but these cases have never had a local origin or focus. For example, an Amish contractor from Ohio who had been placed in the ban by his Old Order church when he joined a nearby New Order fellowship would discover upon moving to the Salem New Order community that neighboring Swartzentruber, Paoli, and Swiss members would feel bound to refuse contracts with him and otherwise honor the discipline of his original church.

The practice of shunning in any form stems from all four groups' common commitment to the 1632 Dordrecht Confession of Faith and related Amish theological tenets. All practice adult baptism, meet biweekly for worship, and observe a threefold ministry of bishops, ministers, and deacons. In all four settlements, worship is in the vernacular—Swiss for the Salem Swiss churches, and Pennsylvania German for the others. The New Order church will use some English if visitors or seekers are present, but even then, they still sing in German. Worship follows a similar format in all four groups, with two-and-a-half to three-hour services. Swartzentruber, Swiss, and Paoli church districts meet in homes, while the New Order church meets in a church meetinghouse next to their school building. The three groups that worship in homes also use the sixteenth-century *Ausbund*—the most commonly used songbook among Old Orders nationwide. The New Orders sing from a version of the 1892 *Unparteiische Liedersammlung* (also called the "Guengerich book"), a modest adaptation of the *Ausbund* used as well by a small number of Old Orders, including the nearby Daviess County, Indiana, Old Order churches.[19] The edition used in Salem includes an appendix of English hymns that the New Order Amish sing at evening gatherings.

Perhaps the religious program that most distinguishes the New Order Amish in Salem from their Old Order neighbors is their practice of holding Sunday school

Illustration 8.2. New Order Amish near Salem worship in a church meetinghouse instead of homes. The meetinghouse is in the foreground; the settlement schoolhouse stands behind it. Source: Courtesy of Thomas J. Meyers.

sessions on the weeks in between regular worship services. A session of Sunday school begins with a hymn, after which a minister reads a chapter of New Testament text, comments on it, and then opens the floor for a general discussion of its meaning and application. Two weeks later the same format addresses the next chapter, until the congregation has worked through the entire New Testament, at which point it starts over. The dynamics are not egalitarian, but the practice of discussing Scripture's meaning and articulating interpretation are things that distinguish New Order religious life and worldview.[20]

Beyond formal churchly ties and worship practice, most Amish settlements communicate with one another through correspondence newspapers, listing ministry names in an Amish-published annual almanac, or assembling church directories. All of these projects are carried on by lay members and serve as conduits for family and business news more than formal ecclesial connection. Yet participation signals something of a group's interest in building or maintaining fraternal ties.

The national edition of *The Budget,* a weekly correspondence newspaper published in Sugarcreek, Ohio, carries columns from Amish and conservative Mennonite "scribes" across the country.[21] Scribes detail who visited their settlement and who traveled elsewhere, marriages, births, and deaths, along with notes on the weather, humorous anecdotes, and general observations on life. The Swiss, New Order, and Swartzentruber churches all have self-appointed *Budget* scribes, and households in all three groups read the paper. Indeed, for those without easy access to telephone communication, the weekly *Budget* is a welcome means of keeping in touch with family in other states. In contrast, no one from the Paoli church subscribes to or writes columns for *The Budget.* Church leaders in that settlement view the paper as frivolous, and one bishop reportedly said that anyone who has time to read *The Budget* should read the Bible instead. The rejection of this common form of Amish communication signals to other Amish something of the separatist outlook of the Paoli church and also helps to insulate these districts from reading about suspect activities, such as vacation travel or tourist trade employment, that go on in other Amish settlements.

Raber's *New American Almanac,* published in Baltic, Ohio, is a privately published annual that facilitates churchly connection and correspondence.[22] The *Almanac* lists the leaders of each Amish church district that chooses to participate. Three of the Orange and Washington counties settlements send relevant information to the *Almanac;* the Paoli church does not—once again indicating its disinterest in such fraternal ties and its suspicion of the very notion of systematized enumeration.

Since the 1960s, many Amish settlements, large and small, have begun to issue church directories.[23] Updated every five to ten years, these volumes are compendia of information on church districts and leaders, area Amish schools, and data on families in the settlement. Compiling the directories (without the aid of computer data bases) is a large undertaking, carried out only because the directories are, in most places, very popular with Amish families who want ready access to addresses, birthdays, and anniversary dates for friends and relatives across the settlement or in other settlements. Among the four settlements around Paoli and Salem, however, only the New Order church participates in a directory—one that combines all New Order churches outside eastern Ohio. Although the large Swiss settlements in Allen and Adams counties issue directories, and some Swiss diaspora communities in other states have directories, the Salem Swiss do not participate in any directory listing, perhaps because of their disinterest in others' ability to contact them. Salem Swiss families do visit family and friends in other places, but no demand has emerged to produce a settlement directory for their own use. Likewise, the Swartzentruber and Paoli churches have not compiled directories. For the Swartzentrubers near Paoli, this decision is consistent with others of their affiliation; no Swartzentruber districts participate in directory projects. For the Paoli church, again, the desire to remain separate and the absence of a demand for the information on the part of other settlements work against directory production. In the case of both the Paoli and Swartzentruber churches, the circle of formal interaction is relatively small, and most members know the addresses and other household information they need for those in the limited circle of fellowship that is important to them.

Within Indiana, one forum that provides an opportunity for Amish of various persuasions to meet one another around common concerns is the meetings of the Amish State School Committee. Participants discuss private school matters—from pending requirements emanating from Indianapolis; to questions of curriculum and pedagogy; to basic reporting on the number of schools, teachers, and students in each settlement. Despite the fact that all four of the Orange and Washington counties settlements are highly committed to Amish schools, none of the groups send representatives to the state meetings. The Paoli and New Order groups are concerned that their attendance might signal approval of other participating groups with whom they differ, while the Swartzentrubers see no reason to attend the gathering, which they view as unnecessary. And although the Allen and Adams counties Swiss Amish are active in the meetings, the Salem Swiss have never bothered to send a representative. Not attending the school meeting is one thing the four settlements discussed in this chapter agree on, but their stance separates them in an important way from other Hoosier Amish (see table 8.5).

TABLE 8.5
Markers of church and fraternal ties, Orange and Washington counties

	Swartzentruber	Paoli	Swiss	New Order
Circle of fellowship	Some Swartzen-truber dis-tricts in other states	Selected districts in Midwest	Some other Swiss districts	About half the New Order districts in the U.S.
Worship	Biweekly in homes	Biweekly in homes	Biweekly in homes	Biweekly in meetinghouse
Strict shunning	Yes	Yes	Yes	No
Sunday school	No	No	No	Yes, biweekly
Hymnal	*Ausbund*	*Ausbund*	*Ausbund*	*Unparteiische Liedersammlung* with appendix of English hymns
Write in *The Budget*	Yes	No	Yes	Yes
List in Raber's *Almanac*	Yes	No	Yes	Yes
Have a church directory	No	No	No	Yes
Participate in state school meetings	No	No	No	No

SITUATING FAITHFULNESS

The Amish in Orange and Washington counties offer a spectrum of Amish prac-tice, but not one that is neatly two-dimensional. Inviting as it would be to arrange the four settlements on a continuum stretching from liberal to conservative, "low" to "high" Ordnung, or sectarian to outward-looking, such linear images fall short of making sense of these communities. If one considers only easily observable uses of technology, it might be possible to align the Amish on a polar schematic of tra-ditional to progressive. But a deeper look at the relationships between these com-munities, their migration histories and reasons for existence, and their ethnic cus-toms complicates the picture considerably.

The Ordnung surrounding technology is one important expression of the Amish worldview, but a limited appropriation of modern gadgetry does not necessarily predict the way in which a church's Ordnung will appraise other issues. The Paoli settlement's districts, for example, are akin to the Swartzentrubers in terms of many occupational and technological choices—in some cases they are more re-strictive than the Swartzentrubers—while at the same time aligning with the technologically progressive New Orders, and against the Swartzentrubers, in reforming matters of personal morality and youth culture.

Likewise, the motives for migration—reactionary in the Paoli case, or with an eye to continuity in the Swartzentruber and Swiss cases—shaped the nature of these settlements. The way in which the Salem New Order church evolved from rather more amorphous Mennonite and Amish roots also has a bearing on its expression of Amish sensibilities. Meanwhile, Swiss ethnicity means that many of the Ordnung choices and cultural customs of that group make them poor candidates for comparison with the other groups on continuous terms. In many ways the Swiss are not more or less inclined to certain practices and temperaments so much as they are simply different.

How to describe where the Amish stand depends a good deal on the sorts of questions one asks and values. Even evaluations of sectarian outlook become tricky when considered carefully. By some measures, the Paoli churches cultivate a highly sectarian stance with their objections to everything from working away from home to avoiding Amish correspondence papers. Yet they have been open to dialogue with serious seekers in ways similar to the more outward-looking and innovative New Orders. Nor does an apparent sectarian stance always correlate with technological recalcitrance. In the case of the Swiss, social reticence may be a cultural trait even among those more open to change.

The location of these settlements in proximity to one another also serves as a reminder that those identities are constructed and construed with other Amish people in mind as much as they are with the wider world. The Paoli churches exist in silent protest against mid-century Amish tendencies in some places; the New Orders seek to offer an alterative Amish witness to a world only familiar with Amish folks who speak little about their faith and indulge in habits the New Orders denounce. Swartzentrubers perpetuate an affiliation that exists in defiance of change-minded Ohioans of nearly a century ago, while the Swiss know who they are in part because of their non-Swiss neighbors. The experience of these four settlements— small as they are—is a reminder of the complex factors that comprise Amish identities and outsider's appraisals of them.

As the settlement case studies in this and the previous three chapters illustrate, the Amish social landscape is remarkably varied. Different migration histories, applications of Ordnung, and ethnic understandings mark the Amish experience in distinct ways. Amish cultural identity takes shape as these internal factors combine in specific contexts shaped by their own sets of external social, economic, political, and demographic factors. For example, not only are Swiss and non-Swiss Amish communities different, but Amish life in industrial, suburbanizing, and tourist-textured northern Indiana is necessarily different from that experienced by newly transplanted Lancaster households in mid-state or in the small and remote settlements of Indiana's southern tier. Exploring the many layers of cultural identity, though, begs questions of commonality and unity. In the face of plain diversity, how might we make sense of varied Amish worlds? The final chapters explore that question.

PART THREE

Diversity and Unity

CHAPTER NINE

Diverse Amish Worlds

Sifting the similarities and differences that mark Amish life promises to make sense of more than just the Indiana experience. Stripping away the superficial veneer of uniformity that coats popular perceptions of Amish life, the variegated reality that lies underneath requires us to sort out the common from the coincidental, the central from the circumstantial. Understanding Amish cultural identity demands this double vision that attends to both the general and the particular.

One place to begin mapping the social topography of the Amish world is to examine common tensions within all Amish communities. While the resolution of these tensions varies, the lines of debate are recognizable from place to place. These lines, in turn, suggest the orientation of an Old Order worldview—or, more accurately, clusters of worldviews—that frame how the Amish understand themselves in relation to one another and to the wider world.

TRADITIONAL VERSUS RATIONAL AUTHORITY

One of the tensions within Amish society is between the competing authorities of tradition and rational logic. If this tension exists to some degree in all human societies, it is especially acute among the Amish, given their sensitivity to the wisdom of tradition. Deference to tradition is one of the hallmarks of the Old Order way. Tradition is an authority that stands apart from the individual. Its claims reach from the past in ways that moderate the tyranny of the present and question the promises of progress. Tradition is cautious, patient, and attuned to the experience of the group.

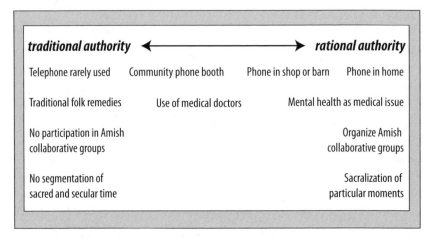

Figure 9.1. Examples of Issues on Traditional-Rational Authority Continuum

The authority of the rational, on the other hand, is calculating and forward thinking. Sizing up each experience as a new challenge or a novel opportunity, those operating in the rational mode welcome innovation, expect change, and anticipate the future. Rationality analyzes, pulls apart, and seeks efficiency. In some ways, all Amish recognize rational authority. Many are ingenious artisans who delight in adapting machinery to accomplish commonplace tasks. Some develop reputations as shrewd business people who understand the logic of markets and profit margins. Nevertheless, the power that rational authority typically commands in Western society is notably checked in Amish experience, and the relationship between its appeal and that of tradition plays out in various ways (see figure 9.1).[1]

Amish responses to technologies such as the telephone illustrate these choices. The authority of tradition upholds the centrality of the home and dictates that phones should be kept away from family life.[2] The traditional mind also values communication as it has always been done—face-to-face—and in a high-context culture, that allows for the entire range of symbols surrounding dress and demeanor to signal one's place in the community. More rational approaches, in contrast, analyze the phone on its own terms and consider ways of separating a person's use of the phone into necessary and unnecessary categories, minimizing the latter. Community phone booths shared by several households, or a phone in a shed or outbuilding and used only for business purposes, fits this second approach. Finally, a highly rational approach—present among only a few horse-and-buggy-driving Amish—allows the phone in the home itself, thereby minimizing inefficiency by saving time in accessing communication. Here the burden of limiting unnecessary phone use rests disproportionately on individual choice and reveals a faith in the individual's power to evaluate each communication opportunity.

The traditional-rational tension expresses itself in other ways too. Traditional Amish responses to health, for example, view medicine and healing as closely tied to ordinary life itself.[3] While the modern patient trusts the professionally trained stranger to provide care that the professional learned through formal education, Old Order people believe that knowing the practitioner as a person is as important as that person's professional credentials. Moreover, tradition-minded Amish favor treating illness with remedies handed down from the past and that typically involve consuming naturally available tonics in a manner that mirrors everyday life processes, rather than seeking treatment through pills, injections, or other therapies that have no analogue in normal life.[4] Most Amish combine these sorts of traditionalist sensibilities with a more modern notion that the human body is complex and may be aided by the insights of medical diagnosis. Many Amish who strike this balance between the rational and the traditional, though, would still be slow to see *mental* health as a medical issue, viewing psychology as a questionable exercise in abstracting thoughts and feelings from soul and spirit, and treating the mind merely as a biological organ. Nevertheless, a minority of Amish accept the modern med-

Illustration 9.1. A shared phone booth in the Elkhart-LaGrange settlement provides telephone access, while keeping the phone out of the home. Source: Courtesy of Dennis L. Hughes.

ical analysis of mental health, for example, viewing depression or anxiety as physical ailments treatable with drugs.[5]

Amish community life itself exhibits a modest spectrum of rational and traditional understandings of organization and coordination. While far from bureaucratic, some Amish church districts within and among some settlements band together to achieve certain goals. Forming revolving loan funds to help newly married couples buy a home or start a business are examples of such activity, as are mutual aid fire and storm damage plans that assess member fees and pay costs as measured by exact documented losses. The most systematized efforts have been those on the part of Amish seeking to negotiate with the state—the epitome of rationality and bureaucracy. In a real sense, the Amish State School Committee and the National Amish Steering Committee are calculated attempts to hold at bay the even more calculating logic of the modern welfare state.[6] Highly tradition-minded Amish, however, choose not to participate in any such systematic or strategic efforts—be they church-state liaisons or formalized mutual aid within the church, preferring strictly local, ad hoc, and spontaneous action.

On a day-to-day basis, the rational world segments time, carving up days and weeks and fitting them to the most efficient use for calculated activity. Amish of a highly traditional bent, however, do not segment time into sacred and secular components. True, biweekly church services and semiannual communion services texture time, but these patterns themselves are the product of tradition and are not reworked to fit changing notions of effective Christian worship. Those accepting the authority of tradition live in a world whose ebb and flow is not governed by human choice. When Swartzentruber Amish children near Paoli begin after-school chores, all the while singing the "Loblied" hymn from the *Ausbund,* they express this sense of time. They sing the old hymn in part because there are no songs in their lives other than these Reformation-era hymns. Nor is there any better time to sing them. Life is lived—and faithfulness transmitted—continually. The songs are not reserved for Sunday morning, nor are there other songs for the rest of the week. In contrast, Amish who have instituted special set-apart time for family devotions or biweekly Sunday school gatherings for instruction in the faith reveal a more rational approach to time and the tasks they see for themselves.

COMMUNAL VERSUS INDIVIDUAL ORIENTATION

Another significant tension in Amish society exists between orientations that are communal and those that accent the individual (see figure 9.2). As with the traditional-rational authority continuum, the communal-individual tension is dis-

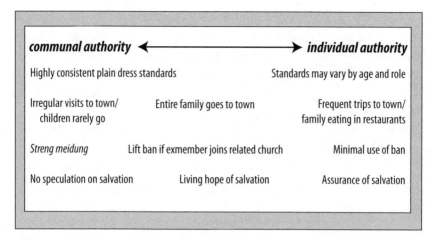

Figure 9.2. Examples of Issues on Communal-Individual Authority Continuum

tinctly Amish insofar as Amish society is much more weighted toward communal sensibilities than is surrounding American culture. Even the most individually oriented Amish person bows to community standards with a frequency that is remarkable by worldly standards that celebrate the autonomous individual as the basis of modern life.

Among the Amish, a communal orientation is one that validates and values social control over individual behavior. It privileges the group and insists that individuals find meaning only within the group. For the Amish, a communal orientation involves giving assent to Ordnung, but it may also be measured in terms of the comprehensiveness and scope of Ordnung. In contrast, an individual orientation—even without partaking of the modern cult of individualism—is a way of being Amish that allows for interpretation of Ordnung in somewhat less comprehensive ways. An individual orientation also gives more weight to private religious experience, seeing at least some expressions as legitimate forms of piety and not necessarily forms of public pride.

Personal and social behaviors as well as theological language and ideas exist in the tension between communal and individual orientations. Amish church districts or settlements with a highly communal orientation exhibit remarkably consistent dress across the age spectrum and between ordained and lay members. Those with fewer such sensibilities allow for some variation, with older members or ordained men adhering to the ideal code of plain living. This means that those with the most social responsibility carry a disproportionate share of the community's character. Dress is still not a matter of arbitrary choice, but there is room for individual discretion on the part of members who live further from the community core—a distinction that in itself suggests a church with somewhat less communal orientation.

A communal orientation also finds expression among those Amish who restrict trips to town, limiting such forays to occasional visits or even encouraging household heads to make any necessary errands without children so as to limit youngsters' interaction with the world. Other Amish, in contrast, permit the hiring of non-Amish drivers for a wide range of trips and excursions, sometimes more often than weekly. As a communal orientation shades toward more individual choice, children are socialized into worldly interaction by being taken along on trips to town, including visits to large shopping centers or evening meals with the family in area restaurants.

The occupational spectrum also mirrors this range of communal-to-individual sensibilities. While some Amish affiliations limit employment of married men strictly to at-home employment, others allow married men a wider range of job locations. Leaving home and working for a non-Amish employer in one's neighborhood represents a move in this direction, and leaving the area completely for work does so even more. The church can also exercise social control, in varying degrees, over the terms and conditions of one's work, restricting technology use, for example.

The practice of church discipline is an expression of a deep-seated communal orientation, but it is not without variations stemming from more individual understandings. Most expressive of a communal orientation is the form of church discipline known as *streng Meidung* (strict shunning), in which excommunication is permanent unless the banned person returns to the church from which he or she separated. An approach that grants more weight to the excommunicated individual's reason for leaving the church operates among those Amish who "lift the ban" on former members who join another "plain church" and subsequently prove to be faithful members there. In such cases, evaluating the disposition of the individual member is as important as the offense against the group; whereas in the case of *streng Meidung,* the excommunicated person's disposition is assumed to be willful pride.[7] As churches shift their evaluation of discipline toward an individual's disposition, the frequency of discipline itself may decline.

Theologically, the concept of salvation—or at least the language used to describe it—also exists in the tension between orientations that are fundamentally communal or individual. Although the 1632 Dordrecht Confession of Faith that sums up Amish beliefs affirms a traditionally orthodox Christian notion of God's saving activity on behalf of humanity, how one describes that salvation has been contested in Amish circles.[8] Those giving more weight to the authority of individual and subjective experience speak of an assurance of salvation—sometimes using the language of the assurance of things hoped for, but assurance on the part of the individual nonetheless. This approach is most common among the New Order Amish but is found in literature read in some other Amish homes. At the other extreme would be those Old Orders who refuse to speculate openly about their own salvation, saying that God alone knows whether one is saved and that any additional claims are vain pride. In this case, the emphasis on divine authority that is beyond human understanding supercedes any individual experiential commentary. The human agency involved is the gathered church community, which serves as the conduit for divine blessing, but salvation is not for lone humans to grasp.

Somewhere in the middle are the Amish who speak of having a "living hope" of salvation. They have much in common with those who refuse any speculation, including the purposeful use of the term *hope* to suggest that authority rests solely in God's hands and that they are not placing individual demands on the Divine. Nevertheless, they resist the functional fatalism they fear could accompany such a blanket statement. By speaking of a living hope, they mean to suggest that those with the hope of salvation hold that hope personally, even if remains something other than assurance.

If these major tensions within the Amish world—traditional versus rational authority, and communal versus individual orientation—seem clear, their relationships are not parallel but intersecting. Those espousing communal authority do not always yield completely to the authority of tradition, nor do those who edge toward a more rational worldview always endorse the value of individual authority. Instead of reinforcing one another, these impulses are crosscutting. The relationship between them, illustrated in figure 9.3, provides one way of locating Amish identities.[9] While some Amish clearly do combine communal and traditional sensibilities, and others tend toward rational-individual combinations, still others link communal and rational approaches in creative ways, and almost all put these elements together with nuance and shades of intensity, given their particular histories, folkways, and local contexts.

AMISH WORLDVIEWS

The curved line in figure 9.3 suggests the direction of an Old Order worldview. Locating the Amish in relation to that worldview requires some generalization and risks simplification but promises to offer a more complex picture than linear models typically have afforded.[10] At least four identifiable worldviews stand out when plotted in this way. Some of these are readily associated with particular settlements

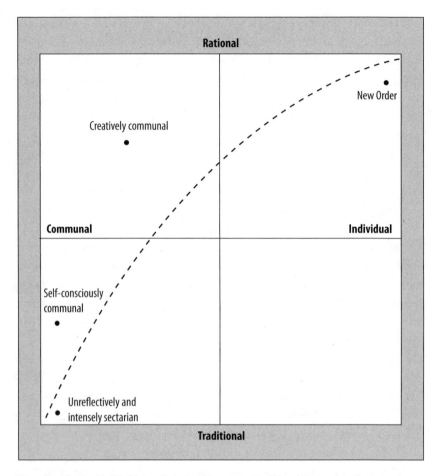

Figure 9.3. The Amish Worldview: Relationship among Traditional-Rational Authority and Communal-Individual Orientation.

or affiliations; others include various affiliations and represent several settlements. Then, too, some larger settlements may include more than a single worldview among their members.

Unreflectively and Intensely Sectarian

The most traditional and communal worldview is perhaps best represented in Indiana by the Swartzentruber settlement and certain segments of and affiliations within the state's Swiss communities. These Amish exhibit little concern for the larger world, including the larger Amish world. When asked how many Amish live in a particular area, members operating with this worldview respond with the size of their own church district or affiliation, ignoring even other Amish groups that live in close proximity. When asked how long a neighboring Old Order affiliation had been in the Paoli area, a Swartzentruber man—otherwise knowledgeable about local topography and agriculture—could only say, "I have no idea." Secure in their sense of separation from the world, they spend little time shoring up their mental boundaries, offering reasoned explanations for why they do things, or analyzing how best to avoid the pitfalls of surrounding society.

Those bearing this worldview carry on past practice in unreflective ways—from traditional dress patterns to styles of buggies. Modern scientific concern about the effects of tobacco fails to sway those who see its use as a part of the way life has always been. The same authority legitimates traditional courting and marriage customs that other Amish may find scandalous. To the degree that traditional businesses and farming practices have a capitalist edge, these Amish can exhibit a rational, calculating side next to an uncritical religious orientation, but the strong impression one generally receives is of an unreflective acceptance of life and faith that has long existed and will endure well after any particular individual's existence. Ironic as it may seem to outsiders, Amish with a worldview so keenly attuned to tradition have little interest in history.

Self-Consciously Communal

Amish holding a self-consciously communal worldview share some things in common with the highly traditional and highly communal Old Orders described above. Yet the self-consciously communal worldview also differs in important ways through its selective appeal to rational authority and its criticism of some forms of tradition. Perhaps best represented by the Paoli settlement, this worldview in some respects is shared by segments of the northern Indiana Amish populations.

Distinctly communal in orientation, these Old Orders accept a comprehensive Ordnung that limits individual choice to a remarkable degree. In principle or in practical fact, they practice a discipline of *streng Meidung,* and they are notably cautious about interaction with the wider world, believing that influences—positive or negative—in one part of life are really challenges to the whole.

It is that sort of somewhat analytic appraisal of themselves, however, that make those who hold this worldview distinct. Interested in history and aware of change over time, these Old Orders critique or defend tradition in ways that do not wholly rely on the authority of tradition itself.[11] Prudently slow to change and resistant to the logic of efficiency or effectiveness, the self-consciously communal very often defer to tradition. But they also reform it in occasional, striking ways. Prohibiting tobacco and alcohol use, and strictly limiting mixed-sex youth activities are two examples of traditions grounded in rural American and Amish life that these Amish reject as nonbinding, corrupting accretions to faithful living.

This particular clustering of ideals has made Amish in this camp somewhat attractive to non-Amish seekers who are interested in joining the Amish and who typically bring a sort of analytical style to their spiritual journey. And to the degree that the self-consciously communal Old Orders have a critical interest in the larger world, they are open to the questions such seekers bring. Yet their highly communal commitments also mean that it is difficult for outsiders successfully to join. Churches do not bend their expectations or modify their customs for the particular needs of the individual—learning Pennsylvania German, for example, is necessary.

Creatively Communal

A third worldview, creatively communal, is one that characterizes many Indiana settlements, including most of the north-central communities, many of the Swiss Amish, and the Kokomo and Milroy groups, as well as the Lancaster transplants, to some extent. This worldview rests close to the center of the matrix that defines Amish life and thought, approaching balance while granting greater credence to communal understandings and a bit more weight to rational analysis and responses.

Communal commitments, significant as they are, bend more easily in the face of individual needs than is the case among adherents of the other two worldviews. Typically, a greater range of practice falls within acceptable Ordnung guidelines, and occupational choices and interaction with outsiders through daily commercial interaction is acceptable. Most do not practice *streng Meidung.*

While these Amish are much more sensitive to the claims of tradition than their non-Amish neighbors, many also think critically about being Amish, divide means from ends, and creatively consider how to support traditional activity in innovative ways. They can theoretically separate life into component parts and sense that change in any one area might or might not effect the whole, and then selectively use information from the world to begin thinking about the relationship between idea and practice. From this slightly more rational approach to life has come a range of creative, if modest, institutions, projects, and ideas that seek to bolster communal life in ways that are somewhat innovative. Broadly cooperative efforts to secure private schools, small business loans to allow fathers to begin at-home businesses, establishing a birthing center, and publications for parents and teachers with tips for passing on the faith are all the fruit of this sort of approach to being Amish.[12]

New Order

Finally, there are a small but significant number of Amish whose worldview lies close to the margins of the Old Order, tilting toward both rational authority and an individual orientation.[13] In Indiana the so-called New Order settlements near Salem and Worthington exemplify this approach.

This worldview assumes much more latitude of individual choice in technology use, details of dress, and so on, than those of other Old Orders; but more importantly, it grants value to the role and experience of the individual in notable ways. Using a nuanced concept of assurance of salvation, stressing the need for personal Bible study and devotional time, and worshiping in English when outsider "seekers" are present are all ways in which communal commitments yield to concern for the needs of the individual. The community surely matters a great deal to such Amish, but in ways that are less structured and more articulated than in other settings.

This worldview is also unusual in its willingness to critique tradition and think critically about being Amish, separating elements into "essential" and "nonessential" categories. They have a clear understanding of how they are the same and different from other churches, express an interest in dialogue on religious matters, and do not shy away from pointed questions and gentle proselytizing.[14] Moreover, these Amish also explain technological change and innovation in rational, practical terms, and in some cases—such as convenient telephone use—place the burden of proof on the more tradition-minded to delineate the distinction between use and ownership. In some ways the tendencies toward rational analysis and individual orientation among these Amish find common expression, such as when adherents speak of specialized roles for individual leaders, describing ministers, for example, in the function of "counselor" and then in another setting acting as "pastor."[15] (A more tradition-defined and communalist understanding of leadership centers simply on leaders embodying an Ordnung-guided life before the watching church.)

CROSSCUTTING AND CONTEXTUAL FACTORS

While these Amish worldviews provide a general map for locating Amish cultural identities, there are other factors that cut across them, distinguishing certain groups or inserting similar themes into otherwise disparate stories. Chief among these is the element of size and scale, with larger settlements accommodating more diversity than smaller ones. The Elkhart-LaGrange and Adams counties communities, for example—despite their different ethnic origins—realize a similar sort of variation in their make-up simply due to the number of church districts in each place. And while Swiss tradition and polity has structured that diversity more sharply in the form of competing affiliations, in contrast to the moderate and congregational Elkhart-LaGrange approach, an underlying common element cannot be ignored.

The age of a settlement is also a critical factor. New settlements may be composed of migrants from various backgrounds and locations, making the establishment of an agreed-upon Ordnung more painstaking—perhaps even resulting in a partially written document. The experiences of the Amish who came together from different places to form the Salem settlement in 1972 or the Rochester community in the late 1990s illustrate this phenomenon. While the Amish in these two places have pursued different paths—a New Order approach versus a more conservative angle—their need for self-conscious discussion of discipline bears some similarities.

Common understandings in older settlements, in contrast, certainly come in for discussion, debate, and change over time as well, but they also exist as generally understood and widely shared commitments that can be caught more than taught. Newcomers to older, established settlements understand that they will assimilate into an existing church order, while those participating in young communities enter a more dynamic—and thus, more self-consciously regulated—environment. Even in daughter settlements that set out to replicate the life of the parent community—such as Parke and Wayne counties' transplanted Lancaster Amish life, or Worthington's extension of the Ohio New Order church—end up being more self-conscious of their choices and practice in the face of neighbors unfamiliar with their customs.

In a related way, the relationship that Amish communities have with their non-Amish neighbors is also an external factor that shapes daily life in ways that transcend different worldviews, ethnicities, or approaches to Ordnung. Settlements with a long history in a given place and long-established relations with neighbors—from local government to area employers—function differently from communities that are relatively new. Participation in public schools is a key example of this dynamic. In places where Old Orders have participated in rural public schools for generations and where they felt they knew the teachers and believed administrators were responsive to their concerns, they have remained public school participants. Although school consolidation and curriculum changes have prompted a majority of parents to enroll their children in Amish schools, the persistence of public school students in Nappanee, Elkhart-LaGrange, and Adams Counties settlements is testimony to the enduring significance of local ties.[16]

In newer settlements, where the Amish had no previous links to the public schools, parents immediately established private schools—even though the local public schools in these remarkably rural places are actually smaller and less consolidated than those in the older, suburbanizing communities that continue to enroll Amish children. This pattern holds whether the new settlement is New Order Amish or ultra-traditional Swartzentruber, off-shoots of mainstream Elkhart-LaGrange and Nappanee settlements (Vallonia and Rochester) or ethnically Swiss (South Whitley, Salem, or Vevay). Lack of longstanding local relationships is the common factor in their commitment to Amish schooling.

Likewise, geographic isolation versus more densely settled environments offers contextual factors that cut across worldview lines. Settlements in relatively remote areas have fewer commercial opportunities for Amish to be producers or consumers. Lack of industry makes factory employment impossible, even if the Ordnung would permit it. A dearth of tourist trade limits interaction with outsiders that might take place in more accessible locations.[17] With fewer economic options, settlements in notably rural areas rely on at-home businesses or agriculture. There is less cash wealth with fewer wage-paying jobs, and the micro-enterprises that do exist may have a more difficult time connecting with markets. In some cases a complex relationship develops between Ordnung and environment, so that church discipline sanctions a particularly plain lifestyle that also may be as much an economic necessity as a choice.

Amish settlements in more heavily populated areas typically have more employment possibilities, easier access to markets, and readily available cash. Tourism in these places offers other job options, while suburbanization boosts property appreciation and population pressures push up wages in other forms of employment. In addition to the opportunity for increased income, such areas also typically are home to varied and sizable retail stores, whether on the edge of the Fort Wayne metropolitan area (Allen County settlement) or in strip malls adjacent to midsize towns like Goshen (Elkhart-LaGrange) or Decatur (Adams). In any case, the possibilities for purchasing a wide range of goods and services, eating in restaurants, and interacting with non-Amish consumer-oriented neighbors are much higher in some areas than others. Whether or not relationships with non-Amish neighbors or co-workers in such places are deeper than in areas where populations are smaller, but time for talking more abundant, the frequency and number of such contacts is clearly more intense in suburbanizing Elkhart and Allen counties than it is in rural Adams, Orange, and Switzerland counties.

Finally, the impact of particular personalities or of unforeseen events is something that can cut across Amish communities of all sorts and spark various re-

Illustration 9.2. Interaction with outsiders is common in the densely populated Elkhart-LaGrange settlement. Here Amish and non-Amish children play together at a Shipshewana park. Source: Courtesy of the Mennonite Historical Library/Dottie Kauffmann.

sponses. A strong-willed leader who becomes entangled in church conflict may precipitate a schism, or a high-profile former member may continue to exert informal influence in a settlement long after being excommunicated. Natural disasters or economic recessions may plunge an area into crisis and produce out-migration or an unplanned shift to other lines of work. A popular personality may push the boundaries of Ordnung and win concessions from the church, or an especially respected voice may restrain innovation for longer than otherwise would be the case.

AMISH DIVERSITY

The Amish worlds that emerge across Indiana and the rest of North America are the product of interacting factors (figure 9.4). Migration histories and the networks of communication and social orientation they provide are a key starting point for these identities. Differing approaches to Ordnung contribute other elements that make up the Amish mosaic, and ethnic attachments figure into the mix as well, with kin connections and culturally sanctioned ways of interacting with the world stemming from such sensibilities.

These internal factors combine not only in different proportions but also in different external contexts, refracted through a particular set of cultural tensions

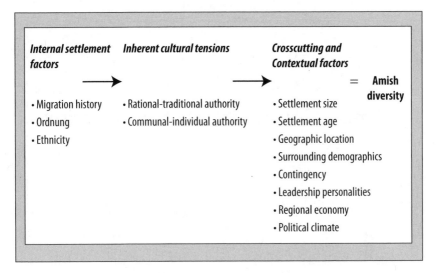

Figure 9.4. Factors Producing Amish Diversity

and worldviews. The tensions within the Amish community between traditional and rational modes of authority or between communal and individual orientations stretch the Amish world in ways that produce different expressions of life and faith. Local contexts further some possibilities and limit others, opening certain avenues to Amish exploration while closing others.

Amid the colors of the Amish mosaic—differing worldviews, clashing contexts, and concerns over cooperation and compromise—what common patterns emerge? Why is it that diverse Amish communities continue to recognize one another as Amish? Even when they know little about or hold negative stereotypes of one another, refuse to publicly join in joint efforts such as the Amish State School Committee, or define themselves in terms of schisms that have ended formal fellowship, they continue to claim one another. In light of the many differences that divide them, how does it make sense to think about them all as Amish? It is to the nature and shape of that emerging image—that community of conversation—that we now turn.

CHAPTER TEN

Amish Community as Conversation

Community is an important word among the Amish. In its German form—
Gemeinde—or its Pennsylvania German derivative—*Gemee*—it refers to the church,
church members, and the regular gathering of those members around religious rituals. From scholarly academics to curious tourists, observers tag community as a
remarkable aspect of Amish life. Marketers and media masters seeking to pinpoint
the distinctive nature of Old Order society home in on community as a salient and
attractive feature of Amish life.[1]

But if Amish community is everywhere, it can also be elusive. It is, first of all,
fragmented. Unity at the level of the local church district is fairly straightforward;
all members repeatedly reaffirm their commitment to a common Ordnung at their
semiannual communion services and function as one another's first line of defense
from financial and natural disasters as they promise practical mutual aid.

But the nature of unity at the level of affiliation, settlement, and ethnic group is
much harder to delineate, given the competing markers to which Amish assign
different meaning in their construction of faithfulness. As previous chapters have
demonstrated, the Amish community is fractured in a host of formal and informal
ways. A comparative consideration of Amish life highlights the fault lines of history,
Ordnung, ethnicity, and context that contour their social landscape, making efforts
to define community by delineating specific customs or practices highly suspect
(table 10.1).

At a general level, efforts to describe an all-encompassing Amish unity or to
define an Amish cultural identity in broadest terms may even seem futile. Modern
analysts look in vain for the bureaucratic apparatus and organizational accou-

TABLE 10.1
Levels of Amish identity

Level	Shared elements	Affinity
Districts	Ordnung, leadership, often immediate and extended family ties	Specific
Affiliation	Some aspects[a] of Ordnung, pool of marriage partners, extended family ties	Moderate
Settlement	Migration history, connection to Steering Committee and School Committee, often extended family ties	Moderate
Ethnic group	Dialect, folkways, genealogical ties	Moderate to General
All Amish	Dordrecht Confession, horse and buggy use, "Loblied" sung, legal recognition from state and federal government, popular perception from tourism	General

[a]Especially those tied to church ritual/discipline; perhaps those tied to lifestyle and technology.

trements they typically use to tag religious and ethnic communities in North American, finding no delegate assemblies, retreat centers, or program budgets. The extremely modest structures that do exist—the National Amish Steering Committee or various state school committees that serve as liaisons to government—take pains to limit their agendas.

For their part, the Amish are also quick to point out the many ways that difference and diversity permeate their collective life, both because they seek to avoid the pride they believe would follow exaggerated claims of unity and because they know—through their everyday experience—that the Amish world is complex and often contested. The Old Order periodical *Family Life* settles for a definition of Amish as all churches that "forbid the ownership of automobiles and use the name 'Amish'"—although that umbrella tells one almost nothing about the groups that huddle under it.[2]

But what if the quest to understand Amish unity amid diversity falters, not because Amish community does not exist, but because those seeking it are looking in the wrong places? What if discovering unity in the midst of diversity did not come from unearthing a list of essential traits, specific practices, or key structures, but from conceiving of community as a conversation? In such a model, diversity serves not to confound communality but to illustrate its presence on a deeper level. If comparative examinations of Amish life undercut simpler definitions of peoplehood, they also reinforce the sense that there are centripetal forces drawing them together. The metaphor of shared conversation reveals these relationships and the community they engender.[3]

COMMUNITY IN CONVERSATION

Imagine any group of people having a meaningful conversation. They may be sharing information, asking questions, revealing opinions. They could have different personalities, communication styles, and life experiences on which to draw. They might disagree on the issues they are discussing—indeed, their conversation may at times turn into an argument. Nevertheless, the conversation continues because the participants hold in common an interest in talking about the same things. Even as they disagree or even argue, they reveal a shared sense of what is worth arguing about. In other words, they disagree in particular ways—ways that point to a underlying common conversation.

Conversations change and evolve, sometimes taking directions the participants would not have predicted. But conversations also have limits. People introducing subjects of no interest to other group members will soon find themselves more at home in another conversation and drift off to another circle of discussion. Those with different ideas about what is worth debating or very different assumptions about how to make a point that others will find intelligible end up with little to say. The conversation defines the community, not because the members agree on everything they are discussing or share the same background, but because they are, in fact, participating in a living conversation that they agree is significant.

Larger human communities develop along similar lines, even if the cultural conversation is metaphorical rather than literal among hundreds or thousands of people. Questions and assumptions about what is important, what is valuable, or what needs to be done define communities even when the answers to those questions vary. Participants sense when they are no longer part of the cultural conversation and have moved out of one community and into another.

For example, Amish parents, grandparents, and other church members have engaged in a conversation—both figuratively and literally—about the content and purpose of eight years of formal schooling. The participants disagree over whether private schools or public schools offer better instruction or over whether Amish or non-Amish teachers more effectively staff Amish schools. They do not find common ground on the question of whether newer Amish-authored textbooks are better than commercial textbooks from several generations ago or whether obtaining a GED credential is helpful for those who have not gone on to high school. But all of these discussions—regardless of the outcome—are part of a conversation with shared assumptions. Not all of these values and assumptions are precisely articulated—and they need not be. Indeed, the conversation continues in the absence of

Illustration 10.1. Conversation is a favorite Amish pastime. Source: Courtesy of Dennis L. Hughes.

that kind of articulation because the cultural conversation is *itself* the embodiment of those values and assumptions in a way that is more real than any delineated outline of ideas could be.

One can imagine other worthwhile conversations about education that would share certain Amish concerns about separation from the world or the value of practical versus theoretical knowledge. For example, groups might nurture discussion on how public high school students could best maintain a particularistic Christian worldview amid non-Christian peers, or the relative merits of church-run colleges, or the relationship of faith to the epistemology of the liberal arts. But these are not Amish conversations; those who engage in them are not part of the Amish community. They may be conversations that define historically related groups, such as the Beachy Amish or the Mennonites, but not the Amish. Amish cultural conversations—while they may defy simple summary—define their community.[4] Paying attention to the contours of this cultural conversation reveals the underlying nature of Amish identity and unity.

CONVERSATION PARTNERS

Asked to sum up what all Amish have in common, or what holds them together despite diversity and a dearth of organizational structures, one LaGrange County

A community defined by dialogue with...		
...the past	**...the world**	**...itself**
• *Ausbund* hymns	• Symbolic separators, such as	• National Steering Committee
• Church discipline/shunning	horse & buggy	• State school committees
• Socially marginal status	• Product perception	• Two-kingdom worldview
• *Dordrecht Confession*	• Tourism	• Truth validated by action
• Ordnung tradition	• Legal definitions/exemptions	• Church district as central

Figure 10.1. Cultural Conversations that Define Amish Unity

bishop thought for some time and then ventured, "We have the eighteen articles [Dordrecht Confession of Faith], and the horse and buggy, and beyond that we interpret it in the church." The thoughtful elder had pointed to the three conversations that define the Amish community: a conversation with the past, with the larger world, and with themselves (figure 10.1). The conversation partners differ in each case, but together they carry on a set of dialogues that have extended over time and that define Amish unity.

Conversation with the Past

Amish identity and unity lies in part in the Amish conversation with the past. While all communities engage in some version of this conversation, the Amish conversation with the past takes a particular shape. The bishop's reference to "the eighteen articles" points to one important piece of that dialogue: the 1632 Dordrecht Confession of Faith—a Dutch Anabaptist theological statement that serves as a touchstone for their church.[5] It sets out the topics the Amish believe are important to discuss, from God, to divine creation, to the atonement of Christ, to nonresistance and peace. Significantly, the Dordrecht Confession discusses the nature of the church and the necessity of a social component to church discipline. Not all Amish agree on what the implications of shunning should be, but all consider it a matter that one cannot ignore.

The conversation runs both ways, and not coincidentally, the Amish have talked little on matters that the Dordrecht Confession does not detail. Dordrecht does not speculate on eschatology, nor does it discuss the exact nature of the authority of the

Bible.[6] Rarely have the Amish given extended consideration to such matters, even though such topics are key to defining conversations among many other American Christian groups.[7] The Amish may not have picked up on every potential Dordrecht theme, but their conversation with this confession has shaped which issues they find worthy and which they avoid.

The Amish conversation with the past is also marked by special attention to the socially marginalized early church, the Anabaptist martyrs of the sixteenth century, and the disputes that led to the divide between the Amish and Mennonites. From the martyr-written hymns they sing to the historical examples and allusions that crop up in sermons and small talk, the past as a point of reference does more than provide a particular heritage; it also helps set the agenda for ongoing discernment.[8] Among some Amish, the martyrs may inspire a meek and submissive personality, while in other Amish ethnic settings they may engender a principled, if not stubborn, tenacity. In either case, the results are different from those that would emerge, say, from dialogue around the implications of the church as cultural custodian for all of society.

Community is also defined by conversations with a more immediate past. Ordnung assumes the prominence that it does in part because Amish value the wisdom they find in the decisions and choices of their forebears in North America. While other American communities draw on historical conversations that highlight the theme of progress, or integration into the social mainstream, or the triumph of the individual, the Amish discussion reveres choices about separation and self-denial. They are hesitant to topple traditions that link them to these predecessors, precisely because the cues they take from the past make them sensitive to the authority that precedent sets. Such sentiments hardly settle all debates in Amish circles, but they provide a key component for the community conversation.

Dialogue with the World

A second important Amish cultural conversation takes place between the church and the larger world. If conversation with the past raises and reinforces the notion of separation from larger society, dialogue with that world is also crucial for understanding who comprises the Amish community.

At the level of popular perception, worldly expectations of the Amish do a great deal to define and reinforce Amish identity. Even if some popular opinions are misplaced, others present powerful parameters for defining who the Amish are. A reticence to adopt every new type of technology, for example, has become an Amish hallmark in part because broader society has come to expect it from the Amish. The

cachet that non-Amish customers and marketers find in Amish-produced goods de-
rives in large part from this perceived margin of difference, and Amish producers
are, at some level, constrained by these images to offer items in publicly acceptable
Amish ways.[9]

Similarly, the use of horse-and-buggy transportation on the road has emerged as
a salient feature of Amish life to a degree that makes sense only from the standpoint
of an ongoing Amish conversation with modernity that sees automatic mobility as
the pinnacle of personal power. The world has responded to Amish automobile reluctance with a range of options—from providing hired drivers to leasing business
vehicles—making the Amish choice to decline direct ownership or operation easier, while also reinforcing the notion that distancing themselves from motor transportation is a nonnegotiable. After all, even the non-Amish world takes their scru-
ples into account. When some Amish request the privilege of driving buggies
without SMV signs, or when tourist brochures feature horses and buggies, all parties are engaged in a social discussion that helps define the Amish community.[10]

In certain ways, the dialogue with larger society is different because the worldly
conversation partner is often demanding, backing the Amish into a legal corner and
making the Amish talk in ways they otherwise would not. Nevertheless, whether
in formal channels that seem more like interrogation or in the more open give-and-

Illustration 10.2. Horse-and-buggy transportation has become a mark of Amish identity in the
modern world. Swartzentruber Amish buggies do not display orange Slow Moving Vehicle
triangles on their buggies. The acceptability of the SMV symbol remains a matter of discussion
and disagreement within the wider Amish community. Source: Courtesy of Thomas J. Meyers.

take arena of daily life, Amish community is defined in part through such interaction, legitimating certain aspects of Amish identity and downplaying others. The 1972 *Wisconsin v. Yoder* U.S. Supreme Court case, for example, enshrined Amish exemption from high school education among the central tenants of the group. But it did so, in part, based on the justices' perceptions that the Amish were backward farmers who had no need for higher learning—perceptions drawn from wider popular preconceptions. Although some of these impressions drew on idealized or outdated images, they became part of the local conversation that still defines the Amish community. In addition, that legal precedent has served as the basis for other exemptions, introducing its language and assumptions into other arenas of interaction.[11] Congress's recent waiver of aspects of child labor codes for Amish businesses, for example, included group definitions built on educational exemptions granted by earlier courts.

Sectarian Ecumenicity

Such interactions, in turn, influence internal Amish discussion, sometimes forcing literal conversation among Old Orders who otherwise might have little contact with one another. The coercive nature of negotiation with government, for example, has placed Amish leaders in formal settings where they are forced to try to speak with one voice. Such conversations are defined, in large part, by public policies that the Amish had no hand in instituting but that channel their internal cultural conversation in particular ways.

In Indiana—as in other states—the Amish State School Committee is one such forum. Transcending Swiss and non-Swiss ethnic lines, bringing together residents from longtime settlements and new Lancaster transplants from the East Coast, and linking representatives from settlements whose approach to Ordnung differs significantly, the State School Committee becomes a place where an Amish community emerges from shared desires to maintain the private school agreement forged decades ago with officials in Indianapolis.[12] The committee oversees the collection of student attendance records, a responsibility that was part of the original 1967 deal with Indianapolis.[13] The committee also discusses curriculum and issues related to recruiting teachers and enforcing discipline, though always in an advisory and nonbinding mode, since the actual management of each school is the responsibility of local parent-composed school boards.

Despite its relatively recent vintage, the State School Committee has become a major source of identity for the Amish, and not only because it concerns itself with matters that both Amish and non-Amish increasingly see as setting the Amish apart in modern North America. Equally important is the fact that the committee's annual meetings rotate among the participating settlements and draw sizable crowds of interested teachers, parents, and local school board members from across the state. Those who otherwise have little interaction with fellow Indiana Old Orders—such as the Parke and Wayne contingents from Lancaster—are enthusiastic participants, and the State School Committee meetings have become the site of interaction for socially distant spiritual kin who have no family ties, few business contacts, or limited churchly relations.[14] A byproduct of conversation with the state, the committee, in turn, has added a new layer to the Amish conversation that reaches beyond immediate educational issues.

True, some Amish do not publicly participate in the State School Committee work, declining to appoint representatives or contacts or to attend the semiannual gatherings. These include the Swartzentrubers and the ultra-conservative Paoli settlement as well as the so-called New Order churches. Some Swiss settlements and subgroups, including those in Steuben County and near Salem and Vevay, also abstain. Yet these nonparticipants hardly dismiss Amish schools or the State School Committee's work; indeed, in every case they are among those who completely avoid public schools and maintain the attendance and other records required by the 1967 agreement. They are committed participants in the cultural conversation about Amish schools even if they decline the literal conversation they find too intrusive to their sense of separatism.

A second forum that has shaped the cultural conversation of identity is the work of the National Amish Steering Committee. This committee grew out of frustrations in 1966 with Selective Service handling of Amish young men liable for the draft. After a group of leaders from several states met with officials in Washington, D.C., they formed a committee to coordinate ongoing interaction with the federal government.[15] Indiana and other Midwestern leaders balked at the Steering Committee's name (said one, "We didn't like the idea of a committee 'steering' the Amish; we were just speaking for the Amish.") and preferred the name Amish Central Committee.[16] But either name—Steering Committee or Central Committee—suggests a constituency with shared interests, something engendered by the need to talk to Selective Service.

In time, the Steering Committee structure expanded to include the appointment of a director for each state or group of states with a sizable Amish population, and local contacts in each officially participating district.[17] The state directors attend the semiannual National Steering Committee meetings to keep abreast of national issues and serve as the channel of communication to local district contacts. State directors also serve as liaison for matters that involve state legislation or regulation

Illustration 10.3. Amish schools have become an increasingly significant site for cultivating and representing Amish identity. Source: Courtesy of the Mennonite Historical Library/Joel Fath.

(except school issues), including workers compensation, building codes, and local safety and health board ordinances.

The School Committee and Steering Committee not only provide forums for formal conversation, but they help define Amish identity. On the one hand, the state itself limits the conversation to those whom the government deems authentically *Amish*—Baptists and Roman Catholics, for example, are not permitted to stand in for special treatment under the Amish rubric, nor are historically connected mainline Mennonites, whom the state considers beyond the Old Order pale. From the Amish side, the conversation draws those who interpret or apply Old Order answers in strikingly different ways. Indeed, the Amish who refrain from making a personal appearance at School Committee and Steering Committee meetings do not necessarily object to the work of the these groups or to the issues the committee has identified as significant.[18] The Swartzentrubers or New Order Amish typically stand by the agreements the committees reach on their behalf with Indianapolis or Washington, D.C., because these Amish—while not part of the literal conversation—are part of the cultural conversation the committees moderate.

CONTOURS OF COMMUNITY

While dialogue with the wider world is an important part of the discussion that forms the contours of community, the Amish cultural conversation ultimately involves the meaning and implications of separation from larger society. Drawing on an Anabaptist concept of "two kingdoms"—the kingdom of God and the kingdom of this world—the Amish see life in terms of alternative and vying collective realities. Following a divine call to be separate from the world and to embody the kingdom of God, they nonetheless know that on some level they remain a part of the surrounding social order. Whether paying income taxes or maintaining polite relations with non-Amish neighbors, all Amish are enmeshed in a world that is larger than their church.

But where does one "kingdom" end and the other begin? Does work away from home compromise a two-kingdom dualism? What of participation in the tourist trade? Or the acceptance of Social Security numbers? The Amish disagree on all of these specifics, but they stand together in viewing them as significant, not trivial, matters. This conversation holds their interest and remains vital because it connects with their most important and immediate choices. Some move to new locations to avoid contacts with the "world," and others pour time and energy into Amish schools. For still others, an array of modest institutions that provide Amish alternatives for securing low-interest mortgage loans or giving birth outside a hospital become ways to contribute to the conversation. Dress, transportation options, technology use, and other matters become symbolic separators in the context of this cultural conversation and are not simply external trappings or persistent traditions as they might be viewed by participants of other cultural conversations.

Amid all the two-kingdom talk, there are important spoken and unspoken assumptions that color the dialogue. For example, the Amish assume the fundamental unity of each person. They do not see people as divided into exclusive and competing "roles" or "functions," but as living integrated lives, even if they sometimes live those lives in the midst of an alien kingdom. Unlike the modern professional, for example, who may place herself in distinct roles as, say, "doctor" or "mother" or "neighbor" or "customer," depending on immediate social expectations, the Amish person assumes that he or she is first and foremost Amish, no matter the situation. This critical assumption means that the Amish conversation about matters such as occupations is notably different from its worldly counterpart, even if the conversation at first sounds somewhat similar. For example, the appropriateness of working in industry will remain highly contested in Amish circles, but the terms of that debate will not hinge—as outsider might assume—on whether someone ceases to be Amish when they step onto the factory floor. Amish assembly-line workers do not find identities in their jobs, which then threaten their sense of being Amish. They may carry away handsome paychecks or paid vacation time that will alter the shape of their lives when they are not at work, but—significant as that possibility is—it is a different sort of problem, a different conversation piece, from that assumed by non-Amish observers. Assumptions such as these, woven deeply into Amish cultural conversation, do as much to define community and mark Amish identity as any physical symbolic separators or legal definitions of membership.

If two-kingdom assumptions mark Amish community life, a second characteristic theme of the dialogue is the conviction that faith and values are valid only to the extent that they are practically embodied in daily life. The Amish cultural conversation is not one marked by extensive theoretical speculation or philosophical reflection. Lengthy apologetics or detailed defenses of decisions command less respect than the quiet demonstration of a consistent pattern of behavior. Indeed, among some Amish, undue attention to the theoretical underpinnings of a particular activity may render it suspect. Talk of assurance of salvation, social responsibility, predestination, or the cultural construction of gender roles gains few listeners and scores no debating points.

In order to be taken seriously in the Amish world, one must recognize that actions not only speak louder than words—in many cases they supercede or replace words. Thus, face-to-face communication is better than telephone chatter, since phones strip away context and nonverbal cues, while personal interaction allows for the expression of body language, demeanor, dress, eye contact, and other features that subtly but significantly convey more than words alone. The distinct forms that such nonverbal elements take vary immensely and cannot be boiled down into a single Amish personality, but the conviction that actions matter is a feature common to all.

Those outside the Amish fold, from evangelical revivalists to political activists, who have tried to persuade the Amish of the ideological value of their causes, have typically met with little success. At times the Amish are not so much opposed to what these purveyors have to offer as they are disinterested in, or even unable to appreciate, the sorts of arguments these agents of theoretical conversation bring. Those who do respond to such appeals and become caught up in this other line of talk inevitably move to the margins of Amish life or exit Amish circles altogether as they find other conversation partners more intelligible and the Amish community increasingly difficult to decipher.

Ultimately, the Amish cultural conversation produces a distinct community because it takes place in the local church district. Members carry on the dialogue that sets the terms of Amish identity, sometimes in the form of a literal discussion, but more often in the form of mundane interaction and ordinary choices. Some Amish traditions accent congregational autonomy more than others, and some tip the balance of discernment toward the opinions of ordained leaders or of the settlement or the affiliation. But for all Amish, the centrality of districts in directing the future of the conversation is key. Onlookers who hope to find someone to "speak for the Amish"—whether to approve a particular public policy or to offer endorsement for certain products—will not find a ready answer, because their request comes in a language that is foreign to that which creates that Amish community in the first place.

For the Amish, this local feature of their community of conversation means that practices that baffle outsiders trouble those in the church very little. What on the surface seem to be frustratingly varied practices that defy simple systematizing share a common foundation from the Amish perspective. Rooted in congregational discernment and decision making, differing choices retain their integrity and receive recognition from other Amish. Churches with profoundly different interpretations of Ordnung respect one another's discipline because of this common conviction. Conversely, those who puzzle over the variety of Amish practice do not share in the conversation and are outside the Amish orbit.

CONTINUING THE CONVERSATION

Moderns have predicted that a locally oriented, decentralized, and ethnically divided people would disperse, assimilate, or otherwise disappear in a North American culture bent on producing homogenized individuals ill-equipped to produce direct or daring dissent. To the degree that onlookers recognize Amish persistence, they often conclude that cultural conformity is the key to delineating boundaries and staving off the inroads of the world. The Amish, many assume, find unity in uniformity.

A closer look belies that image. Engaging the Amish community as conversation reorients the questions and presuppositions that spring from such notions about unity. The Amish remain distinct—and united—not by demanding total conformity or papering over deep historical, ethnic, and churchly difference. They exist as community to the degree that they carry on a distinct conversation, in a different social grammar that is separate from the cultural mainstream. They do not accept the dominant discourse as the only reality, nor do they seek to become fluent in its vocabulary or pick up its accent. They may at times talk *about* the same subjects as their non-Amish neighbors, but they talk in a way that carries a profoundly different set of meanings, shaped by—and shaping—alternative concerns and identities.

The Amish dialogue with a particular past, with outsiders, and among themselves, allows them to remain in the world but not fully of it, to balance tradition and reason, and to mediate individual and communal concerns. The Amish conversation does not cancel the importance of context or dampen the reality of diversity. Community, in fact, exists through the differences that keep the conversation dynamic and durable. And yet, the Amish do not pursue this sort of unity for its own sake. As one elder with contacts across a diverse Amish world summed up what he saw as his people's common cause, "We hope to live our lives so that we have nothing to be proud of and much to be thankful for." In that humble recognition resides much of the spirit of Amish community.

Extinct Indiana Amish Settlements

At least eleven Amish settlements that once existed in Indiana dissolved for one or more reasons, including economic collapse, internal church conflicts, and pressure from external forces. They are listed below in chronological order.

1. Rossville-Edna Mills (Clinton County). Begun c.1843, in 1866 this Amish church affiliated with the so-called Egly Amish movement that evolved into the Evangelical Mennonite Church.

2. Newton-Jasper Counties, 1873–1955. There were one hundred families in two Old Order church districts at the height of the settlement.

3. Cleona (Brown County) 1896–1911. A few settlers from Elkhart County lived here for several years; most moved back to Elkhart County.

4. Littles-Oakland City (Pike-Gibson Counties) 1903–1914. Settlers from Daviess County moved here but suffered repeated flooding and bad weather.

5. Portland (Jay County) 1936–1958. A notably conservative group, it experienced internal disputes and had extended difficulties with state school officials.

6. Ashley (Steuben County) 1953–1978.

7. Carlisle (Sullivan County) 1955–1960. This small group adopted tractor farming methods and most members affiliated with the Beachy Amish Church.

8. Mitchell (Lawrence County) 1958–1967.

9. Kendalville (Noble County) 1974–1993. Only a handful of families ever lived here; failing to attract more members, the settlement disbanded.

10. English (Crawford County) 1977–1990.

11. Liberty (Union County) 1996–1998. Only three families (from Ohio) ever lived in this New Order Amish settlement.

Sources: David Luthy, *The Amish in America: Settlements That Failed, 1840–1960* (1986), 94–112; David Luthy, *Why Some Amish Communities Fail: Extinct Settlements, 1961–1999* (2000).

Notes

1. Meyers, "Amish Tourism."

2. Weaver-Zercher, *The Amish in the American Imagination,* explores the commodification of Amish life in American popular and academic culture.

3. "UPN in 'Amish' country again; Reality skein rides onto sked," *Daily Variety,* 7 July 2004.

4. Surveys of the Anabaptist movement, with interpretation, include Snyder, *Anabaptist History and Theology;* and Weaver, *Becoming Anabaptist.*

5. Thieleman J. van Braght, *Der blutige Schauplatz, oder, Märtyrer-Spiegel der Taufgesinnten, oder, Wehrlosen Christen* . . . . The English edition is *The Bloody Theater, or, Martyrs Mirror of the Defenseless Christians* . . . . *Martyrs Mirror* was first published in the Netherlands, in the Dutch language, in 1660.

6. The full title is *Ausbund: das ist, Etliche schöne Christliche Lieder.* English translations of *Ausbund* hymns are available in *Songs of the Ausbund,* vol. 1, and in Peters, ed., and Riall, trans., *The Earliest Hymns of the Ausbund.* Most Old Order Amish—including almost all those who live in Indiana—use the *Ausbund.* The Indiana exceptions are the Daviess County settlement, which uses a variation of the *Ausbund* entitled *Unparteiische Liedersammlung,* and the Salem ("New Order") church, which uses a variation of the *Unparteiische Liedersammlung.* Among the Amish, the *Unparteiische Liedersammlung* is commonly known as the "Guengerich book" since it was edited by Kalona, Iowa, Amishman Samuel D. Guengerich (1836–1929).

7. Documentation and interpretation of this schism is found in Roth, trans. and ed., *Letters of the Amish Division.*

8. Ammann pointed to passages in the New Testament and parts of several early Anabaptist confessions of faith that endorsed the practice. The key document in this regard was the Dutch Anabaptist-Mennonite confession of faith known as the Dordrecht Confession of 1632, which remains the standard doctrinal statement for the Amish. The text is most readily available in Leith, ed., *Creeds of the Churches,* 292–308. For a current Old Order Amish interpretation of Dordrecht, see Stoll, *How the Dordrecht Confession Came Down to Us.*

9. Mennonite immigration began in 1683 but involved only a handful of individuals until 1707, when numbers increased notably.

10. The Canadian Amish all live in Ontario, although there were a few families in British Columbia from 1969 to 1972. Small Old Order Amish settlements existed briefly in Mexico (1923–1929), Paraguay (1967–1978), and Honduras (1968–1979). A historically related group,

the car-driving and evangelically oriented Beachy Amish Mennonites, have congregations in other parts of the world, including Latin America, East Africa, and Europe.

11. A significant, though uncommon, exception to the general pattern of dividing districts only when they grow too large is the occasional division of districts as a means of resolving conflict within a district. This phenomenon, given more attention later, occurs especially among the so-called Swiss Amish. As a result, an increase in the number of church districts in a Swiss settlement does not always indicate numeric growth as it does in other settlements.

12. Church leaders are chosen by a process that combines members' nominations of candidates and casting lots, a process through which the Amish believe the divine will is revealed. For a brief explanation of the process, see Kraybill, *Riddle of Amish Culture*, 128–31.

13. Proximity alone, however, does not define a settlement, since settlements may be geographically adjacent or even overlapping but still constitute different settlements if each has a distinct origin and history in the area. Conversely, schism may subsequently divide a settlement into non-fellowshipping *affiliations* (defined below), but all such parties continue to see themselves as heirs of the original church districts in that place and thus continue to consider themselves a single settlement.

14. Recognition and respect are key: not necessarily sharing the same discipline, but respecting it. Thus, an individual under discipline in one group is considered under discipline by most other groups even if those other groups would not exercise discipline in the same way or for the same matters.

15. The term the Amish use to for such fellowship is *dien,* from the German word *Diener,* which they use in ministerial titles (bishop, *Völliger Diener;* minister, *Diener zum Buch;* deacon, *Armendiener*). The Amish use the term *dien* even in English conversation, noting for example, that "We *dien* with them" or "Those groups *dien* together." The use of this term signals the symbolic importance of ministerial reciprocity in establishing and marking affiliation.

16. "The Ordnung as agreed on when top buggies came in," *Die Kurier,* 10 February 1998. From 1869 to 1990 the Daviess County settlement had used "open buggies" (i.e., unenclosed; without tops or sides to enclose the riders). Since then, the districts in the settlement have allowed enclosed buggies. Such an abrupt change in a longstanding practice resulted in the buggy Ordnung being worked out in this sort of detail—scripted specifics that otherwise would be highly unusual in the Ordnung of older settlements where understandings are passed on orally and informally. However, in some newer communities that draw members from various places and for whom the creation of a new settlement identity cannot rely on common tradition and shared memory, a written list of basic Ordnung provisions is not unknown. This Daviess County buggy Ordnung, in fact, was printed in 1998 as a reminder to church members, perhaps because some residents were flouting its provisions or because it was still so new as to require repetition.

17. For case studies, see Kraybill and Nolt, *Amish Enterprise,* 125–40.

18. For a discussion of the meaning and implications of the concept of identity as used by historians, sociologists, and psychologists, see Gleason, "Identifying Identity." The use here relies on these historical and sociological understandings. Our approach to describing and analyzing cultural identity also draws on the theories and cultural analysis that asserts the real role of culture in shaping social organizations. See Hall and Neitz, *Culture: Sociolog-*

ical Perspectives; Hunter and Ainley, eds., *Making Sense of Modern Times;* Wuthnow, *Meaning and Moral Order;* and Wuthnow et al., *Cultural Analysis.*

19. See Appendix for list of extinct Indiana Amish settlements.

20. The Sarasota, Florida, Amish community exists within that municipality's city limits, but its highly unusual Amish profile—mostly elderly retired or seasonal residents wintering from the North—make it unique and without parallel to the sorts of community interactions and issues that mark other settlements.

CHAPTER 2: MIGRATION

1. But see the exceptional Gingerich, *Wer will die Lueken Verzaunen und der Wege Bessern? Or Who Will Repair the Breach and Stand in the Gap?* 3–6.

2. Cayton, *Frontier Indiana,* 261–316. For migration data, see Madison, *The Indiana Way,* 58–62. Indiana's net migration rate dropped from 54.56 percent in the 1830s to 1.32 percent in the 1840s before moving into negative territory in the 1850s.

3. The towns of Nappanee and Kokomo did not exist when the first Amish located in the areas that would eventually take on these settlement names. These names are used here to identify Old Order Amish geographic communities widely known by these names today.

4. Nolt, *A History of the Amish,* 72–95, 118–56, provides more details and citations for these immigration waves.

5. From a narrative by John E. Borntreger (1837–1930), son of one of the land scouts, published as *Geschichte der Ersten Ansiedelung der Amischen Mennoniten* in 1917, and translated by Elizabeth Gingerich as *A History of the First Settlers of the Amish.* The quotation is on p. 5.

6. On details of location, correcting widely believed oral tradition, see Hochstetler, "Where Was the First Amish Mennonite Worship Service in Clinton Township Held?" 3–4.

7. Wenger, *Mennonites in Indiana and Michigan,* 183–85.

8. From chapter 3, "The Amish from 1840 through 1851," in Habegger and Adams, *The Swiss of Adams and Wells Counties.*

9. Widower Richer later married Barbara Hilty Klopfenstein.

10. Stoll, "The Eichers of Adams County, Indiana," 22–28.

11. Ringenberg, "Development and Division," 117, 120.

12. For a description of similar dynamics in a different ethno-religious story, see Don Yoder, "The 'Dutchman' and the '*Deitschlenner.*'" Yoder describes cultural differences between descendants of eighteenth-century Pennsylvania Germans and nineteenth-century German immigrants who settled in the Midwest. His examples come from German Reformed and Lutheran communities.

13. Klopfenstein, *Marching to Zion,* 77–198.

14. On the Egly Amish, see Paton Yoder, *Tradition and Transition,* 180–86.

15. The Amish here formed a so-called Egly Amish church in 1866. They constructed a meetinghouse near Edna Mills in 1885. The Egly Amish eventually took on the name Defenseless Mennonite Church, and in 1948, Evangelical Mennonite Church. The Edna Mills Defenseless Mennonite Church moved into the city of Lafayette in 1942, where it existed as the Lafayette Evangelical Mennonite Church until it closed in 1995.

16. For a detailed discussion of the complex origins of what became the Nappanee set-

tlement, see the genealogical and settlement strands unraveled in Stutzman, "Religious Separatism and Economic Participation."

17. Bontrager's life is detailed in Eli J. Bontrager, *My Life Story* (1982).

18. On nineteenth-century Amish economics and market forces, see anecdotes in Luthy, *Amish in America: Settlements that Failed;* and the community case study of Reschly, *Amish on the Iowa Prairie.*

19. In some cases, the Lancaster Amish migrants to Indiana did not move directly from Lancaster County but came from other Lancaster "daughter" settlements. In addition, the Parke County settlement attracted a few households who came from Mifflin County, Pennsylvania, but who immediately adapted to the Parke-Lancaster Ordnung. See chapter 7.

20. *Amish Directory: Feather Your Nest,* 166–72. The other households form two other extended families.

21. Borkholder, comp., *Nappanee Amish Directory,* 286–89.

22. Stoll, *Amish in Daviess County,* 7–19.

23. "Worthington," in *New Order Amish Directory,* 1999, 24–25.

24. Bontrager, *My Life Story,* 20, 22; and Pratt, *Shipshewana,* 72–78, 81–86. For a comprehensive assessment of Amish schools, see Johnson-Weiner, *Train Up a Child.*

25. Farmwald, *History and Directory of Indiana Amish Parochial Schools,* 16–31.

26. Statistics were calculated using known Amish private school enrollments and closely estimated Amish school-age populations drawn from settlement directories. Estimated percentage of Amish children who attended public schools for 2001–2002 in the Nappanee settlement was 21 percent; in Elkhart-LaGrange, 39 percent; and in Adams County, 22 percent. Because of the particular history of school issues in Allen County, that longstanding settlement has very few children enrolled in public schools, providing an exception to the general pattern, discussed in chapter 6.

27. However, the process of consolidation has enlarged these schools and changed the student body composition so that Amish students are a minority—sometimes small minority—in these now sizable institutions.

28. E.g., teachers quoted in "Schools Respect Amish Culture," *The* [Elkhart] *Truth,* 27 August 2004, A-10; and conversations between authors and public school teachers with Amish students.

29. Farmwald, *History and Directory of Indiana Amish Parochial Schools,* 32–150; quote, p. 400 (Minutes of the Annual Indiana Directors Meeting 2001). See also pp. 390–91 for minutes of the 1997 directors meeting in which Wells was the honored guest.

30. "Families Establish Amish Community in Rural Mount Zion" and "Amish Plan to Build One-Room Schoolhouse," *South Bend Tribune,* 7 September 1998, B3.

CHAPTER 3: ORDNUNG

1. Exceptions to this generalization occur in newer settlements where the population may be made up of migrants from several different communities who carry different understandings of Ordnung. In such cases, residents sometimes produce a written Ordnung covering certain basic or potentially contentious points to make sure everyone understands

the working assumptions that may differ from those that prevailed in their respective settlements of origin. Yet even such a written Ordnung is only partial and does not cover every possible application. One early example of such a written Ordnung was that produced by the Daviess County settlement (founded in 1869) in 1871. That community included families from Allen County, Indiana, as well as Ohio, Missouri, and Ontario. See "The *Ordnungsbrief* of [Nov. 27] 1871," in Stoll, *Amish in Daviess County, Indiana*, 20–30.

2. For a concise statement by an Amish minister (from the Lancaster, Pennsylvania, settlement), see [Beiler], "Ordnung," 382–84.

3. See the discussion in Schlabach, *Peace, Faith, Nation*, 201–29; and Beulah Stauffer Hostetler, "The Formation of the Old Orders," 5–25. On Old Order movements in other Anabaptist-related groups, see Kraybill and Bowman, *On the Backroad to Heaven*.

4. For more material on the cultural developments discussed here, see Bushman, *Refinement of America*. Of course, the promise of creating one's own persona through popular refinement was tied up with notions of race, and these possibilities were only open to those deemed white.

5. Foster, *An Errand of Mercy;* Griffin, *Their Brothers' Keeper;* and Johnson, *Redeeming America*.

6. Nolt, "Plain People and the Refinement of America."

7. The Indiana meetings were those of 1864, held at the Daniel Schrock farm in Clinton Township, Elkhart County; and 1872, held at the Samuel S. Miller farm in the Forks area of LaGrange County. For more detailed history of those meetings and mid-nineteenth-century Amish life, see Paton Yoder, *Tradition and Transition*. Yoder introduced the terms "tradition-minded" and "change-minded" to describe these groups. The minutes of the gatherings are available in English as Yoder and Estes, *Proceedings of the Amish Ministers' Meetings, 1862–1878*.

8. Yoder, *Tradition and Transition*, 117–21; Pratt, *Shipshewana*, 26–32.

9. Yoder and Estes, *Proceedings of the Amish Ministers' Meetings*, 391–93.

10. This movement and its impact on Old Order identity is detailed in Nolt, "The Amish 'Mission Movement.'"

11. Local Protestants came to the home to hold Sunday morning worship services for the elderly residents, but it was never assumed that the Amish volunteers were accountable to these churches. Hershberger and Hochstetler, eds., *History and Memories of Hillcrest Home*, 26.

12. The Old Order volunteers in Arkansas were seen as temporarily separated from their home communities. The situation is similar to that which prevails today among Amish seniors from various settlements who spend winter months in Sarasota, Florida. The atypical Sarasota Amish community exists in ways that transcend any one local discipline and in which the temporary nature of one's association with the "settlement" allows one, in some cases, to live provisionally outside the boundaries of the one's home church discipline without challenging that discipline or implying that one will not submit to it after returning home.

13. For more detail on all these points, see Nolt, "The Amish 'Mission Movement.'"

14. Not surprisingly, in 1965 Old Order Amish churches withdrew their formal representation on the umbrella organization Mennonite Central Committee, which had previously

spoken publicly on their behalf, and the following year organized the National Amish Steering Committee to speak to the state from a more sectarian stance. On Pathway publishers, see John A. Hostetler, *Amish Society*, 378–81.

15. Between 1953 and 1961 five ministers and a group of lay members from LaGrange County relocated to Kenton, Ohio. Other settlements in this network drew members from a broader range of other communities. Already in 1956 mission movement supporter Harvey Graber had noted a common impulse behind this neoconservative Old Order development and his own more progressive movement; see Graber, "Spiritual Awakening in the Old Order Amish Church," 24.

16. Nolt, "The Amish 'Mission Movement,'" 35–36. The best detail on New Order origins is Kline and Beachy, "History and Dynamics of the New Order Amish."

17. Midwestern Amish worship follows a lectionary printed in *The New American Almanac* (Baltic, OH: Ben J. Raber, annual), and in German as *Der Neue Amerikanische Calender* (Baltic, OH: Ben J. Raber, annual); these publications are popularly known as "Raber's Almanac." The Lancaster, Pennsylvania, Amish and their daughter settlements use a lectionary formulated by Jonathan Kauffman in 1896 that differs slightly from that observed in the Midwest: *Ein Register von Lieder und Schriften die in der Amischen Gemeinde gebraucht warden* (S.l: Pequea Brüder, 1979). On the lectionary, see Oyer, "Is There an Amish Theology?"

18. For more details on different worship practices, see Scott, *The Amish Wedding*, 82–90. Those Amish churches in which all members remain seated for the scripture reading are the ethnically Swiss Amish (see chapter 4). The description of members facing the reader or standing with their backs toward the reader merits some logistical explanation. In the order of Amish worship, the congregation kneels for a lengthy silent prayer immediately prior to the scripture reading. Amish worshipers kneel by turning around and kneeling against the bench on which they have been sitting—thus positioning themselves in such a way that when the prayer is over and they stand up, they are facing backward. In Lancaster Amish worship services, the congregation rises from kneeling prayer to hear the Scripture, but no one turns around and sits down until the reading is finished, which means that everyone is still facing away from the deacon who is reading the text. In most non-Swiss Midwestern Amish churches, the congregation rises from kneeling prayer to hear the Scripture, but the men turn around and face the minister who is reading, while the women stand but do not turn, and thus are facing away from the reader. The origins of these customs are obscure; for discussion of folk explanations for practices surrounding scripture reading in Amish worship, see Beck, *MennoFolk*, 60–61.

19. For historical background, see Yoder, *Tradition and Transition*, 111, 272–74, 279. On current practice of *streng Meidung*, see Kraybill, *Riddle of Amish Culture*, 137–41.

20. The Lancaster, Pennsylvania, Amish experience is an exception to this phenomenon. As early as 1969 that settlement accepted refrigerated bulk milk tanks as a way of allowing farmers to stay competitive in the Grade A market even though it marked a decided shift in Amish dairy practice. See Kraybill, *Riddle of Amish Culture*, 202–6. Few other Amish settlements made such a collective move, and those that did—later and on a district-by-district basis—often found it was too little and too late to stem the shift away from farming. In 1972 the Arthur, Illinois, Old Order bishops approved the use of bulk milk tanks, but dairying in that settlement continued to decline, and today the community includes very few full-time farmers; see Stoltzfus, "Amish Agriculture."

21. See, e.g., Umble, *Holding the Line.*

22. Kraybill and Nolt, *Amish Enterprise,* 228-41.

23. Kraybill, *Riddle of Amish Culture,* 94, 98-101. The Lancaster settlement is composed of a single affiliation, with the exception of one small New Order Amish district that exists on the settlement's northeastern edge; its presence is insignificant in the context of some 154 thriving Old Order churches.

24. The four major affiliations are Swartzentruber, Andy Weaver, mainline Old Order, and New Order. See the historical chart showing the emergence of affiliations in this settlement in the front matter of the *Ohio Amish Directory* (various editions). For discussion, see Kraybill, "Plotting Social Change across Four Affiliations," though the relationship between the four is more complex than the essay's linear alignment suggests.

CHAPTER 4: ETHNICITY

1. See, e.g., Meyers, "The Old Order Amish," 378-95; Greksa and Korbin, "Key Decisions in the Lives of the Old Order Amish," 373-98; and Stevick, *Growing Up Amish.*

2. For one academic appraisal of the Amish as an ethnic group, see Redekop and Hostetler, "The Plain People: An Interpretation."

3. The individual elements that mark ethnicity are not necessarily unique—indeed, some may be common to many different groups—but the particular composition or constellation of elements gives ethnicity its distinctive character. The literature on ethnicity is vast. One starting point for the definition offered in this chapter is Petersen, "Concepts of Ethnicity," in *Harvard Encyclopedia of American Ethnic Groups,* 234-42; and Conzen et al., "The Invention of Ethnicity."

4. On high-context culture, see Hall, *Beyond Culture,* esp. 74-77, 91-93.

5. Oboler, *Ethnic Labels, Latino Lives.*

6. In some times and places, Old Order Amish men have been permitted to obtain drivers licenses and operate trucks as part of their jobs for non-Amish employers. This was the case in the Nappanee settlement in the 1930s to 1950s, but it is no longer permitted. A few men still hold this exceptional privilege in the Arthur, Illinois, settlement—though not as many as was the case in the 1970s.

7. See, e.g., "Amish" in *Gale Encyclopedia of Multicultural America* (Detroit, MI: Gale Research, 1995), 1:55-70, which simplistically assumes a single Amish ethnicity, especially in terms of dialect or folkways such as holidays and wedding customs.

8. Although today *Pennsylvania Dutch* is often considered a misnomer (i.e., assumed to be a corruption of Pennsylvania *Deutsch*), it was actually the typical eighteenth-century English term for Rhine Valley immigrants. *Dutch,* according to the *Oxford English Dictionary,* was the English term for the Rhine Valley inhabitants as far south as Switzerland. Thus the English spoke of *Dutch* immigrants, whereas later sources often spoke of the *Germans.* (The English also spoke of the *Holland Dutch* or *Low Dutch* to refer to those today known as *Dutch.*) On the etymology, see Don Yoder, "Palatine, Hessian, Dutchman."

9. From the authors' fieldwork notes; see also the similar sense in Thompson, "Languages of the Amish of Allen County, Indiana."

10. On the dialect, see Seifert, "The World Geography of Pennsylvania German," 14-42.

For a concise overview of early Pennsylvania German immigration, settlement, and cultural evolution, see Nolt, *Foreigners in Their Own Land,* 11–46.

11. Technically, an enclosed vehicle is a *carriage,* while an open vehicle is a *buggy.* A few older Amish people, particularly in Lancaster, Pennsylvania, continue to make this nominal distinction. For most people—Amish and non-Amish—the terms are interchangeable, and enclosed horse-drawn vehicles are also buggies.

12. Although his study does not focus specifically on Amish immigrants or the particular themes of this chapter, Delbert L. Gratz's book *Bernese Anabaptists and Their American Descendants* (1953), provides some background and context.

13. There are eighteen Swiss settlements, including ninety two church districts, in seven states: Indiana, Kentucky, Michigan, Missouri, New York, Ohio, and Pennsylvania. See chapter 6, n. 4 for a list of Swiss settlements.

14. A detailed study of this Swiss dialect is Wenger, "A Swiss-German Dialect Study."

15. Both dialects differ from standard German not only in vocabulary and phonetic pronunciation but also in grammar. Pennsylvania German, for example, does not have a dative case, while the so-called Swiss dialect does.

16. The Amish describe Adams County Swiss speech as "flat" in comparison to that spoken in Allen County. Thompson, "Languages of the Amish of Allen County, Indiana," argues that the Swiss dialect in Allen County is actually an Alsatian dialect. On Adams County, see Humpa, "Retention and Loss of Bernese Alemannic Traits in an Indiana Amish Dialect." Anecdotal evidence suggests that the Allen County Swiss mix more English with their dialect than do the Adams County Swiss.

17. A few Swiss settlements have adopted enclosed carriages: Linesville, Pennsylvania; Bowling Green, Missouri; Norfolk, New York; and Prattsburg, New York. The large Daviess County, Indiana, settlement, many of whose members are of nineteenth-century Swiss extraction, adopted enclosed buggies in 1990.

18. Popularly known among the Amish by the English name "kid box," the small enclosed seat is also known as a "coupe box." It is attached to the back of a buggy with two wing nuts and in the summer can be removed and replaced with another seat. The Allen County–related settlements at South Whitley, Indiana, and Quincy, Michigan, also use kid boxes in the winter, but other Allen County daughter settlements do not.

19. Happily for historians, Roman D. Schwartz reconstructed, through local memories, the records of burials in one major Adams County cemetery where many wooden stakes have disintegrated. He began the project in 1964, tapping the memories of the oldest area residents. See his comments in *History and Records of Internment, 1865–1995,* 3–6.

20. *Schwartzs' Song-Book,* compiled by Christian and Elizabeth N. Schwartz, includes English yodels (text only) on pp. 180–85, and Swiss yodels (text only) on pp. 186–91.

21. Thompson, "Yodeling of the Indiana Swiss Amish." On yodeling more generally, see Plantenga, *Yodel-Ay-Ee-Oooo.*

22. Lambright was a German Lutheran immigrant to America before joining the Amish church. The Chupp family had been United Brethren (a German-speaking Methodist-related denomination). Whetstone was an English orphan adopted into an Amish home. Individual published genealogies on various Amish families give more surname background.

23. See Luthy, "New Names Among the Amish," in *Family Life* (August/September 1972):

31–35; (October 1972): 20–23; (November 1972): 21–23; (February 1973): 13–15; (June 1973): 13–15.

24. One exploration of this dynamic with examples from Pennsylvania German Mennonites is Nolt, "Finding a Context for Mennonite History." On the specific example of Second Christmas (December 26), see Shoemaker, *Christmas in Pennsylvania*.

25. Keiser, "Language Change Across Speech Islands," notes the "unusual homogeneity of Midwestern Deitsch" and the emergence of regional variations as markers of "a distinct regional social identity" (ii–iii).

26. Stoll, *Amish in Daviess County, Indiana*, 7–66.

27. Between 1994 and 2002, twenty Swiss households moved to the Pennsylvania German–speaking Elkhart-LaGrange settlement, where they concentrated in several districts on the settlement's eastern edge. This mini-migration—while significant for the sending Swiss communities (discussed in chapter 6) is relatively unimportant for Elkhart-LaGrange, as the twenty Swiss households comprise a numerically insignificant percentage of the population. In the Nappanee community, no analogous mini-migration has taken place. The high profile of the Adams County–derived Schwartz name appears to stem from the unusually large number of descendants the Nappanee Schwartz settler had. In the 2001 *Nappanee Amish Directory*, Schwartz was the fifth most common surname, inching ahead of Chupp, the surname that had traditionally held the fifth place in this settlement.

28. There is an extensive literature on onomastics (naming patterns and practices). For four historical examples of onomastics, with explorations of the cultural biases they reveal, see Fischer, *Albion's Seed*, 93–97, 306–10, 502–7, 683–86.

29. Some individuality comes by way of nicknames. See Enninger, "Amish By-Names."

30. Schrock, *The Amish Christian Church*. A notable example of a church conflict that crossed ethnic lines is the 1953 schism in Adams County. In that case, the Swiss settlement was embroiled in a complicated church discipline case with roots in northeastern Ohio's non-Swiss Holmes-Wayne counties settlement. When an Ohioan under discipline moved to Adams County, the Swiss church's response to his situation and the use of the ban in Ohio divided many Swiss churches. Significantly, the several delegations of church leaders who sought to make peace in this case included ministers and bishops from several states and from both ethnic groups. See documents in Gingerich, *Wer will die Lueken Verzaunen?* A more recent example of inter-ethnic interaction around church issues was the 1990s appeal of some Adams County Swiss districts to certain Nappanee leaders. The Adams churches asked Nappanee bishops to offer counsel in resolving controversies, and in at least one case, a Nappanee bishop temporarily provided bishop oversight for an Adams district torn by conflict. Significantly, it was the distant—even outsider—status of the Nappanee bishops that made them appealing parties for possible conflict resolution in these cases.

31. Swiss families who move to Pennsylvania German–speaking settlements may retain a Swiss accent, but they soon switch to the prevailing dialect. Pennsylvania German speakers who move to Swiss communities, in contrast, often retain their Pennsylvania German dialect longer. See Thompson, "Languages of the Amish of Allen County," 72–74.

32. Data from the 2002 *Indiana Amish Directory: Elkhart, LaGrange, and Noble Counties*. Listings for twenty households indicate arrival from Swiss settlements (seventeen from Adams County; one, Allen County; two, other locations). Nineteen of the families lived in seven

church districts on the eastern edge of the settlement: District 13–1, six families; District 4, four families; Districts 5 and 6, three families each; and Districts 2, 3, and 13, one family each. Seven of the families moved in 1998, three in 1997, and two each in 1999 and 2002; one household arrived each year in 1994–1996, 2000–2001; one family, related to the others and moving next to them, undoubtedly migrated during this period but did not list a moving date in their entry.

33. Anecdotal stories attest to some Swiss bishops having excommunicated individuals whom they baptized, even though the offending parties have moved elsewhere and no longer were members of the bishops' districts—suggesting an implied authority tied to baptism, whereby the one who baptizes holds spiritual authority over those he baptized for as long as they live, no matter where they move. This is not typical Amish polity or disciplinary procedure; typically discipline is a matter reserved for the local church in which one is a resident member, regardless of where one was raised or baptized.

CHAPTER 5: ELKHART-LAGRANGE AND NAPPANEE SETTLEMENTS

1. "Amish Country: Northern Indiana. 2005 Vacation Planner" (Elkhart County Convention and Visitors Bureau, 2004).

2. See the analysis in Meyers, "Amish Tourism," which is based on surveys of area tourists conducted in 2000.

3. Jones et al., eds., *Churches and Church Membership in the United States, 2000,* 164, 397–98. In 2000 the Old Order Amish were the largest religious denomination in LaGrange County; in Lancaster County, they ranked sixth. (Note that the figures for Amish church membership in LaGrange County in this Glenmary study are too low, although the relative size and ranking are correct.)

4. Although these individuals could come from any settlement, that Elkhart-LaGrange is the largest Hoosier settlement and that committee members typically serve undefined terms and find their own successors suggest that the position is likely to remain in that region.

5. Indeed, the Elkhart-LaGrange settlement directory is entitled simply *Indiana Amish Directory,* with "Elkhart, LaGrange, and Noble Counties" in a subtitle.

6. Edmunds, *Potawatomis, Keepers of the Fire,* 240–43, 267–71.

7. Borntreger, *A History of the First Settlers of the Amish,* 5.

8. On details of location, correcting widely held oral tradition, see Hochstetler, "Where Was the First Amish Mennonite Worship Service Held?" 3–4.

9. Pratt, *Shipshewana,* 26–32.

10. See the historical narrative and chart of church district formation in Miller, comp., *Indiana Amish Directory: Elkhart, LaGrange, and Noble Counties,* 8–28, 35, 41, 59, 65, 75, 95, 101, 107, 113, 119. Hereafter, this source is listed as *2002 Elkhart-LaGrange Directory.*

11. For many years the date 1839 was associated with the beginning of the Nappanee settlement. However, this date, popularized by its use in the work of historical geographer James E. Landing, was not based on archival data. It appears to be rooted in a passing comment about 1829 immigrants who "after living ten years in Ohio," moved to Indiana, that was included in an unreferenced 1937 entry in Kauffman, *Mennonite Cyclopedic Dictionary,* 354, which was repeated in the later 1950s *Mennonite Encyclopedia,* and in turn cited by Landing.

Stutzman's "Religious Separatism and Economic Participation" offers a carefully detailed discussion of the arrival of Amish families in the future Nappanee area, which he documents as being no earlier than 1842 (though these arrivals had non-Amish relatives in the area from the 1830s onward). The paper's Appendix A includes much data on the early families.

12. The town of Nappanee did not exist when the first Amish located in the area; the name is used here to identify the settlement that now goes by that name.

13. Stutzman, "Religious Separatism."

14. The Yoders arrived in 1849 from Tuscarawas County, Ohio; the Hochstetlers, the same year from Holmes County, Ohio. In the 1850s, Holmes County Hochstetlers and Schlabachs moved to the future Nappanee area.

15. Landing, "The Spatial Development and Organization of an Old Order Amish-Beachy Amish Settlement," 38–94, offers some discussion of the geographic growth of the Nappanee settlement from the 1850s to the 1960s, with historical maps. See also Rechlin, *Spatial Behavior of the Old Order Amish of Nappanee, Indiana*, 38–57.

16. Stutzman, "Religious Separatism," Appendix C, provides some helpful correctives to the sometimes confused story of the schism in the Nappanee settlement.

17. See the historical narrative and chart of church district formation in Borkholder, comp., *Nappanee Amish Directory, including Rochester, Kokomo, and Milroy Communities, 2001*, 5, 16–24, 54–68. Hereafter, this source is listed as *2001 Nappanee Directory*.

18. The first Beachy Amish church in Indiana was the Maple Lawn congregation near Nappanee, organized in 1940 by one-time Old Order bishop David O. Borkholder (1886–1959). On the Beachy Amish movement in the 1940s here, see Elmer S. Yoder, *Beachy Amish Mennonite Fellowship of Churches*, 129–31, 151, 190–91, 316–24; and Landing, "Spatial Development," 141–44. On the mission movement, see Nolt, "The Amish 'Mission Movement,'" 7–36.

19. *2001 Nappanee Directory*, 9.

20. On the Christner church, see *2001 Nappanee Directory*, 22; and Landing, "Spatial Development," 138–41.

21. While Christner and a fellow deacon provided the initial local leadership, they appealed to the ultra-conservative Buchanan County, Iowa, settlement for bishop oversight. However, Christner performed the ordination even though he was not a bishop, in violation of Amish polity. For a brief discussion of Kemp's varied career in Amish circles, especially after his association with Christner, see Luthy, "Erlis Kemp and 'Atomic Bibles' for Russia."

22. See Cong, "Amish Factionalism and Technological Change," though this essay mistakenly presents the story entirely in terms of tensions over technology use. For a more complete discussion of the issues involved, see "Geschichten und Begebenheiten in der Nord East Barrens."

23. For examples of varied uses of household appliances in Nappanee in the 1970s, see Rechlin, *Spatial Behavior*, 112–18.

24. Certainly there are modifications in Ordnung that would signal a separation from the Old Order mainstream—the adoption of automobiles or the abandonment of shunning, for example—but in such cases it has been the subsequent affiliation with another group such as the Beachy Amish that has cemented the formal divide as much as the precipitating innovations themselves.

25. In very recent years, the Lancaster settlement has begun to see some diversity of prac-

tice in regard to using bicycles, power lawn mowers, and self-propelled corn harvesters. The gathered Lancaster bishops have begun agreeing to permit diversity on such items, but this is a new phenomenon in the settlement.

26. *The Devil's Playground* (Wellspring Media Inc.) featured the stories of four Amish teens and young adults from the Elkhart-LaGrange settlement engaged in highly deviant (and sometimes illegal) behavior. The film, which also aired on cable television, was embarrassing to the Amish community and prompted some church leaders to admonish parents to maintain greater oversight of their children's activities. The stories presented in the film were authentic, though they presented biographies that were less than typical in key respects. For example, all four characters had attended public school, and only one ended up joining the Amish church; whereas a majority of children in the Elkhart-LaGrange settlement attend Amish parochial schools, and more than 90 percent join the church in young adulthood.

27. Significantly, even the origins of the Elkhart-LaGrange *Dienerversammlung* point to a desire to maintain amity in the settlement rather than to impose strict uniformity. According to Eli E. Gingerich (1915–2005), a minister who attended nearly every meeting and often served as recording secretary, the gathering began because "there was a minister who moved into the settlement from elsewhere who was a bit outspoken, and he got into an argument with another minister. No one could do anything about it. Some shook their heads. Some wept. Finally, [Bishop] Henry Miller [1908–1978] said there should be something we can do about this. Thus, began the regular *Dienerversammlung*, as an effort to address the conflict between two ministers and successfully bring an end to the quarrel. They chose two leaders who in turn chose a third to assist them." Gingerich emphasized that there is equality among the older and younger ministers. It was important that the group gathered each year and not only for special circumstances, "otherwise people would wonder, What is this all about? But having it regularly allowed people to bring up issues before there was a crisis." Although some people complain that the ministers from the more progressive Clinton and Shipshewana districts come to the *Dienerversammlung* and "then go home and do as they please," Gingerich (who served in a more conservative district), concluded, "I think the ones that come are doing the best that they can. They want to hold together." Interview, 7 October 1999.

28. Observations of various contemporary Amish interviewees. See also Landing, "Spatial Development," 154–65.

29. The Amish were overrepresented in wheat production and did own disproportionately more cows and swine than their neighbors. In addition, because they were heavily ensconced in farming, they also were overrepresented in terms of land ownership; in 1860 the Amish represented 28 percent of the population but controlled 49 percent of the real estate value (see Pratt, *Shipshewana*, 12–14). Stutzman, "Religious Separation," 11–13, provides a similar set of data for the Nappanee settlement, based on the 1850 and 1860 Agricultural Census. He found that the Amish there were slightly wealthier and held slightly more land than their neighbors, produced proportionately less corn, and owned proportionately more animals for meat.

30. Landing, *American Essence: A History of the Peppermint and Spearmint Industry.*

31. Luthy, *Amish in America: Settlements that Failed,* 95–100, 177–81, 221–28, 305–25, 393–96. Nappanee families had begun the Newton County, Indiana, settlement in 1873, but migration there continued for several decades.

32. Ibid.

33. See memories in Freeman L. and Lizzie Yoder, comps., *Echoes of the Past;* also information from authors' interviews.

34. In 1940, Mennonite Central Committee sent a survey to all Amish bishops, asking them to report data, including employment, of conscription-age men in their churches. Though the return was incomplete, the results did document that some Amish men were employed in factories and a handful in government-funded work jobs. See Peace Section Census, 1940, Questionnaires: Old Order Amish, Indiana, IX-7–1, Box 1, Folder 7, Archives of the Mennonite Church USA—Goshen, Indiana.

35. Landing, "Spatial Development," 116–28, documents Nappanee settlement factory work and industrial impact in the 1960s; Rechlin, *Spatial Behavior,* 78–96, in the 1970s.

36. The cheese plant was completed and took in its first milk in December 1979. In 2002 the company was purchased by Canadian agribusiness giant Agropur.

37. The 1980 Elkhart-LaGrange directory showed 54 percent of household heads under 65 were full-time farmers and 28 percent worked in factories; the 1988 directory reported 37 percent were farmers and 43 percent factory workers. For more detail, see Meyers, "Population Growth and Its Consequences in the Elkhart-LaGrange Old Order Amish Settlement."

38. On Geauga settlement occupations, see Greksa and Korbin, "Key Decisions in the Lives of the Old Order Amish."

39. For their part, local factory owners, including sizable recreational vehicle companies that employ hundreds of Amish men—Keystone, in Goshen; Newmar, in Nappanee; Jayco, in Middlebury—have made modest adaptations to the Amish holiday schedule, closing production lines on Ascension Day, for example. See "Amish Don't Work on Ascension Day," *The* [Elkhart] *Truth,* 19 May 2004, A-1, 7.

40. Meyers, "Lunch Pails and Factories," 173–74.

41. "[Ohio] Shop Support Committee Meeting," minutes, 6 October 1999, citing Steering Committee correspondence.

42. Meyers, "The Old Order Amish: To Remain in the Faith or to Leave"; Greksa and Korbin, "Key Decisions in the Lives of the Old Order Amish," 373–98. Greksa and Korbin found that farmers' children had slightly higher defection rates.

43. Kraybill and Nolt, *Amish Enterprise,* 228–41.

44. Pratt, *Shipshewana,* 72–78, 81–86, details the 1920s conflicts with public school authorities in LaGrange County.

45. See the school history sections in the *2002 Elkhart-LaGrange Directory,* 1–3; and the *2001 Nappanee Directory,* 25–49; as well as Farmwald, *History and Directory of Indiana Amish Parochial Schools.*

46. Borkholder, comp., *A History of the Borkholder School District No. 1.*

47. For many years the Honeyville School (built in 1930, closed in 2001) was a public school with an almost entirely Amish student body, even after the Westview District consolidation. In 2001 the Westview District closed Honeyville, opened a new elementary known as Meadow View, and redistricted its elementary divisions so that no elementary school would have an exclusively Amish student body.

48. On Amish Acres, see Ramirez, *This Wooden O.* For a brief history of the 800-vendor Shipshewana Flea Market, see J. B. Miller, "Trading Places: 30,000 People a Week Come to

Shipshewana," *Mennonite Weekly Review,* 6 January 2000, 7. The cattle auction that predated the flea market had begun in 1922.

49. Meyers, "Amish Tourism."

50. A comparison of the "Amish County: Northern Indiana" and "Lancaster County: The Heart of Pennsylvania Dutch Country"—official published visitors guides for the convention and visitors bureaus in each place—reveal 237 businesses listed in the Indiana guide and 554 listed in the Lancaster guide. Twenty-three (4 percent) of the Lancaster entries included *Amish* in their name, while fourteen (6 percent) of Indiana entries did. Fifty (9 percent) of the Lancaster entries included the word *Amish* in their advertisement copy; fifty-four (23 percent) of the Indiana entries did. While 169 (71 percent) of entries in the Indiana guide made no reference to *Amish,* 481 (87 percent) of the Lancaster entries made no reference to *Amish.*

51. See, e.g., photos and text in "Amish Country: Northern Indiana."

52. *Economic Impact of Elkhart County's Tourism* (Lexington, KY: Certec, Inc., 1998).

53. The ABC Fund of the Arthur, Illinois, Old Order Amish settlement was the first such revolving loan fund in the country.

54. AMMF was later imitated elsewhere: the Tri-County Land Trust, which serves the Elkhart-LaGrange (and Noble) counties settlement area, was patterned after it.

55. A parallel but organizationally independent program in the Lancaster settlement is known as Helping Hand and was organized in 1998. The Hillsboro, Wisconsin, and Aylmer, Ontario, settlements have similar initiatives, though they are organized somewhat differently.

56. Allen, "My Birth, My Way," describes the New Eden Center. The birthing center is based on the model of the Amish-affiliated Mount Eaton Care Center in Holmes County, Ohio. See Huntington, "Health Care," 174–75. A handful of non-Amish women also give birth at New Eden each year.

57. "New Mental Health Clinic Tailored to Amish Values," *Goshen News,* 14 February 2002. In July 2005 a similar facility opened in the Lancaster, Pennsylvania, settlement, patterned on Rest Haven. Known as Green Pastures, the Lancaster center follows the model pioneered in Elkhart County in almost every detail and is associated clinically with the Mennonite-sponsored Philhaven Hospital in Mount Gretna, Pennsylvania. See "Coming Out of the Shadows: New Center will help Plain People Deal with Mental Illness," [Lancaster] *Intelligencer Journal,* 21 April 2005, B-1; "Amish Facility Planned at Philhaven: Churches Creating Home for Mentally Ill," *Lancaster New Era,* 8 April 2005, A-1.

58. Data from *1995 Elkhart-LaGrange Directory,* calculated by Thomas J. Meyers. Of 92 bishops, 179 ministers, and 83 deacons, two-thirds of those over age sixty-five had been farmers, while less than a fifth of those under age thirty fell into that category. Leaders under forty were more than 60 percent factory employees. Of the ordained men fifty and older (180), the average age at ordination had been forty; for men under fifty (174), the average age at ordination had been thirty-two. The percentage of ordained men whose father or grandfather was in the ministry, by age cohorts, was: ages 65 and older, 49 percent; ages 50–64, 48 percent; ages 40–49, 51 percent; ages 30–39, 54 percent; and ages 20–29, 69 percent.

59. The process of choosing leaders in the Old Order church involves both nominations from the congregation and a final selection based on the candidates drawing lots and thus leaving the choice in God's hands; however, the declining age of those ordained indicates an apparent decline in the ages of candidates members are willing to nominate.

60. Factors here include life in and around town, high rates of public school attendance, and a loose Ordnung (especially since a key leadership transition in 1979). Defection has been notably high in this area for some time. In the 1995 *Elkhart-LaGrange Directory*, of the adult children of church members in the Shipshewana district, 54 percent were not Amish; in the 1980 directory, 62 percent were not Amish. So while the rate of defection in the immediate Shipshewana area dropped, it was still much higher than for the settlement as a whole.

CHAPTER 6: SWISS SETTLEMENTS OF EASTERN INDIANA

1. An exception is the highly journalistic rendering of Allen County in Längin, *Plain and Amish*. The rare cases of media representation of Swiss Amish illustrate the obscuring of Swiss Amish distinctiveness. The 1988 made-for-TV movie, *A Stoning in Fulham County*, was based on events in Adams County, Indiana, in 1979, when non-Amish teens threw a tile into a Swiss Amish buggy and killed an infant passenger. However, the television dramatization stripped any specifically Swiss context, set the story in North Carolina, and played on popular images of the Amish drawn from the Lancaster, Pennsylvania, settlement. From 1991–2002 the nationally syndicated newspaper column "The Amish Cook," by Elizabeth Coblentz (1936–2002), included not only recipes but also weekly descriptions of life around Coblentz's home near Geneva, Indiana, in the Adams County settlement. However, since the column did not identify Coblentz's settlement by name (the only address offered was that of the Ohio-based syndicator), the widely read column did not focus attention on the Swiss settlements. Among scholarly works, John A. Hostetler's *Amish Society* makes only a few references (65–66, 110, 241–42) to Swiss Amish. Stephen E. Scott, in several of his popular treatments of Old Order life and practice, describes the Swiss in some detail: *Plain Buggies* (1981); *Living Without Electricity* (1990); and *The Amish Wedding and Other Special Occasions* (1988). Interestingly, one of the first Amish-themed romance novels, Cora Gottschalk Welty's *The Masquerading of Margaret* (1908), was set among the Indiana Swiss Amish.

2. This Swiss informant, who had a remarkably wide range of other-than-Swiss contacts, believed that the Lancaster, Pennsylvania Amish exhibited an even stronger sense of being prototypically Amish, noting that when he goes to Lancaster and says he is from Indiana, Amish people there often assume he means Indiana County, Pennsylvania—not the Midwestern state of Indiana!

3. Thompson, "The Languages of the Amish of Allen County, Indiana," 72–74.

4. Enumerating Swiss settlements is not as straightforward as it might at first seem, since some settlements of Swiss background (such as Daviess County, Indiana) have evolved away from some Swiss customs and the use of the Swiss dialect. Amish historian David Luthy considers "any settlement 'Swiss' where most of the families speak Swiss at home" (Correspondence, 2 June 2004). Using that criteria, Swiss settlements are: in Indiana: Adams County (40 church districts), Allen County (17), Steuben County (2), South Whitley (1), Salem (2), and Vevay (2); in Kentucky: Mays Lick (1); in Michigan: Camden (2), Branch County/California (5), Branch County/Quincy (3), and Reading (2); in Missouri: Seymour (8); in New York: Norfolk (1), Prattsburgh (1), and Clyde (1); in Ohio: DeGraff (2); and in Pennsylvania: Linesville (2) and Emlenton/Sligo (1).

5. Ringenberg, "Development and Division in the Mennonite Community in Allen

County, Indiana," 116–18. See Habegger and Adams, *The Swiss of Adams and Wells Counties, Indiana, 1838–1862*, 44–67 (for Amish settlement from 1840–1851), and 96–131 (for Amish arrivals beginning in 1852).

6. As noted in chapter 4, the Swiss settlements have assimilated outsiders into their ranks—both those of non-Amish background and a few Pennsylvania German speakers who have married into the communities.

7. Interestingly, even the few Allen County Swiss Amish who did align with the change-minded faction in the 1860s and 1870s did so in unusual ways that did not integrate them into the large, progressive Amish Mennonite movement. See Ringenberg, "Development and Division in the Mennonite Community in Allen County," 124, on the Leo Amish Mennonite Church.

8. Fifteen Adams County Old Order men participated in Civilian Public Service, and all remained with the church throughout that experience and in the decade and a half that followed. Only one later defected, joining the Beachy Amish after about 1960. The Allen County retention rate for CPS participants was also very high. Such rates stand in contrast to the experience of Amish in the Elkhart-LaGrange and Nappanee settlements, where about one-third of CPS participants left the Old Order church during or soon after CPS.

9. For details on this group and some primary source documents, see Schrock, *The Amish Christian Church: Its History and Legacy*. This book reports quite frankly the opposition that the group engendered. During the leadership of Schwartz (1894–1936), the group was not particularly "plain" in lifestyle. After Schwartz was himself excommunicated from the group for immorality, the church reorganized in 1937 under the name Reformed Amish Christian Church and reoriented itself toward a dramatically "plain" way of life. Ten years later it moved, as a body, to Lawrence County, Tennessee; and in 1952 it relocated again, this time to Snyder County, Pennsylvania, where it affiliated with a very conservative and tiny Mennonite group. Many members returned to Tennessee in 1965, and other scattered.

10. These bishops were Joseph Schwartz (1834–1920), Joseph A. Schwartz (1867–1949), and Joe L. Schwartz (1893–1982). In addition, this leadership line featured son, brother, and uncle relationships that linked these men to the Amish Christian Church's head.

11. Promotional material is modest; one key brochure advertising the Amish connections of the town of Grabill ("Welcome to Grabill, Our Friendly Little Town") reminds visitors: "Because of their religious beliefs, Amish people prefer not be photographed. Please respect their wishes."

12. Habegger and Adams, *Swiss of Adams and Wells Counties*, iv, 68–95. The 1,000-member First Mennonite Church, located in the center of Berne, is another prominent community institution well-known for its Swiss ethnic character.

13. Amishville, which opened in 1968, was the first Amish-themed attraction in Indiana. Its simulated Amish house and farm had been owned by an Old Order family who that year moved to Seymour, Missouri, and sold their acres to three local businessmen. Literature issued by the Berne Chamber of Commerce mentions the Amish, but it tends to highlight a non-Amish Swiss ethos (see, e.g., the brochure "Berne, Indiana: A Bit of Old Switzerland"). See also "Former Cheese Factory will Become a Museum Honoring Swiss, Amish," Associated Press, 15 February 2001, which describes the efforts of the area's Swiss Heritage Society

to open a tourist attraction that clearly subordinated the Amish to a more general Swiss theme.

14. The Daviess County settlement was from the start a heterogeneous group, mixing the Allen County body with arrivals from Ohio, one family from Missouri, and a few Mennonites. The Davies settlement remained in church fellowship with the Allen County church, however. Perhaps because of the composite nature of the Daviess County group, the church there drew up a written Ordnung in 1871. This *Ordnungsbrief* suggested high ideals for new settlement; see Stoll, *Amish in Daviess County,* 20–30.

15. The Linesville settlement is known for having adopted enclosed buggies, in contrast to other Swiss communities.

16. Virtually all the South Whitley families moved from Allen County, though one came from Adams County. The original South Whitley settlers wanted to farm and were more open to innovation in dairy technology than those in Allen county were, accepting bulk milk tanks in about 1976, more than fifteen years before Allen County did.

17. The three original Salem households were among those who moved to Vevay. The Vevay group was later joined by others from Salem, some from Branch County, Michigan, and a few directly from Adams County, Indiana.

18. Some Amish also cite the use of alcohol among the Swiss in ways that violate the temperate use (or occasional teetotalism) most other Amish espouse. For a recent example of Swiss Amish alcohol use (by middle-aged, married people—not rowdy teens), see the police report of a Sunday afternoon drag race near the Adams County town of Decatur reported as an AP story in *The* [Elkhart] *Truth,* 15 April 2003, A-15.

19. There is some variation in how Swiss settlements and affiliations relate to Pennsylvania German (or "High German") churches that do not practice *streng Meidung.* Members in Allen County will "sit under the preaching" of ministers from churches that do not practice *streng Meidung,* but Allen County ministers will not preach in their churches, nor will they take communion together or ask those ministers for counsel in addressing church conflicts. In some other Swiss churches—such as those in the Steuben County settlement—the separation is sharper, and the Swiss will not sit under the preaching of the other ministers.

20. [David L. Schwartz], "Articles of Faith of the Old Order Amish Mennonite Church, Berne, Indiana."

21. The first Steering Committee secretary was from Allen County, and the first treasurer was from Adams County. (The first chair was from the Lancaster, Pa., settlement.) All three of the initial members served lengthy terms. On the Steering Committee, see Olshan, "The National Amish Steering Committee," and "Homespun Bureaucracy." For details on a variety of Amish conflicts with government, see the entire set of case studies in Kraybill, ed., *Amish and the State.* Interestingly, one Amish-owned Allen County manufacturing shop sells copies of *The Amish and the State* (and has even included the title in its wholesale catalogue) simply because the owners feel so strongly about the importance of the issues the book discusses and of Amish independence from state interference.

22. Curiously, since the break-away Amish Christian Church in Adams County had established a parochial school that operated through the early 1930s, a few Adams County Old Orders initially were cool to the idea of parochial schools, not wanting to do anything that

might link them in the public mind with the disgraced Amish Christian Church or any of its activities.

23. The other significant confrontation over high school attendance and the legitimacy of Amish parochial schools occurred in Jay County, Indiana, in 1948–50, and centered on a Gingerich family. This crisis was diffused in court but the Jay settlement soon disbanded anyway. For details, see Luthy, *The Amish in America: Settlements that Failed*, 109–10.

24. The first in Allen County (Amish School #1) was only for grades 7–8, then grade 6 was added, and then grade 5. Later grades 1–4 were added at the same time. For detail, see Farmwald, *History and Directory of Indiana Amish Parochial Schools*, 52–95.

25. Farmwald, *History and Directory*, 130–45. Years later, Indiana Amish school leaders continue to remark on Superintendent Wells's understanding and sympathetic spirit, contrasting him with other inflexible and prejudiced officials they encountered during the period. The breakthrough came in the mid-1960s when Wells proposed a state-wide plan, realizing that negotiating with each local district would prove unwieldy. As a first step, Wells approved the so- called vocational school plan for students who had completed 8th grade, which had been pioneered in Pennsylvania in 1955. Next the state granted legitimacy to the parochial schools themselves. David Schwartz drafted what became the frequently reprinted *Regulations and Guidelines for Amish Parochial Schools in Indiana*. Wells and Schwartz then collaborated on *Articles of Agreement Regarding the Indiana Amish Parochial Schools and the Department of Public Instruction*. On the Pennsylvania vocational school plan, see Hostetler and Huntington, *Amish Children*, 40–41, 67–68.

26. From the public school side of the metaphorical negotiating table, the key issue is money and the need to maintain enrollment numbers so as to keep up funding from the state capital. At times, local school administrators have tried to persuade Amish parents to send their children to public schools for just a few hours per week in order to boost official enrollments and gain more dollars from Indianapolis. See Zehr, "Allen County, Indiana School Movement," 67–68, for a description of such an attempt in Allen County.

27. At first the district charged the Amish schools a transportation fee per mile, which amounted to about $600 year total; later the service became free. In Adams County the public schools also provide bussing, but the Amish must still pay for it. Until 1999, the Amish in Allen County were bused on the same buses as the public school children—the Amish being taken to Harlan and then changing buses to go to their own schools. But in September 1999, the district began to runs two bus shifts—first picking up and delivering the Amish children, and then public school children. In the afternoon they do the same double run, taking the Amish home first and then the others.

28. For discussion of Amish school structure more generally, see Johnson-Weiner, *Train Up a Child*.

29. The newest school (opened in 2003) has only two rooms and is the smallest in the settlement; Allen County informant and *Blackboard Bulletin*, December 2005, 10–11.

30. Among some Swiss Amish, one occasionally hears categorical language otherwise unusual in Amish circles, such as "The devil's in the calculator," or similar statements assigning ultimate moral value to aspects of Ordnung prohibition.

31. See, e.g., the theory and example of Charles Tilly, "Contentious Repertoires in Great Britain, 1758–1834."

32. Ringenberg, "Development and Division in the Mennonite Community in Allen County," 125–27. Now known as the Ridgeview Amish Mennonite Church, the Lengacher church name derived from leader Clarence Lengacher. The church was in fellowship with the so-called Joshua King Amish affiliation of churches until the Lengacher/Ridgeview church accepted automobile ownership. Stark County, Ohio, "King Amish" bishop Seth Byler organized the Lengacher church in 1943; the group built a meetinghouse in 1964.

33. The explanation here is highly abbreviated. See primary sources reproduced in Gingerich, *Wer will die Lueken Verzaunen und der Wege Bessern?* and *Begebenheiten von die Alte Amischen Gemeinde von Holmes und Wayne County, Ohio und Adams County, Indiana.*

34. One small but symbolic example: At one time, women moving into a Joe L. church district from another part of the country—often because they had married an Adams County man—did not immediately need to adopt the distinctive black head covering worn by Adams County women, but could continue wearing their white coverings (white is worn by virtually all other Amish) until they wore out. The Joe L. group now requires all members, regardless of their origin, immediately to adopt its dress Ordnung, even if that means discarding almost-new clothing. Reacting in part to such changes, a small number of families from the Joe L. affiliation left in the late 1970s, and about five years later joined with the Shetler group. That sort of defection, however, only renewed and reaffirmed the differences between the groups.

35. The Pete J. Eicher church, whose members mostly live east of Geneva, left the Joe L. affiliation; the settlement's most technologically liberal group, the David N. Wengerd church, split from the Shetler group.

36. *Indiana Amish Directory: Adams County and Vicinity Amish Directory, 1992* included two maps showing the overlapping church districts of the Joe L. and Shetler affiliations. Five years later, the *Indiana Amish Directory: Adams and Jay Counties and Vicinity Amish Directory, 1997* contained no such affiliation maps, likely due to the fact that the mid-1990s witnessed a new round of schisms that were not entirely sorted out, and the mapping would undoubtedly have been quite complicated. Nevertheless, the individual district maps in the 1997 directory demonstrated the geographically overlapping distribution of districts in the settlement.

37. As recently as 1979 the building of a brick home in Allen County was mildly controversial because there were no Amish bricklayers, so the family needed to hire outsiders to do the work.

38. Verizon official quoted in "Communication Station," [Fort Wayne, Ind.] *News-Sentinel,* 25 June 2001, F-1, 5.

39. This work parallels that in north central Indiana in that it is also in modular homes, such as Decatur's All American Homes Corp. A few Amishmen also work in furniture plants, such as Smith Brothers Furniture in Berne. This limited factory work began in the 1950s. A few Allen County men work in a Grabill factory that makes countertops.

40. In 1996 some ninety-eight frustrated Allen County Old Orders had registered to vote in local elections. See *Mennonite Weekly Review,* 29 February 1996, 9.

41. "Ind. Weighs Amish Zoning District," [Lancaster, Pa.] *Intelligencer Journal,* 18 February 1995, B-14.

42. The Steuben settlement Ordnung is generally conservative. Homes are sparsely furnished, with no use of area rugs, stuffed furniture, curtains, or indoor plumbing. Families

use large dry sinks for washing (carrying water indoors), kerosene cook stoves, and wood-stoves for heating. Those involved in dairying milk by hand and transport milk in cans (rendering it grade B quality). Houses may be painted white, but all other outbuildings are to be gray.

43. In 2000 only one family was involved entirely in agriculture, raising about 100 acres of vegetables. Some households retain 10–20 cows. There were six pallet shops, six saw mills, and three cabinet shops.

CHAPTER 7: TRANSPLANTS FROM LANCASTER, PENNSYLVANIA

1. For an analysis and interpretation of the settlement, see Kraybill, *Riddle of Amish Culture*. The settlement includes districts in Lancaster and adjacent Chester and York counties. On tourism and the Lancaster Amish in the popular mind of media and tourism, see Weaver-Zercher, *Amish in the American Imagination*. The geographic implications of the tourist region are purposefully loose since the tourist industry is centered in Lancaster County but encompasses many tourist destinations outside the county, from Gettysburg, to Hershey, to Chad's Ford. In another sense, however, the designation is narrow and betrays the way in which the Lancaster Amish have become the focus of tourism over time, since from a historical-cultural standpoint, Pennsylvania Dutch Country should also include at least a dozen other counties north and northwest of Philadelphia.

2. On Lancaster's peculiar polity, see Kraybill, *Riddle of Amish Culture*, 94; on the schisms, 25–26.

3. See *Church Directory of the Lancaster County Amish* (2002), and earlier editions (1996, 1988, 1980, 1973, and 1965; titles vary). The 1988 edition was titled *Amish Directory of the Lancaster County Family*.

4. The Lancaster settlement birthed two daughter settlements in 1940 (St. Mary's County, Md.) and 1941 (Lebanon County, Pa.), and then none until 1960, when a few families moved to Gettysburg, Pa. (the settlement there dissolved in 1995). Lancaster Amish families launched a spate of small settlements between 1967 and 1978—all located within Pennsylvania, mostly in the northern and central parts of the state. Some of those communities, in turn, often begun on marginal land, quickly maximized their capacity and spun off new settlements as early as 1981 (Romulus, N.Y.), but mostly in the 1990s (in Virginia, Missouri, and Wisconsin). No Lancaster County–based Amish left the old settlement to begin new out-of-state settlements until 1989 (Hopkinsville, Ky.) and 1991 (Parke County, Ind.), followed by Wayne County, Indiana (1994). Since 1940—and including all daughter settlements of daughter settlements—the network of Lancaster diaspora Amish by 2002 counted nearly thirty settlements. Nevertheless, despite the out-migration these communities represent, the total number of migrants has remained small relative to the Lancaster settlement's total population and has never made a dent in the continuing demographic growth of the old settlement itself. For a listing of settlement beginnings, see the 2002 *Church Directory of the Lancaster County Amish* 1:xliii–xlv; Kraybill, *Riddle of Amish Culture*, 18, graphs the number of families migrating out of the Lancaster settlement, 1970–2000.

5. Not all the Wayne County, Indiana, families came directly from Lancaster County itself. Some came from Lancaster "sister settlements" in other parts of Pennsylvania—Centre

County, Brush Valley, and Gettysburg—but all were part of the larger Lancaster network. (The Gettysburg settlement disbanded in 1995, and several households moved to Wayne County rather than return to Lancaster County.) The vast majority of Parke County, Indiana, Amish residents came directly from Lancaster County, but a few, curiously, came from Mifflin County, Pennsylvania, a very old settlement, but not one tied directly to Lancaster. However, the Mifflin families immediately adopted the Lancaster Ordnung upon arrival in Parke County.

6. On teen behavior in larger settlements, see Stevick, *Growing Up Amish.*

7. The formal limit on the number of milking stanchions was later lifted, but that move has not sparked a flurry of large dairies.

8. Local farmers often were taken aback by the Amish practice of plowing and planting right up to the edge of a field or the road, since the more common Indiana convention had been to allow a fallow strip of several yards as a border around all fields. This sort of minor but noticeable difference in farming practices were the sort of things that longtime residents mentioned when asked how the Amish have changed area agriculture.

9. On the situation in Wayne County, see AP wire story, "Wayne County Considering Fee for Amish Vehicles," 4 October 2002. Since 1954 Indiana has permitted counties the option of licensing buggies; some counties have adopted the option, but others have not. No other state requires or allows buggies to be licensed. (Since 2003, townships in Illinois have the option of charging a $50 per driver buggy fee, but not licensing per se.) The implications of Indiana's county-option license law varies, with some counties requiring an annual fee and others a one-time registration charge; some counties insist that buggies bear license plates, while a few require only a license document to be kept in the buggy. The diversity of requirements is particularly noticeable in the Nappanee, Indiana, settlement, which spans four counties, not all of which have the same regulations. Some buggies in the Nappanee settlement have license plates; others do not.

10. Chamber of Commerce and tourist bureau materials in both counties mention the Amish but do not promote Amish-theme tourism. For its part, Parke County has long promoted tourism around its many covered bridges—a strategy it has continued.

11. The vast majority of Wayne and Parke counties Amish farms are dairy operations, though many specialize in produce alongside dairy. In 2002 Parke County's Amish farms also included one chicken farm, one hog farm, and one that dealt in produce only.

12. The Parke County Amish forbid tobacco growing and use; the Wayne County churches, while discouraging tobacco use, have not made it a principle of Ordnung. Nevertheless, the Wayne County Amish do not grow tobacco, since Wayne County does not have a quota base for tobacco price support. Tobacco was grown in Wayne County at one time and still is in the Indiana counties immediately to the south, but it cannot be profitably marketed from Wayne County.

13. For details on this situation, see Kraybill and Nolt, *Amish Enterprise.*

14. *Blackboard Bulletin,* December 2005, 11.

15. Establishing a school, for example, required subdividing the property on which the school was to be built, not simply leasing the land to the school as had been the Lancaster pattern. School attendance regulations differ in Indiana too, which in a round-about way has made some details of record keeping and school administration in Indiana different from

Pennsylvania practice. For example, the Lancaster pattern is to have five-member school boards that each oversee three one-room schools. In Wayne County, the Amish have adopted the prevailing Indiana Amish pattern of having three-person school boards each oversee a single school. The Parke County Amish have retained the Lancaster pattern.

16. For example, among the Lancaster Amish, the deacon reads the morning scripture text aloud at the appropriate time in the worship service. Among most other Amish in the Midwest, one of the ministers reads the text.

17. See, e.g., 1 Timothy 3:5. This restriction is not iron-clad, and there are times when bishops have been chosen who have teenage children who are not yet in the church but who offer a consistent witness of obedience.

18. See discussion of declining age of ordination in the Elkhart-LaGrange settlement in chapter 5.

19. Traditionally, in the Lancaster settlement, ordained men were not to move away from the church district in which they were ordained; to do so was seen as shirking one's divine mandate to serve the district for which one had been chosen. Nevertheless, the migrants leaving Lancaster to establish daughter settlements elsewhere have included a few ministers and deacons—though not bishops, who are still expected to give a lifetime of service to the district in which they were ordained. The presence of migrating ministers and deacons meant that the Parke and Wayne settlements, almost from the beginning, could conduct a regular regimen of bi-weekly Sunday morning worship services. Four ministers and three deacons moved to Parke County during that settlement's first five years, and three ministers and one deacon were among the early settlers in Wayne County. These men often were assisted by visiting ministers, deacons, or bishops from Lancaster (or occasionally another settlement), who made trips to Indiana to "help the churches" there. A bishop's presence was essential for communion, baptisms, or weddings. The first ordinations in the Indiana settlements were in Parke County, where a layman was ordained minister in 1993, and two more ministers were ordained in 1996.

20. For example, in 2002 the Lancaster settlement was larger (143 districts in 2002) than the Elkhart-LaGrange, Indiana settlement (114 districts in 2002), but had fewer bishops (79 vs. 106).

21. See Kraybill, *Riddle of Amish Culture*, 98–101 for a description. While the Lancaster Ordnung is not entirely uniform in all its particulars across the entire settlement, the degree of uniformity, and the narrow range of difference across its more than 150 districts (in 2006) is striking, especially when compared with other large Old Order Amish settlements in Ohio and Indiana that do not attempt such settlement-wide consensus.

22. Exceptional settlements in the Lancaster diaspora—such as that near Romulus, New York—do not attend the Lancaster *Dienerversammlungen*. In the case of the Romulus, the districts there are in fellowship with more conservative settlements in western Pennsylvania, who object to what they perceive to be Lancaster's technological permissiveness (though they are not offended by the Romulus community itself). So the Romulus church abstains from the Lancaster bishop conference so as not to offend the other groups with which it is in fellowship or jeopardize its relationship with them. Nevertheless, the Romulus group maintains basically the same Ordnung as the Lancaster settlement, or one slightly less permissive on technological innovation. This sort of situation has not developed among the

Lancaster-linked settlements in Indiana, and observers do not foresee it moving that direction.

23. One anomaly was that a few of the Parke County settlement's early residents hailed from central Pennsylvania's "Big Valley" (Mifflin and adjacent counties), though they moved to Parke with the express understanding that they would adopt the Lancaster Ordnung, including initially converting their black buggies to gray.

24. See n. 5 above for more detail on settlement members' geographic origins.

25. See Kraybill, *Riddle of Amish Culture*, 101–3, on these plans. One Parke County resident reported some discomfort with his settlement's participation in the Lancaster-based Church Aid Plan that shares medical costs, since he believes much of the charity alms coming from Lancaster coffers stem from profits earned from tobacco farming. Since the Parke settlement has taken a stand against tobacco, he wonders if it is consistent for him and others to accept as charity, money earned in such pursuits. His concern—while sincere—has not stopped the Parke Amish churches from participating in this practice of mutual aid with other Lancaster-linked Amish.

26. Farmwald, *History and Directory of Indiana Amish Parochial Schools*, 390, 400.

CHAPTER 8: THE PAOLI-SALEM COMMUNITIES

1. Kraybill, "Plotting Social Change across Four Affiliations," see esp. n. 24 on "high-low" language. For other examples of this one-dimensional model, see also Driedger, "The Anabaptist Identification Ladder"; and Baehr, "Secularization among the Mennonites of Elkhart County, Indiana." *The Mennonite Encyclopedia* also uses a linear organization with its spectrum chart of Amish and Mennonite groups of Swiss origin; see "Conservative Mennonites (Swiss-High German, Pennsylvania)," *Mennonite Encyclopedia*, 5:200. One scholar has taken exception to linear models: Olshan, "Affinities and Antipathies: The Old Order Amish in New York State," asserts, "An analysis of each community's distinctive combination of beliefs and practices will not yield a neat ranking of communities on a continuum from most conservative to most liberal" (p. 1). Since this paper was not published, its insight on this point has not shaped other scholarship.

2. In some cases, such as an analysis of a single settlement, it may be possible to arrange Amish practice along such a continuum, if one could assume that certain factors are not variable, such as ethnicity or migration history, and the local context is the same. When these and other elements move into play, however, one-dimensional continua are not complex enough to be useful tools.

3. Since 1996 there has been a very small settlement on the north central edge of Washington County, known as the Vallonia settlement (Vallonia being the mailing address, even though the town of Vallonia is actually in Jackson County, to the north). This new, small settlement is composed of families originally from the Elkhart-LaGrange settlement. Although the Vallonia group is relatively close to the four settlements discussed in this chapter, it is not geographically proximate in the same way, and since interaction between its members and those of the four described here is much less frequent, we have not included the Vallonia settlement. It should be noted, however, that if one were to include them, they would add another, more complex layer to the comparison.

4. Non-Amish Orange County locals sometimes use other names for these two settlements nestled next to Paoli. The group we are calling the Paoli settlement (following the name suggested in Luthy, "Amish Settlements Across America: 2003," is locally sometimes known as the "Bromer group" because of its proximity to the crossroads community of Bromer, Indiana. Locals sometimes tag the Swartzentruber Amish as the "Orleans group" because of its proximity to the village of Orleans.

5. See Bodnar, *Our Towns*, 1–46, for a description of Paoli on the eve of Amish arrival, and underscoring the area's rather isolated character in the mid-twentieth century.

6. Over time, the church took on more Amish-style worship patterns too. For example, virtually all Amish churches sing *Ausbund* hymn 130, the so-called Loblied, as the second hymn at each worship service. Initially, the Salem church did not sing the "Loblied" with this sort of regularity, but in the early 1980s they began to do so, following the pattern of other Amish churches. After that they also began to use as the basis for sermons the prescribed New Testament lectionary texts that other Midwestern Amish use. Especially after a key early leader who was of Mennonite background left the Salem community in the mid-1980s, the church took on more decidedly Amish ritual patterns and practices, while underscoring its New Order sensibilities.

7. In 1974 the Salem group began meeting for worship in their schoolhouse. In part the move was not controversial because one of the group's early leaders was of Mennonite background and was accustomed to worshiping in a meetinghouse. In addition, the move was understood as a by-product of municipal regulation. When a woman who was a member of the church died in 1974, the group inquired about beginning a cemetery, only to be told that rural cemeteries could be started only with proof that the burial ground had a board of trustees with a $35,000 maintenance endowment. The only exception was for new cemeteries adjacent to church buildings. Without the funds to establish the required endowment, the Salem church began a burial ground next to their school house and, wanting to be "good to our word," started meeting for worship in the schoolhouse so it would be a church building. After the school became too small for the growing group's Sunday morning use, they met for worship in homes for one year (1978–1979) while they built a new, larger meetinghouse next to the school. Since 1979 they have maintained both a school building and a church building on the same property. In 1980 the person ordained as the settlement's new bishop was a man who had grown up in the Oakland, Maryland, Amish settlement—an old (founded 1850) but unusual Old Order Amish settlement whose members also meet for worship in a simple church building. Thus, Salem's bishop is also accustomed to meetinghouses, though he was not the one who instigated the practice.

8. The best narrative of New Order Amish origins is Kline and Beachy, "History and Dynamics of the New Order Amish of Holmes County, Ohio."

9. See, e.g., the New Order theological statement, *The Truth in Word and Work*.

10. Salem's settlers were part of the "Joe L." affiliation. The symbolic issue in Salem was the use of large motorized fans for ventilating large turkey houses. Without such fans, operations are necessarily much smaller; with the fans, farmers can have larger houses and more birds. The use or non-use of fans was really about the size and scale of commercial farming, even though the argument itself centered on the permissibility of a particular piece of machinery.

11. Luthy, " Origin and Growth of the Swartzentruber Amish."

12. As the settlement has grown it, has spilled into Lawrence County to the north with some families living there.

13. About half the New Order churches in North America permit tractor farming; the Salem church is among those that do not.

14. Arguably, the Swiss-style open buggies symbolize the most traditional approach to transportation, since the enclosed style now used in Indiana's other settlements is an early-twentieth-century innovation. All buggies were unenclosed until then, at which point the non-Swiss began to permit enclosures—see Scott, *Plain Buggies*, 60, 72.

15. Bed-courtship, popularly known as "bundling," involves the nighttime visiting of dating couples in the young woman's bedroom. Presumably both individuals remain fully clothed, but the popular inference—and anecdotally acknowledged fact—of premarital sex has given the custom a bad reputation among many Amish, including New Orders and the Paoli group. For highly tradition-guided people, such as the Swartzentrubers, bundling is simply the way young people have always gotten to know one another, and self-critical reflection on the practice is not entertained. For general comment on bundling, see Hostetler, *Amish Society*, 148. For a sharp critique of bundling that has the endorsement of New Order leaders, see Stutzman, *A Call to Repentance*. It should be noted that bundling does not necessarily imply unrestrained sexual relations. For example, the colonial American Puritans, whose young people engaged in bundling as a matter of course, had dramatically lower rates of premarital pregnancy than did colonial "backcountry" settlers who did *not* practice bundling. See Fischer, *Albion's Seed*, 79–80, 681–82.

16. The Kenton, Ohio settlement, which is one of the few in fellowship with the Paoli group, do permit married men to work away from home, though in a narrow range of actual options. A few Paoli households, unable to support themselves in Orange County, have relocated to Kenton.

17. This route existed for many years and then was cut, only to be reinstated in 2001 and then discontinued in June 2005. Because the route was established for the convenience of students going to Indiana University in Bloomington, the schedule was inconvenient for Amish riders wanting to go to Louisville, yet they were deeply grateful for the access under any circumstances. Special concessions on the part of the bus company include the Amish privilege of "flagging" a ride along Rt. 56 and not having to go to the Paoli terminal itself, and the ability to pay for the trip after arriving at the destination terminal rather than obtaining a prepaid ticket.

18. Kenton, Ohio; Chesterhill, Ohio; the Becks Mills districts in Holmes County, Ohio; Gladwin, Michigan (not the Gladwin-Swartzentruber group); and perhaps the Stanwood, Blanchard, and Coral, Michigan churches.

19. Luthy, "Replacing the *Ausbund*."

20. Sunday school is very rare among the Amish outside of New Order circles. Exceptional cases of Old Order districts with Sunday school include a couple districts in the Elkhart-LaGrange settlement, the non-Swiss Vevay settlement, and a handful of other places across North America.

21. Luthy, "A History of *The Budget*."

22. Luthy, "A History of Raber's Bookstore."

23. Two early directories appeared in the 1940s: Mennonite minister Herbert N. Troyer

compiled and published *Ohio Amish Directory* and Old Order Amishman Levi D. Christner of Topeka, Indiana compiled and published *Old Order Amish Church Districts of Indiana*. Both of these directories included maps identifying all Amish residents of their respective states. The Troyer directory included the three Swartzentruber districts that existed at that time; since then the Swartzentrubers have declined to be included in directories. A new era of settlement-specific Amish directory publication began in 1954, when Ohio Amishman Ervin Gingerich issued *Ohio Amish Directory: Holmes, Tuscarawas, Coshocton, and Wayne Counties*, which has been the basis for periodic revisions ever since. Other large settlement directories followed: Lancaster, Pennsylvania, in 1965 and Elkhart-LaGrange, Indiana, in 1970. After 1970 many smaller settlements followed suit, sometimes combining several smaller settlements with a larger one in a single volume (e.g., Nappanee-Kokomo-Milroy, Indiana). The *New Order Amish Directory, 1999* is unusual in being an affiliation-based directory. Its publisher, Abana Books, has made a business of producing Amish directories.

CHAPTER 9: DIVERSE AMISH WORLDS

1. Kraybill and Nolt, *Amish Enterprise*, discusses the role of rationality—and cultural limits placed on it—among Amish entrepreneurs.

2. For more discussion (though within a Pennsylvania context), see Umble, *Holding the Line*.

3. For extended discussion, see A. Frances Z. Wenger, "The Phenomenon of Care in a High Context Culture."

4. Some Amish gravitate toward chiropractic because of its practitioners' claims to being holistic and because treatment through manipulation of the body makes sense to many Amish; such treatment is direct and physical, not indirect or secondary. A similar reactive, direct-application understanding of medicine is also at the heart of conservative Amish disinterest in preventive medicine. Members of the Swartzentruber affiliation and the Paoli settlement, for example, do not routinely accept immunization, even though they would readily agree to have a broken bone set or a wound tended. Levi Miller, in "The Role of the *Braucher*-Chiropractor in an Amish Community," describes how interest in folk medicine is today often linked to interest in alternative care, such as chiropractic. Some Amish are also drawn to alternative medicine such as reflexology and iridology. See also John A. Hostetler, "Folk Medicine and Sympathy Healing Among the Amish." Other philosophical issues surrounding health care, life, and death have led to Amish conflict with traditional medical providers, as evidenced in Huntington, "Health Care." At the same time, many Amish patronize family physicians in cooperative and mutually respectful ways.

5. See the example of Rest Haven or Pleasant Haven in chapter 5. The "People's Helpers" movement is a loose network of Amish interested in counseling at a lay level and unconnected in a formal way to professional centers (though some sympathetic ties exist in certain communities). Those interested in People's Helpers meet annually, usually in an Amish community in Michigan. Some northern Indiana Old Orders are supportive of People's Helpers, and the two group homes it supports—one for men and one for women—both located in Michigan settlements. See n. 15, below.

6. For one theoretical perspective, see Olshan, "Homespun Bureaucracy," 199–213.

7. Of course, the very act of church discipline remains, in an important sense, a communal one, since the church still decides and approves the charge.

8. For a presentation of typical Old Order understandings, see Oyer, "Is There an Amish Theology?" 278–302. See also the New Order theological statement, *The Truth in Word and Work*.

9. A different two-dimensional model that measures social control and social separation to compare the "social texture" of Old Order groups is Kraybill and Bowman, *On the Backroad to Heaven*, 213–26.

10. E.g., Kraybill, "Plotting Social Change across Four Affiliations," 53–74; Kraybill and Hostetler, *Anabaptist World USA*, 55–64; and "Conservative Mennonites (Swiss-High German, Pennsylvania)," *Mennonite Encyclopedia* 5:200.

11. For example, a key leader in the Paoli settlement explains his group's practices with reference to historical developments, referring at times to academic works of history such as Paton Yoder's *Tradition and Transition* to suggest patterns of declension and renewal and faithfulness that his group understands.

12. See the various publications—textbook curriculum, fiction, and periodicals—issued by Pathway Publishers, an Old Order publisher based in Aylmer, Ontario, and LaGrange, Indiana. See also some of the modest institutions cited in chapter 5.

13. While the presentation here suggests that this fourth worldview is somewhat marginal to the Old Order world, it is clear that adherents see themselves as standing in the center of Amish life, equally critical of worldly society on one hand, and of unreflective tradition and communalism on the other.

14. The New Order Amish have produced a range of remarkably articulate booklets and pamphlets outlining their beliefs. These have been published under the Amish Brotherhood Publications imprint.

15. This ability to distinguish roles is perhaps most pronounced at Harmony Haven Home, an Evart, Michigan, Old Order Amish center with some Indiana Amish support. Harmony Haven offers residential counseling "for emotionally, spiritually, and mentally troubled" Amish men and boys of any affiliation. The center opened in 1997 (see *Michigan Amish Directory 2002*, 126; see also other literature in authors' files).

16. Allen County is an exception in this regard. The particular history of school conflicts and church support for private schools here has meant that almost all Amish students attend Amish schools. In Lancaster, Pennsylvania, a similar situation prevails, with all Amish children attending private schools despite the long history of that community and generations of Amish attending public schools through the 1950s. The complete preference for private schools there no doubt stems from the Lancaster practice of attempting settlement-wide consistency in Ordnung—a pattern otherwise uncommon in the Amish world.

17. Remarkably, Amish-theme tourism seems to have emerged, to some degree, even in settlements that are apparently remote from major visitor destinations. An Amish-owned retail outlet—The Swiss Trading Company—caters to tourists in the Milroy settlement; bus tours visit Amish back roads in Daviess County, and even small Swartzentruber basket and bucket shops and general stores receive tourists in rural Orange County, in part due to very modest Swartzentruber roadside advertising signs.

CHAPTER 10: AMISH COMMUNITY AS CONVERSATION

1. John A. Hostetler, in his classic text, *Amish Society,* 3–24, describes several social science models of community that scholars have used.

2. This practical definition appears in the introduction to Luthy, "Amish Settlements Across America," 17.

3. One example of this theory at work is Sabean's *Power in the Blood,* 27–30. The well-known theory of nationalism presented in Anderson's *Imagined Communities,* employs this concept to some degree as well.

4. The conversation model operates on both literal and metaphorical levels. In some cases, the Amish maintain actual, verbal discussions of certain topics. In other cases, "conversation" describes the shared values and choices that comprise a tradition that can be understood as a metaphorical conversation over time. It is important to note that our use of conversation does not imply that verbal discourse is at the heart of Old Order tradition. Indeed, the conversation model is compatible with key observations on the importance of silence in Amish culture as presented in John A. Hostetler, *Amish Society,* 387–90, and "Silence and Survival Strategies among the New and Old Order Amish," 81–91.

5. The best translation of the Dordrecht statement is Irvin B. Horst, *Mennonite Confession of Faith, Adopted April 21st, 1632 at Dordrecht, the Netherlands.* The text is most widely available in Leith, ed., *Creeds of the Churches,* 292–308.

6. Article eighteen presents a fairly straightforward discussion of "The Resurrection of the Dead and the Last Judgment." The Dordrecht Confession contains no article on the Bible as such, although the document is filled with biblical quotations and assumes a sort of authority for the Bible. A similar sort of atmosphere prevails in Amish settings today, where there is an assumed or implied biblical authority, but little or no theoretical explanation or defense of the Bible's authority.

7. E.g., Boyer, *When Time Shall Be No More.* The very rare Amish exceptions prove the rule; see, e.g., Hartzler-Miller, "'Der Weiss' Jonas Stutzmann: Amish Pioneer and Mystic," 4–12.

8. See the remarkable commentary on history, theology, and contemporary Amish life woven into the Amish-authored Blank, *The Amazing Story of the Ausbund;* and *Creation to Resurrection.*

9. Among the many examples, see the text and description in "Amish Country: Northern Indiana. 2005 Vacation Planner" (Elkhart County Convention and Visitors Bureau, 2004).

10. On one of the limits of that discussion, see Zook, "Slow-Moving Vehicles," 145–60.

11. See Ball, "First Amendment Issues," and "Building a Landmark Case: *Wisconsin v. Yoder*"; and Peters, *The Yoder Case.* One may discern a limit to this conversation in the context of the post-2001 "war on terrorism" in which the U.S. Department of Homeland Security is less inclined to allow Old Order Amish who refuse to pose for photographs to cross the U.S. border to and from Canada without a photo ID. See "Amish who Refused Immigration Photos Sue," Associated Press, 3 April 2004.

12. The State School Committee is composed of representatives from most of the Amish

settlements in Indiana; the larger settlements also have designated local contacts who communicate with individual school boards.

13. See *Articles of Agreement Regarding the Indiana Amish Parochial Schools and the Department of Public Instruction* and *Regulations and Guidelines for Amish Parochial Schools in Indiana.*

14. Occasionally, support for schools has led to direct inter-settlement connection via teachers from one settlement who are hired by schools in another. Although a rare occurrence, such inter-settlement hiring has happened—e.g., the Allen County settlement's first Amish teacher was Edwin Kuhns from the Nappanee settlement—and is testimony to the power of parochial education in contemporary Amish life. Few other endeavors would engender inter-ethnic, inter-settlement interaction of this sort.

15. Olshan, "National Amish Steering Committee," 67–85, and "Homespun Bureaucracy," 199–213. For the first National Steering Committee chairman's account of the group's origins, see Kinsinger and Kinsinger, *A Little History of Our Parochial Schools*, 221–66.

16. The chairman, Andrew S. Kinsinger (1920–1995), from the weighty Lancaster, Pennsylvania, settlement, insisted on the name Steering Committee. As a Lancaster resident, Kinsinger also may have been somewhat more sensitive not to use Amish Central Committee because of the similarly named Mennonite Central Committee that is headquartered in nearby Akron, Pennsylvania and with whom the Lancaster Amish had a closer relationship than did their Midwestern counterparts. Kinsinger served as Steering Committee chair until 1989.

17. There are fourteen state directors, one each for Pennsylvania, Ohio, Michigan, Indiana, Wisconsin, Iowa, Missouri, Illinois, Maryland, Delaware, New York, and Minnesota, plus one representative for Kentucky and Tennessee (combined) and one for Kansas and Oklahoma (combined). For an example of a state director's communication with his constituents, see "From the Steering Committee," *Die Blatt*, 4 January 1990, [10]. (*Die Blatt* is a northern Indiana Amish newsletter.)

18. The same groups that avoid direct participation in the State School Committee also avoid formal ties to the National Steering Committee, though the committee continues to consider their concerns. If an issue arises in a community that does not publicly participate—such as the Steuben County settlement—a Steering Committee representative from another settlement may pay an informal visit to gather information and offer counsel. The Steering Committee also has been involved in discussions with various states regarding conflicts such as the non-use of SMV signs on buggies, which involve the Swartzentruber Amish.

References

Allen, Rebecca R. "My Birth, My Way: Reproductive Agency among Three Generations of Amish Women in Elkhart-LaGrange and Nappanee Settlements." Unpublished paper, Mennonite Historical Library, Goshen, Ind., 2004.

Anderson, Benedict. *Imagined Communities: Reflections on the Origin and Spread of Nationalism.* London: Verso, 1991.

Articles of Agreement Regarding the Indiana Amish Parochial Schools and the Department of Public Instruction. Gordonville, Pa.: Gordonville Print Shop, [reprint] 1984.

Ausbund: das ist, Etliche schöne Christliche Lieder. Lancaster, Pa.: Verlag von den Amischen Gemeinden in Lancaster County, Pa., 2003. First known edition was 1564.

Baehr, Karl. "Secularization among the Mennonites of Elkhart County, Indiana." *Mennonite Quarterly Review* 16 (July 1942): 131–60.

Ball, William B. "Building a Landmark Case: *Wisconsin v. Yoder.*" In *Compulsory Education and the Amish: The Right Not to be Modern,* ed. Albert N. Keim, 114–23. Boston: Beacon Press, 1975.

———. "First Amendment Issues." In *The Amish and the State,* 2nd ed., ed. Donald B. Kraybill, 253–64. Baltimore: Johns Hopkins University Press, 2003.

Beck, Ervin. *MennoFolk: Mennonite and Amish Folk Traditions.* Scottdale, Pa.: Herald Press, 2004.

Begebenheiten von die Alte Amischen Gemeinde von Holmes und Wayne County, Ohio und Adams County, Indiana, von 1938 bis zu 1958. Gordonville, Pa.: Gordonville Print Shop, 1968.

[Beiler, Joseph F.] "Ordnung." *Mennonite Quarterly Review* 56 (October 1982): 382–84.

Blackboard Bulletin. Aylmer, Ont.: Pathway Publishers, 1957-.

Blank, Benuel S. *The Amazing Story of the Ausbund.* Narvon, Pa.: B. S. Blank, 2001.

———. *Creation to Resurrection: A History of Bible Times.* Narvon, Pa.: B. S. Blank, 2005.

Die Blatt. Shipshewana, Ind.: s.n., 1977-.

Bodnar, John E. *Our Towns: Remembering Community in Indiana.* Indianapolis: Indiana Historical Society, 2001.

Bontrager, Eli J. *My Life Story.* [Goshen, Ind.: Manasseh E. Bontreger], 1982.

Borkholder, Owen E., comp. *A History of the Borkholder School District No. 1, German Township, Marshall County, Indiana, 1857–2000.* Nappanee, Ind.: Owen E. Borkholder, 2000.

Borntreger, John E. *Geschichte der Ersten Ansiedelung der Amischen Mennoniten.* Elkhart, Ind.: Mennonite Publishing Co., 1917. English: *A History of the First Settlers of the Amish . . .* Translated by Elizabeth Gingerich. Topeka, Ind.: Dan. A. Hochstetler, 1988.

Boyer, Paul S. *When Time Shall Be No More: Prophecy Belief in Modern American Culture.* Cambridge, Mass.: Harvard University Press, 1992.

Braght, Thieleman J. van. *Der blutige Schauplatz, oder, Märtyrer-Spiegel der Taufgesinnten, oder, Wehrlosen Christen. . . .* Aylmer, Ont.: Pathway Publishers, 1990. First edition, the Netherlands in 1660. English: *The Bloody Theater, or, Martyrs Mirror of the Defenseless Christians. . . .* Scottdale, Pa.: Herald Press, [reprint] 1998.

Buffington, Albert F., ed. *Ebbes fer Alle-Ebber Ebbes fer Dich: Something for Everyone- Something for You.* Breinigsville, Pa.: Pennsylvania German Society, 1980.

Bushman, Richard L. *The Refinement of America: Persons, Houses, Cities.* New York: Alfred A. Knopf, 1992.

Cayton, Andrew R. L. *Frontier Indiana.* Bloomington: Indiana University Press, 1996.

Cong, Dachang. "Amish Factionalism and Technological Change: A Case Study of Kerosene Refrigerators and Conservatism." *Ethnology* 31 (July 1992): 205–18.

Conzen, Kathleen Neils, David A. Gerber, Ewa Morawska, George E. Pozzetta, and Rudolph J. Vecoli. "The Invention of Ethnicity: A Perspective from the U.S.A." *Journal of American Ethnic History* 12 (Fall 1992): 3–63.

The Devil's Playground/Stick Figure Productions. [New York]: Wellspring Media, Inc., 2002.

The Diary. Gordonville, Pa.: Donald V. Carpenter, Jr., 1969–.

Driedger, Leo. "The Anabaptist Identification Ladder: Plain-Urbane Continuity in Diversity." *Mennonite Quarterly Review* 51 (October 1977): 278–91.

Edmunds, David R. *The Potawatomis, Keepers of the Fire.* Norman: University of Oklahoma Press, 1978.

Enninger, Werner. "Amish By-Names." *Names* 33 (1985): 243–58.

———., ed. *Internal and External Perspectives on Amish and Mennonite Life.* Essen, Ger.: Unipress, 1984.

Farmwald, Delbert. *History and Directory of Indiana Amish Parochial Schools, 2004.* Topeka, Ind.: Study Time Publishers, 2004.

Fischer, David Hackett. *Albion's Seed: Four British Folkways in America.* New York: Oxford University Press, 1989.

Foster, Charles I. *An Errand of Mercy: The Evangelical United Front, 1790–1837.* Chapel Hill: University of North Carolina Press, 1960.

"Geschichten und Begebenheiten in der Nord East Barrens." Five-page typescript, Heritage Historical Library, Aylmer, Ont.

Gilbert, Glenn G., ed. *The German Language in America: A Symposium.* Austin: University of Texas Press, 1971.

Gingerich, Eli E. *Wer will die Lueken Verzaunen und der Wege Bessern? Or Who Will Repair the Breach and Stand in the Gap?* S.l.: Die Committee von 1968, 1978.

Gleason, Philip. "Identifying Identity: A Semantic History." *Journal of American History* 69 (March 1983): 910–31.

Goshen News. Goshen, Ind.: Goshen News, 1837-.

Graber, Harvey. "Spiritual Awakening in the Old Order Amish Church." Unpublished paper. Mennonite Historical Library, Goshen, Ind., 1956.

Gratz, Delbert L. *Bernese Anabaptists and Their American Descendants.* Goshen, Ind.: Mennonite Historical Society, 1953.

Greksa, Lawrence P., and Jill E. Korbin. "Key Decisions in the Lives of the Old Order Amish: Joining the Church and Migrating to Another Settlement." *Mennonite Quarterly Review* 76 (October 2002): 373–98.

Griffin, Clifford S. *Their Brothers' Keeper: Moral Stewardship in the United States, 1800–1865*. New Brunswick, N.J.: Rutgers University Press, 1960.

Habegger, David L., and Karen C. Adams. *The Swiss of Adams and Wells Counties, Indiana 1838–1862*. Fort Wayne, Ind.: D. L. Habegger, 2002.

Hall, Edward T. *Beyond Culture*. Garden City, N.Y.: Anchor Press, 1976.

Hall, John R., and Mary Jo Neitz. *Culture: Sociological Perspectives*. Englewood Cliffs, N.J.: Prentice Hall, 1993.

Hand, Wayland W., ed. *American Folk Medicine: A Symposium*. Berkeley: University of California Press, 1976.

Hartzler-Miller, Gregory. "'Der Weiss' Jonas Stutzmann: Amish Pioneer and Mystic." *Mennonite Historical Bulletin* 58 (October 1997): 4–12.

Hershberger, Ervin, and Daniel E. Hochstetler, eds. *History and Memories of Hillcrest Home, 1953–1978*. [Harrison, Ark.: Daniel Nisley, 1978?].

Hochstetler, Daniel E. "Where was the First Amish Mennonite Worship Service in Clinton Township Held?" *Michiana Anabaptist Historians News and Notes*, Spring 2001, 3–4.

Horst, Irvin B., ed. and trans. *Mennonite Confession of Faith, Adopted April 21st, 1632 at Dordrecht, the Netherlands*. . . . Lancaster, Pa.: Lancaster Mennonite Historical Society, 1988. Adopted by a gathering of Dutch Anabaptists in 1632.

Hostetler, Beulah Stauffer. "The Formation of the Old Orders." *Mennonite Quarterly Review* 66 (January 1992): 5–25.

Hostetler, John A. *Amish Society*, 4th ed. Baltimore: Johns Hopkins University Press, 1993.

———. "Folk Medicine and Sympathy Healing Among the Amish." In *American Folk Medicine: A Symposium*, ed. Wayland W. Hand, 249–58. Berkeley: University of California Press, 1976.

———. "Silence and Survival Strategies among the New and Old Order Amish." In *Internal and External Perspectives on Amish and Mennonite Life*, ed. Werner Enninger, 81–91. Essen, Ger.: Unipress, 1984.

Hostetler, John A., and Gertrude Enders Huntington. *Amish Children: Education in the Family, School, and Community*, 2nd ed. Fort Worth: Harcourt, Brace, Jovanovich, 1992.

Humpa, Gregory J. "Retention and Loss of Bernese Alemannic Traits in an Indiana Amish Dialect: A Comparative-Historical Study." Ph.D. dissertation, Purdue University, 1996.

Hunter, James Davidson, and Stephen C. Ainlay, eds. *Making Sense of Modern Times: Peter L. Berger and the Vision of Interpretive Sociology*. New York: Routledge, 1986.

Huntington, Gertrude Enders. "Health Care." In *The Amish and the State*, 2nd ed., ed. Donald B. Kraybill, 174–75. Baltimore: Johns Hopkins University Press, 1993.

Intelligencer Journal. Lancaster, Pa.: Lancaster Newspapers, 1794-.

Johnson, Curtis D. *Redeeming America: Evangelicals and the Road to Civil War*. Chicago: Ivan R. Dee, 1993.

Johnson-Weiner, Karen M. *Train Up a Child: Old Order Amish and Mennonite Schools*. Baltimore: Johns Hopkins University Press, 2006.

Jones, Dale E., et al., eds. *Churches and Church Membership in the United States, 2000.* Nashville, Tenn.: Glenmary Research Center, 2002.

Kauffman, Daniel, ed. *Mennonite Cyclopedic Dictionary: A Compendium. . . .* Scottdale, Pa.: Mennonite Publishing House, 1937.

Keim, Albert N., ed. *Compulsory Education and the Amish: The Right Not to be Modern.* Boston: Beacon Press, 1975.

Keiser, Steven Hartman. "Language Change Across Speech Islands: The Emergence of a Midwestern Dialect of Pennsylvania German." Ph.D. dissertation, Ohio State University, 2001.

Kinsinger, Andrew S., and Susan A. Kinsinger. *A Little History of Our Parochial Schools and Steering Committee from 1956–1994.* Gordonville, Pa.: S. A. Kinsinger, 1997.

Kline, Edward A., and Monroe L. Beachy. "History and Dynamics of the New Order Amish of Holmes County, Ohio." *Old Order Notes* 18 (Fall-Winter 1998): 7–19.

Klopfenstein, Perry A. *Marching to Zion: A History of the Apostolic Christian Church of America, 1847–1982.* Fort Scott, Kans.: Sekan Printing Co., 1984.

Kraybill, Donald B. *The Amish and the State,* 2nd ed. Baltimore: Johns Hopkins University Press, 2003.

———. "Plotting Social Change across Four Affiliations." In *The Amish Struggle with Modernity,* ed. Donald B. Kraybill and Marc A. Olshan, 53–74. Hanover, N.H.: University Press of New England, 1994.

———. *The Riddle of Amish Culture,* rev. ed. Baltimore: Johns Hopkins University Press, 2001.

Kraybill, Donald B., and Carl F. Bowman. *On the Backroad to Heaven: Old Order Hutterites, Mennonites, Amish, and Brethren.* Baltimore: Johns Hopkins University Press, 2001.

Kraybill, Donald B., and C. Nelson Hostetter. *Anabaptist World USA.* Scottdale, Pa.: Herald Press, 2001.

Kraybill, Donald B., and Steven M. Nolt. *Amish Enterprise: From Plows to Profits,* 2nd ed. Baltimore: Johns Hopkins University Press, 2004.

Kraybill, Donald B., and Marc A. Olshan, eds. *The Amish Struggle with Modernity.* Hanover, N.H.: University Press of New England, 1994.

Die Kurier. Montgomery, Ind.: n.p., 1997-.

Lancaster New Era. Lancaster, Pa.: Lancaster Newspapers, 1877-.

Landing, James E. *American Essence: A History of the Peppermint and Spearmint Industry in the United States.* Kalamazoo, Mich.: Kalamazoo Public Museum, 1969.

———. "The Spatial Development and Organization of an Old Order Amish-Beachy Amish Settlement: Nappanee, Indiana." Ph.D. dissertation, Pennsylvania State University, 1967.

Längin, Bernd G. *Plain and Amish: An Alternative to Modern Pessimism.* Scottdale, Pa.: Herald Press, 1994.

Leith, John H., ed. *Creeds of the Churches: A Reader in Christian Doctrine from the Bible to the Present,* 3rd ed. Louisville: John Knox Press, 1982.

Luthy, David. *The Amish in America: Settlements that Failed, 1840–1960.* Aylmer, Ont.: Pathway Publishers, 1986.

———. "Amish Settlements Across America: 2003." *Family Life,* October 2003, 17–23.

———. "Erlis Kemp and 'Atomic Bibles' for Russia." *Family Life,* August/September 1990, 17–20.

———. "A History of Raber's Bookstore." *Mennonite Quarterly Review* 58 (April 1984): 168–78.

———. "A History of *The Budget.*" *Family Life,* June 1978, 19–22; July 1978, 15–18.

———. "New Names Among the Amish." *Family Life,* August/September 1972, 31–35; October 1972, 20–23; November 1972, 21–23; February 1973, 13–15; June 1973, 13–15.

———. "The Origin and Growth of the Swartzentruber Amish." *Family Life,* August/September 1998, 19–22.

———. "Replacing the *Ausbund.*" *Family Life,* November 1981, 21–23.

———. *Why Some Amish Communities Fail: Extinct Settlements, 1961–1999.* Aylmer, Ont.: Pathway Publishers, 2000.

Madison, James H. *The Indiana Way: A State History.* Bloomington: Indiana University Press, 1986.

The Mennonite Encyclopedia. 5 vols. Hillsboro, Kan.: Mennonite Brethren Publishing House; Newton, Kan.: Mennonite Publication Office; Scottdale, Pa.: Mennonite Publishing House, 1955–1959; Scottdale, Pa.: Herald Press, 1990.

Mennonite Weekly Review. Newton, Kan.: Herald Publishing Co., 1923-.

Meyers, Thomas J. "Amish Tourism: 'Visiting Shipshewana is Better than Going to the Mall.'" *Mennonite Quarterly Review* 77 (January 2003): 109–26.

———. "Lunch Pails and Factories." In *The Amish Struggle with Modernity,* Donald B. Kraybill and Marc A. Olshan, 165–81. Hanover, N.H.: University Press of New England, 1994.

———. "The Old Order Amish: To Remain in the Faith or to Leave." *Mennonite Quarterly Review* 68 (July 1994): 378–95.

———. "Population Growth and Its Consequences in the Elkhart-LaGrange Old Order Amish Settlement." *Mennonite Quarterly Review* 65 (July 1991): 308–21.

Meyers, Thomas J., and Steven M. Nolt. *An Amish Patchwork: Indiana's Old Orders in the Modern World.* Bloomington: Indiana University Press/Quarry Books, 2005.

Miller, Levi. "The Role of the *Braucher*-Chiropractor in an Amish Community." *Mennonite Quarterly Review* 55 (April 1981): 157–71.

Nolt, Steven M. "The Amish 'Mission Movement' and the Reformulation of Amish Identity in the Twentieth Century." *Mennonite Quarterly Review* 75 (January 2001): 7–36.

———. "Finding a Context for Mennonite History: Pennsylvania German Ethnicity and the (Old) Mennonite Experience." *Pennsylvania Mennonite Heritage* 21 (October 1998): 2–14.

———. *Foreigners in Their Own Land: Pennsylvania Germans in the Early Republic.* University Park: Pennsylvania State University Press, 2002.

———. *A History of the Amish,* rev. ed. Intercourse, Pa.: Good Books, 2003.

———. "Plain People and the Refinement of America." *Mennonite Historical Bulletin* 60 (October 1999): 1–11.

Oboler, Suzanne. *Ethnic Labels, Latino Lives: Identity and the Politics of (Re)Presentation in the United States.* Minneapolis: University of Minnesota Press, 1995.

Olshan, Marc A. "Affinities and Antipathies: The Old Order Amish in New York State." Paper presented at the American Anthropological Meeting, New Orleans, 1990.

———. "Homespun Bureaucracy: A Case Study in Organizational Evolution." In *The Amish Struggle with Modernity,* ed. Donald B. Kraybill and Marc A. Olshan, 199–213. Hanover, N.H.: University Press of New England, 1994.

———. "The National Amish Steering Committee." In *The Amish and the State,* 2nd ed., ed. Donald B. Kraybill, 67–85. Baltimore: Johns Hopkins University Press, 2003.

Oyer, John S. "Is There an Amish Theology?" In *Les Amish: Origine et Particularismes, 1693–1993,* ed. Lydie Hege and Christoph Wiebe, 278–302. Ingersheim: Association Française d'Histoire Anabaptiste-Mennonite, 1994.

Peters, Galen A., ed., and Robert A. Riall, trans. *The Earliest Hymns of the Ausbund: Some Beautiful Christian Songs. . . .* Kitchener, Ont.: Pandora Press, 2003.

Peters, Shawn Francis. *The Yoder Case: Religious Freedom, Education, and Parental Rights.* Lawrence: University Press of Kansas, 2003.

Petersen, William. "Concepts of Ethnicity." In *Harvard Encyclopedia of American Ethnic Groups,* ed. Stephan Thernstrom, 234–42. Cambridge, Mass.: Harvard University Press, 1980.

Plantenga, Bart. *Yodel-Ay-Ee-Oooo: The Secret History of Yodeling Around the World.* New York: Routledge, 2003.

Pratt, Dorothy O. *Shipshewana: An Indiana Amish Community.* Bloomington: Indiana University Press/Quarry Books, 2004.

Ramirez, Frank. *This Wooden O: The Story of Amish Acres, Plain and Fancy, and the Round Barn Theatre.* Nappanee, Ind.: Amish Acres, 2000.

Rechlin, Alice Theodora Merten. *Spatial Behavior of the Old Order Amish of Nappanee, Indiana.* Ann Arbor: University of Michigan Department of Geography, 1976.

Redekop. Calvin W., and John A. Hostetler. "The Plain People: An Interpretation." *Mennonite Quarterly Review* 51 (October 1977): 266–77.

Ein Register von Lieder und Schriften die in der Amischen Gemeinde gebraucht warden. S.l: Pequea Brüder, 1979.

Regulations and Guidelines for Amish Parochial Schools in Indiana. Middlebury, Ind.: Middlebury Graphic Arts, [ca. 1979].

Reschly, Steven D. *The Amish on the Iowa Prairie, 1840 to 1910.* Baltimore: Johns Hopkins University Press, 2000.

Ringenberg, William C. "Development and Division in the Mennonite Community in Allen County, Indiana." *Mennonite Quarterly Review* 50 (April 1976): 114–31.

Roth, John D., trans. and ed., with Joe Springer. *Letters of the Amish Division: A Sourcebook.* Goshen, Ind.: Mennonite Historical Society, 1993.

Sabean, David. *Power in the Blood: Popular Culture and Village Discourse in Early Modern Germany.* New York: Cambridge University Press, 1984.

Schlabach, Theron F. *Peace, Faith, Nation: Mennonites and Amish in Nineteenth-century America.* Scottdale, Pa.: Herald Press, 1988.

Schrock, Frederick J. *The Amish Christian Church: Its History and Legacy.* Monterey, Tenn.: Fredrick J. Schrock, 2001.

Schwartz, Christian, and Elizabeth N., comps. *Schwartzs' Song-Book.* [Gordonville, Pa.]: Gordonville Print Shop, 1980.

[Schwartz, David L.] "Articles of Faith of the Old Order Amish Mennonite Church, Berne, Indiana." [Berne, Ind.: the author, 194–].

Schwartz, Roman D. *History and Records of Internment, 1865–1995, Schwartz Cemetery, Berne, Indiana.* Berne, Ind.: R. D. Schwartz, [1995?].

Scott, Stephen E. *The Amish Wedding and Other Special Occasions of the Old Order Communities.* Intercourse, Pa.: Good Books, 1988.

―――. *Living Without Electricity.* Intercourse, Pa.: Good Books, 1990.

―――. *Plain Buggies: Amish, Mennonite, and Brethren Horse-Drawn Transportation.* Intercourse, Pa.: Good Books, 1981.

Seifert, Lester W. J. "The World Geography of Pennsylvania German: Extent and Causes." In *The German Language in America: A Symposium,* ed. by Glenn G. Gilbert, 14–42. Austin: University of Texas Press, 1971.

Shoemaker, Alfred L. *Christmas in Pennsylvania: A Folk-Cultural Study.* Kutztown, Pa.: Pennsylvania Folklife Society, 1959.

Snyder, C. Arnold. *Anabaptist History and Theology: An Introduction.* Kitchener, Ont.: Pandora Press, 1995.

Songs of the Ausbund, v. 1: History and Translations of Ausbund Hymns. Millersburg, Ohio: Ohio Amish Library, 1998.

South Bend Tribune. South Bend, Ind.: South Bend Tribune, Inc., 1872-.

Stevick, Richard A. *Growing Up Amish: The Teenage Years.* Baltimore: Johns Hopkins University Press, 2007.

Stoll, Joseph. *The Amish in Daviess County, Indiana.* Aylmer, Ont.: Joseph Stoll, 1997.

―――. "The Eichers of Adams County, Indiana." *Family Life,* May 1987, 22–28.

―――. *How the Dordrecht Confession Came Down to Us.* Aylmer, Ont.: Pathway Publishers, 2000.

Stoltzfus, Victor E. "Amish Agriculture: Adaptive Strategies for Economic Survival of Community Life." *Rural Sociology* 38 (Summer 1973): 196–206.

Stutzman, David J. *A Call to Repentance.* Millersburg, Ohio: D. J. Stutzman, 1955.

Stutzman, Karl N. "Religious Separatism and Economic Participation: The Nappanee-area Amish Community and the 'World' in the 19th Century." Unpublished paper. Mennonite Historical Library, Goshen, Ind., 2002.

Thompson, Chad L. "The Languages of the Amish of Allen County, Indiana: Multilingualism and Convergence." *Anthropological Linguistics* 36 (1994): 69–91.

―――. "Yodeling of the Indiana Swiss Amish." *Anthropological Linguistics* 38 (1996): 495–520.

Tilly, Charles. "Contentious Repertoires in Great Britain, 1758–1834." *Social Science History* 17 (1993): 253–80.

The Truth. Elkhart, Ind.: Truth Publishing Co., 1889-.

The Truth in Word and Work: A Statement of Faith by Ministers and Brethren of Amish Churches of Holmes Co., Ohio, and Related Areas. Baltic, Ohio: Amish Brotherhood Publications, 1983.

Umble, Diane Zimmerman. *Holding the Line: The Telephone in Old Order Mennonite and Amish Life.* Baltimore: Johns Hopkins University Press, 1996.

Unparteiische Liedersammlung zum Gebrauch beim oeffentlichen Gottesdienst und zur häuslichen Erbauung. Arthur, Ill.: Echo, 1998. First edition, Elkhart, Ind.: Mennonitische Verlagsanstalt, 1892.

Weaver, J. Denny. *Becoming Anabaptist: The Origin and Significance of Sixteenth-century Anabaptism.* 2nd ed. Scottdale, Pa.: Herald Press, 2005.

Weaver-Zercher, David L. *The Amish in the American Imagination.* Baltimore: Johns Hopkins University Press, 2001.

Welty, Cora Gottschalk. *The Masquerading of Margaret.* Boston: C. M. Clark, 1908.

Wenger, A. Frances Z. "The Phenomenon of Care in a High Context Culture: The Old Order Amish." Ph.D. dissertation, Wayne State University, 1988.

Wenger, John C. *The Mennonites in Indiana and Michigan.* Scottdale, Pa.: Herald Press, 1961.

Wenger, Marion R. "A Swiss-German Dialect Study: Three Linguistic Islands in Midwestern U.S.A." Ph.D. dissertation, Ohio State University, 1969.

Wuthnow, Robert. *Meaning and Moral Order: Explorations in Cultural Analysis.* Berkeley: University of California Press, 1987.

Wuthnow, Robert, James Davidson Hunter, Albert Bergesen, and Edith Kurzweil. *Cultural Analysis: The Work of Peter L. Berger, Mary Douglas, Michel Foucault, and Jürgen Habermas.* Boston: Routledge, 1984.

Yoder, Don. "The 'Dutchman' and the '*Deitschlenner*': The New World Confronts the Old." *Yearbook of German-American Studies* 23 (1988): 1–17.

———. "Palatine, Hessian, Dutchman: Three Images of the German in America." In *Ebbes fer Alle-Ebber Ebbes fer Dich: Something for Everyone-Something for You,* ed. Albert F. Buffington, 107–29. Breinigsville, Pa.: Pennsylvania German Society, 1980.

Yoder, Elmer S. *The Beachy Amish Mennonite Fellowship of Churches.* Hartville, Ohio: Diakonia Ministries, 1987.

Yoder, Freeman L., and Lizzie, comps. *Echoes of the Past: Experiences of the Plain People 1920's through 1940's, during the Depression Years and More.* Middlebury, Ind.: F. L. and L. Yoder, 1998.

Yoder, Paton. *Tradition and Transition: Amish Mennonites and Old Order Amish, 1800–1900.* Scottdale, Pa.: Herald Press, 1991.

Yoder, Paton, and Steven R. Estes, trans. and eds. *Proceedings of the Amish Ministers' Meetings, 1862–1878.* Goshen, Ind.: Mennonite Historical Society, 1999.

Zehr, John. "Allen County, Indiana School Movement." *The Diary* (January 1998), 67–68.

Zook, Lee J. "Slow-Moving Vehicles." In *The Amish and the State,* 2nd ed., ed. Donald B. Kraybill, 145–60. Baltimore: Johns Hopkins University Press, 2003.

SETTLEMENT DIRECTORIES

The Mennonite Historical Library, Goshen, Indiana, houses a complete collection of Amish church directories for settlements across the United States and Ontario. The list below includes only those that appear in the notes, and not all the titles consulted.

Amish Directory: Feather Your Nest with . . . Allen County, South Whitley, Quincy Michigan, Camden Michigan, 2000. S.l.: s.n., 2000.

Borkholder, Owen E., comp. *Nappanee Amish Directory, including Rochester, Kokomo, and Milroy Communities, 2001.* Nappanee, Ind.: Owen E. Borkholder family, 2001. [*2001 Nappanee Directory*].

Brandenberger, Enos, comp. *Indiana Amish Directory: Allen County and Vicinity.* [New Haven, Ind.: E. Brandenberger, 1970. Included Daviess, Steuben, and DeKalb counties.

Christner, Levi D., comp. *Old Order Amish Church Districts of Indiana.* Topeka, Ind.: L. D. Christner, [1949].

S

Church Directory of the Lancaster County Amish, 2 vols. Gordonville, Pa.: The Diary, 2002; and earlier editions (1996, 1988, 1980, 1973, and 1965; titles vary).

Eicher, Willis, comp. *Daviess-Martin County Directory: Directory of the Old Order Amish.* Loogootee, Ind.: W. Eicher, 1994.

Gingerich, Ervin, comp. *Ohio Amish Directory: Holmes, Tuscarawas, Coshocton, and Wayne Counties.* Millersburg, Ohio: E. Gingerich, 1954.

Indiana Amish Directory: Adams and Jay Counties and Vicinity Amish Directory, 1997. Monroe, Ind.: Hilty Home Sales, 1997.

Indiana Amish Directory: Adams County and Vicinity Amish Directory, 1992. Monroe, Ind.: Hilty Home Sales, 1992.

Michigan Amish Directory 2002. Millersburg, Ohio: Abana Books, 2002.

Miller, Jerry E., comp. *Indiana Amish Directory: Elkhart, LaGrange, and Noble Counties.* Middlebury, Ind.: J. E. Miller, 2001. [*2002 Elkhart-LaGrange Directory*].

New Order Amish Directory, 1999. Millersburg, Ohio: Abana Books, 1999.

Troyer, Herbert N., comp. *Ohio Amish Directory.* Millersburg, Ohio: H. N. Troyer, 1940.

Index

Steven M. Nolt is an associate professor of history at Goshen College. His books include *A History of the Amish* (Good Books, 1992; rev. ed., 2003), *Amish Enterprise: From Plows to Profits,* with Donald B. Kraybill (Johns Hopkins University Press, 1995; rev. ed., 2004), and *Foreigners in Their Own Land: Pennsylvania Germans in the Early Republic* (Penn State University Press, 2002).

Thomas J. Meyers is the associate academic dean, the director of international education, and a professor of sociology at Goshen College. He has published numerous articles and book chapters on Amish life and is the author of *An Amish Patchwork: Indiana's Old Orders in the Modern World,* with Steven M. Nolt (Indiana University Press, 2005).